THE UNIVERSITY OF MICHIGAN
CENTER FOR CHINESE STUDIES

MICHIGAN PAPERS IN CHINESE STUDIES
NO. 15

Printed in the United States of America

Of course it was necessary to give them [women]
legal equality to begin with! But from there on, everything still remains to be done. The thought, culture,
and customs which brought China to where we found her
must disappear, and the thought, customs, and culture
of proletarian China, which does not yet exist, must
appear. The Chinese woman does not yet exist either,
among the masses; but she is beginning to want to exist. And then to liberate women is not to manufacture
washing machines--and to liberate their husbands is
not to manufacture bicycles but to build the Moscow
subway.

Mao Tse-tung to André Malraux
c. 1958 (from Anti-mémoires)

Contents

Contents

"Oh, so that's what it was all about," we murmur in surprise when we read of the beating of Goldflower's vicious father-in-law. These women break the bonds of all the old definitions: they retaliate against a man, an elder, an in-law. And they do it together. This is social change with a vengeance.

Focusing our attention on women in China does more than just strengthen our still tenuous grasp on the texture of revolution. It also raises an enormous variety of questions. What were the roots of the women's movement in China? How did that movement relate to the Communist Party? What were (and are) the contradictions between social revolution and militant feminism? What happened to the urban feminists who did not join the Communists? And what was the fate of those who did? How long does it take for social transformation to make its effect felt on the status of women? Curiously, today the Chinese find themselves called upon to answer unexpected questions from sympathetic young Americans. Instead of the uneasy queries about particular bourgeois freedoms (of speech, press, etc.), they confront a barrage of questions about women. Nor are statistics about the number of women crane operators entirely satisfying, however gratifying it is to know they exist.

This volume draws together some recent essays on women so that students may have, in a convenient form, a sense of the range of problems, answers, and questions. The authors share neither a common ideology nor methodology, but only the central query: what about women?

We begin with two important essays by Roxane Witke. The first, a consideration of Mao Tse-tung's early response to the women's issue, underlines the conjunction between the position of women and the key issues of social revolution in China. Passionate, outraged, eager for the struggle, Mao's articles on the suicide of three young girls still speak to us across the decades and the changes. But what were women themselves saying and doing? Professor Witke's essay on women in politics offers both an overview of the feminist movement in the early Republic and a study of the socialist critique of that movement. In particular, she draws our attention to Hsiang Ching-yü, considered by her contemporaries "as perhaps the most outstanding woman revolutionary of her time." Hsiang's insistence that social revolution was the absolutely essential pre-condition for women's liberation has been the accepted position of socialist radicals in virtually all times and places. For Hsiang, and thousands

like her, it was not merely a matter of rhetoric.   In 1928 she gave
her life for it.

    But what of the contradictions?   Suzette Leith's fascinating
study of the 20s and early 30s forces us to confront them.   In the
1920s, peasant women responded with remarkable alacrity to the
organizing efforts of women cadres under the general direction of
P'eng P'ai in the south of China.   Mobilized in a separate women's
union, these peasants performed magnificently in the development of
a communications network.   Much of their ardor for the cause rested
on their awareness that the Communists stood for equality between
men and women and would support the efforts of women to be re-
leased from arranged marriages and brutal husbands.   According to
one leader, "some hated the organization because it defended the
rights of women and took care of the divorce problem."   Thus the
women's issue was seen as a potentially divisive one at the same
time that it was acknowledged to be one which could unleash the
righteous anger of millions of peasants -- who were women -- for
the revolution.   Ms. Leith's essay points to other contradictions
as well: the choice between power in the women's department of
the Party and competition for influence within the Party as a whole,
between the desire to pursue non-sex-linked careers and the tendency of the Party to place prominent women in charge of "women's
work."

    Delia Davin's careful study of women in the liberated areas of
China before 1949 is especially valuable for its detailed discussion
of Party policy towards women in the crucially formative years of
the Kiangsi Soviet and the Yenan period.   How policy changed, what
it was intended to accomplish, how it affected the actual lives of
peasant women, are all systematically examined.   Two fundamental
Party resolutions shape the framework within which one must approach
the changing position of women as viewed by the revolutionary leadership.   The first, in 1943, states unequivocally that "the mobilization
of women for production is the most vital factor in safeguarding
their special interests."   The second, published in 1948, insists
that the struggle against oppressive feudal forms "is an ideological
struggle amongst the peasants, and should be radically different
from the class struggle against the feudal landlords."   Ms. Davin's
informed and sensitive discussion of what these resolutions meant
for Chinese women is an enormously important contribution to our
knowledge of the subject.

The editorial work, production skill, and critical intelligence of Penny T. Greene and Linda H. Erwin have been crucial to the preparation and distribution of this issue of the <u>Michigan Papers in Chinese Studies</u>.

Marilyn B. Young
Ann Arbor
July 1973

Mao Tse-tung, Women and Suicide

Roxane Witke

There was nothing particularly out of the ordinary about the facts of Miss Chao's suicide. It happened this way. Miss Chao Wu-chieh, of Nanyang Street, Changsha, was engaged to marry Wu Feng-lin, of Kantzuyuan, on November 14, 1919. As a matter of course the match had been arranged by her parents and the matchmaker. Although Miss Chao had had only the brief ritual encounters with the fiancé, she disliked him intensely and was unwilling to marry him. Her parents refused both to undo the match and to postpone the wedding date. On the day of the wedding, as Miss Chao was being raised aloft in the bridal chair to be delivered to the home of the groom, she drew out a dagger which she had previously concealed in the chair and slit her throat.[1]

While in ordinary times this incident might have passed unnoticed, during the time of the cultural catharsis of the May Fourth period it was blown up to become one of Changsha's biggest news stories of the year. Miss Chao's suicide was the subject of at least nine impassioned articles by Mao Tse-tung which set the style of the "case study," a new genre of May Fourth polemical literature. Mao's series of articles specifically on Miss Chao but more generally on the role of women and the family in modern China reflected changes already in process and fomented still more radical action. Written in the autumn of 1919, before his thinking began to show the laboured and dogmatic effects of Marxism, the style itself bristled with the bite and pungency of Hunanese argot. Mao's literary executors, striving to keep afloat the myth that he was born Marxist, have excluded these writings from the Collected Works, presumably because they document the heterogeneous phases prior to

Reprinted with permission from The China Quarterly, No. 31, July-September, 1967.

energies which might have been turned outward and made to serve
the public good were channelled inward and dissipated in the useless
prolonging of feudal family lines. While Yang's ideas were by no
means the only ones influencing Mao in his adolescent years, Yang
occupied the unique position of being at once philosopher, teacher,
friend and finally father-in-law.

The unprecedented participation of girl students in Hunan's internal political struggles awakened Mao to the revolutionary potential
of women. From the very beginning of the student movement in Hunan, girl students were swept up into the student activist organisations. In the autumn of 1917 Mao and Ts'ai Ho-sheng began laying
plans for the New People's Study Society (Hsin-min hsueh-hui). Within a year this became one of the most radical student organisations
existing in China at the time, and the bulk of its members eventually
joined the Socialist Youth Corps and the Communist Party.[5] When
the Society was formally organised in April 1918, Ts'ai Ho-sheng's
sister, Ts'ai Ch'ang, who was destined to become one of the foremost leaders of women in Communist China, was the first female
member.[6] According to Ts'ai Ch'ang, Mao, her brother and she
herself so hated the tyrannies of the traditional marriage system
that when the Society was founded they swore never to marry. This
understanding, amusing in retrospect since they all married (Mao
three times), was the basis of their early friendship.[7] In the same
vein of puritanical dedication Mao told Edgar Snow that when the New
People's Study Society was being formed he and his friends had no
time for "love and romance"; the times were far too critical and the
needs for knowledge too urgent to discuss women or personal matters.[8] The Society's membership consisted mostly of activist students and teachers from the leading Changsha schools: the First
Normal School, Chou-nan Girls' Middle School and several other
middle schools, the School of Commerce and the School of Law.
By the eve of the May Fourth Movement it had about 80 members
who met every month or two. Mao is said to have drafted the manifesto which resolved to "reform China and the world" and opposed
prostitution, gambling, concubinage and lewdness of any sort.[9] The
New People's Study Society was explicitly concerned with the woman
problem and particularly with instilling in women a consciousness of
their potential social and political roles.

Mao and Ts'ai Ho-sheng also joined forces in setting up the
Society for Work and Study in France (Liu-Fa ch'in-kung hui). Because Mao was eager to see girls join the programme in France,

he organised the Girls' Society for Work and Study in France (Nü-tzu liu-Fa ch'in-kung hui).[10] Although Mao himself never went abroad with these programmes, he was continuously involved in promoting them in China. At the same time that the overseas programmes were being set into motion, Ts'ai Ch'ang and Hsiang Ching-yü extended the same pattern of organisation to the Women's Work and Study Group which they founded in Changsha.[11] Hsiang Ching-yü, also a native Hunanese, was a graduate of Changsha Girls' Normal School. By this time Hsiang had become the foremost female leader of May Fourth activities in Changsha.[12] When Hsiang Ching-yü and Ts'ai Ch'ang, along with 14 other Hunanese girls and a larger number of male students and teachers, were on the point of embarking for France, Mao said to Hsiang Ching-yü: "I hope that you will be able to lead a large group of female comrades abroad, for each one you take with you is one you save."[13] Ts'ai Ho-sheng also favoured sending as many women as possible to France. It was the consensus of the New People's Study Society that women should be encouraged to go because they were extremely dependable.[14] Hsiang Ching-yü married Ts'ai Ho-sheng and Ts'ai Ch'ang married Li Fu-ch'un while they were in France with the Work-Study Programme.

The Incident of May 4, 1919 lent cohesion and significance to the desperate local struggles which were already under way. In Hunan, as soon as the students were dismissed for summer holidays in June, they channelled all their pent-up outrage and energy into forming a network of student alliances throughout the province. Mao was instrumental in the formation of the overall co-ordinating body called the United Students' Alliance which began functioning on June 3, 1919. From its inception the Alliance included girls as well as boys. At first the girls took cues from the boys, but they soon gained their own revolutionary momentum. T'ao Yüan Girls' School was highly spirited and its administration liberal. In the latter half of May several hundred of its students with the help of their principal, P'eng Shih-ti, organised themselves into "Committees of Ten to Save the Nation." These committees served as pilot groups which were dispatched to various areas of the city to give lectures on how to "save the nation." Occasionally the Committees of Ten had primary school children attached to them, carrying white "save the nation" flags. Their messages typically ran like this: "Dear compatriots, everyone must awaken to the fact that China is about to be lost and we shall become enslaved just as happened to the Koreans, and our women will suffer extreme humiliation. Taiwan is another example [of Japanese colonisation]. Let us all be aware of China's predica-

on August ., 1919 when it was confiscated by the Hunan warlord Chang Ching-yao. Mao supplied most of the articles and the contents covered a broad spectrum--international, national and human events, vernacular literature and the "New Culture." In general the magazine's views were radical and inflammatory. The first issue contained an article signed by Mao and entitled "The Women's Revolutionary Army," but regrettably no parts of this have been preserved in later collections.[19] In "The Great Union of the Popular Masses" (issues 2, 3 and 4) Mao urged peasants, workers, women, teachers and students to join together in opposing the reactionary forces of aristocrats and capitalists.[20] While Mao recognized that superstition, fatalism and slavish devotion to living authorities was practised by all classes, he singled out women as being a vast repository of the old habits of thinking. In the third issue he called upon women specifically to unite to abolish "man-eating feudal morality" . . . and to sweep away the coolies (that destroy) physical and spiritual freedom."[21] Mao insisted that women belonged to "jen," in effect the human race, as opposed to some sub-human species for which special restrictions and a restrictive morality had to be confined. He argued that women should be granted suffrage and the freedom to move outside of the home and to circulate in society on an equal footing with men." He said: "As we are all human beings, why not grant us all suffrage? And as we are all human beings, why not allow us to mix freely with one another?"[22]

Unequal demands for chastity was one of the most bitterly attacked points of the double standard. While prostitution, remarriage and concubinage cost men no social disgrace, the demands of chastity on woman were so rigorous that prenatal or actual loss of chastity became a major cause of female suicide. In the third issue of Hsiang River Review Mao attacked the idea of chastity as a measuring-stick for morality. "What sort of chastity is this, completely confined to women with shrines for female martyrs everywhere? Where are the shrines for chaste boys?"[23]

In a desperate attempt to stamp out all student protest associations and their journals, Chang Ching-yao confiscated Hsiang River Review in October 1919. Mao immediately found outlets in other journals. One was New Hunan, a monthly founded on June 5, 1919 as the successor to Chiu-kuo-chou l'an (Save the Nation Journal). Mao became its editor after the seventh issue, published in August 1919. After the tenth issue in October it was banned.[24] Its aims

on August 4, 1919 when it was confiscated by the Hunan warlord
Chang Ching-yao.   Mao supplied most of the articles and the contents covered a broad spectrum--international, national and Hunanese events, vernacular literature and the "New Culture."   In
general the magazine's views were radical and inflammatory.   The
first issue contained an article signed by Mao and entitled "The
Women's Revolutionary Army," but regrettably no parts of this
have been preserved in later collections.[19]   In "The Great Union
of the Popular Masses" (issues 2, 3 and 4) Mao urged peasants,
workers, women, teachers and students to join together in opposing the reactionary forces of aristocrats and capitalists.[20]   While
Mao recognised that superstition, fatalism and slavish devotion to
living authorities was practised by all classes, he singled out
women as being a vast repository of the old habits of thinking.
In the third issue he called upon women specifically to unite to
abolish "man-eating feudal morality . . . and to sweep away the
goblins [that destroy] physical and spiritual freedom."[21]   Mao insisted that women belonged to "jen," in effect the human race, as
opposed to some sub-human species for which special restrictions
and a retributive morality had to be contrived.   He argued that
women should be granted suffrage and the freedom to move outside
of the home and to circulate in society on an equal footing with
men.   He said: "As we are all human beings, why not grant us
all suffrage?   And as we are all human beings, why not allow us
to mix freely with one another?"[22]

Unequal demands for chastity was one of the most bitterly attacked points of the double standard.   While prostitution, remarriage and concubinage cost men no social disgrace, the demands of
chastity on women were so rigorous that potential or actual loss of
chastity became a major cause of female suicide.   In the third issue of Hsiang River Review Mao attacked the use of chastity as a
measuring-stick for morality: "What sort of chastity is this, completely confined to women with shrines for female martyrs everywhere?   Where are the shrines for chaste boys?"[23]

In a desperate attempt to stamp out all student protest associations and their journals, Chang Ching-yao confiscated Hsiang River
Review in October 1919.   Mao immediately found outlets in other
journals.   One was New Hunan, a monthly founded on June 5, 1919
as the successor to Chiu-kuo chou-k'an (Save the Nation Journal).
Mao became its editor after the seventh issue, published in August
1919.   After the tenth issue in October it was banned.[24]   Its aims

included undermining the theory of the "three bonds" (san kang: to ruler, father and husband) which was the basic formula of the old Confucian ethics of loyalty, filial piety and strict chastity in women; promotion of individualism, independence and sexual equality; and reform of the clan and family system.[25] Mao's contributions most likely included articles on the woman problem; however, the journal's contents have not been made available.

A third journal to which Mao contributed was Women's Bell, published by the student union of Chou-nan Girls' Middle School. When Women's Bell was founded in July 1919 its manifesto read: "Aim: liberty and equality; means: struggle, creativeness and solution of the woman problem by women." Most of the articles were written by students of the Chou-nan school; their subjects were the problems of women's emancipation and female labour.[26] Some of Mao's articles on the suicide of Miss Chao are said to have been published here[27]; however, the only ones to which we presently have access are from Changsha's Ta Kung Pao, which survived Chang Ching-yao's repressive policies more successfully than other contemporary left-wing journals.

Mao's series of nine articles prompted by Miss Chao's suicide were published swiftly one after another in Ta Kung Pao. The first article appeared on November 16, two days after the event, and the last on November 30. While the exact publication date of some of those in between is not known, they are presented here in the order in which they appeared originally. All sections of the articles quoted directly by the Chinese editors are quoted in full. When helpful the editor's paraphrasing of parts which have not been quoted directly is transmitted.

In the first article, "A Critique of Miss Chao's Suicide," one can note Mao's habit of attributing the causes of all events to the "environment," "circumstances" or "society"--terms he uses interchangeably in opposition to the individual. This pattern may reflect the influence of Ibsen and his confrontation of the individual and society. It is most likely that Mao, who avidly read New Youth (Hsin ch'ing-nien), had seen its June 1918 issue, which was wholly devoted to translation of Ibsen's works and studies of "Ibsenism" (I-po-sheng-chu-i). A second notable feature is a streak of determinism in his thinking which leads him to say that had particular conditions of the environment (circumstances or society) not obtained, then the suicide surely could not have come about. He fails to raise the possibility

well; her running off like this with her lover shows that
she has no sense of face." . . . But if you bide your
time, the family which produced this sort of girl would
truly die of humiliation.

This young girl has acted as an extremist. Not only
did she not fear great suffering, but also she risked her
life in struggling with the devil. Yet what did she have
to gain? As I see it there were only three things she
could achieve: one, to be "pursued"; another, to be
"beaten"; and the third, to be "mocked." . . . Because
society possesses the "means" of bringing about Miss
Chao's death, this society is an extremely dangerous
thing. If it can cause the death of Miss Chao, then it
could as well cause the deaths of Miss Ch'ien, Miss Sun
and Miss Li. And if it can bring about the deaths of
"women," then it can also bring about the deaths of "men."
We numerous potential victims must be on our guard
against this dangerous thing that can inflict a mortal blow
upon us. We must cry out to warn our fellow human
beings who are not yet dead. We must condemn the ten-
thousand evils of our society.

From the article "Advice to Boys and Girls on the Marriage Problem"[30] we have only a fragment to the effect that Mao warned boys
and girls all over China about "this tragic event in the bloody city
of Changsha . . . which should arouse them to the depths of their
souls and make them thoroughly aware [of its implications] ."
Moreover, the editor paraphrases, they should exert total effort
in destroying this ten-thousand evil society and in establishing a
new society.

"The Problem of Superstitions about Marriage"[31]

the greatest superstition is the "doctrine of predestined
marriages." . . . As soon as a person drops out of his
mother's belly it is said that his marriage has been settled. When he grows up and it is necessary for him to
marry, he himself would never dare to raise the issue
of marriage. He merely calls upon his parents and the
matchmaker to arrange it. One way is for him to discuss the marriage with his parents and the matchmaker,

but even so it has already been settled previously and
unquestionably it is all to the good. . . . All those
couples whose homes are said to be utterly tranquil have
their chests puffed up with the four big characters which
make up "predestined marriage" (hun-yin ming-ting).
Hence they remember such aphorisms as "marriages
made in heaven" and so forth. . . . This sort of marriage which complies with the doctrine of predestined
marriage accounts for approximately 80 per cent of
all Chinese marriages. . . . Because of this doctrine
of predestined marriage they have other irrational beliefs such as "marriages made in the womb" and "making a match with babe in arms"; all arise from the
same basic superstition. Everyone regards this as a
sort of "beautiful destiny." No one has ever imagined
that it is all a mistake. If you question someone's
reasons he'll feed back "predestined marriage." . . .

"Predestined marriage is a sort of comprehensive superstition.
Besides it there are a number of minor ones." Examples of the
minor superstitions are "the casting of horoscopes," "exchange of
betrothal documents," "selection of a lucky day [for the wedding],"
"mounting the bridal sedan chair," "the greeting of the god of happiness" and the "marriage ceremony in the ancestral temple."[32]
These superstitions are used as a sort of rope whereby couples are
bound together so tightly that they cannot breathe, with the result
that in the end they are an absolutely "perfect match." Mao called
upon the people to uproot completely the basis of the thinking of
this senseless marriage system--the doctrine of predestined mar-
riage--and to carry out a family revolution.

If we launch a campaign for the reform of the marriage
system, we must first destroy all superstitions regarding marriage, of which the most important is destruction
of belief in "predestined marriage." Once this belief
has been abolished, all support for the policy of parental
arrangement will be undermined and the notion of the "in-
compatibility between husband and wife" will immediately
appear in society. Once a man and wife demonstrate in-
compatibility, the army of the family revolution will arise
en masse and a great wave of freedom of marriage and
freedom of love will break over China.

physically in campaign to boycott Japanese imports and spiritually
in the struggle to define his own identity. On November 17, 1919
he committed suicide. His suicide spawned numerous articles,
replies and rebuttals in several journals. Most of these maintained
that suicide was symptomatic of a whole spectrum of social ills
which could be cured by various degrees of reform and revolution.
At this juncture Dewey predicted to Chiang also-tta that what he
termed the "intellectual revolution" would bring about the suicides
of a great many Chinese young people.[28]

Dewey was right. The several hundreds of articles in the May
Fourth literature on suicide and related topics showed that the ava-
tars of the New Thought had developed a nose for youthful suicides
for modern causes and a fascination for dissecting the morbid sui-
cidal streak in the old thought and disintegrating culture. Other
studies of suicide took shape as fiction. Many sketches and short
stories in this vein were part of the May Fourth-inspired movement
to establish "vernacular literature".[29] Four cases taken from contemporary journals and based on actual events not only help to put
Mao's writings on suicide in perspective, but also provide internal
evidence for the validity of his writings to which we have access
only through secondary sources. The first three, Miss Chao Ying,
Miss Li Chao and Miss Yüan Shang-ying, died. The fourth, Miss
Li Chi-ts'un, represents the revolutionary and modern alternative
for she rejected suicide and resolved to lead her own life in defiance of social convention.

At two a.m. on the morning of September 14, 1919 Miss Chao
Ying jumped from the upper-storey of her Shanghai home, suffered
multiple fractures and died in the hospital three weeks later. Because of tremendous public concern her correspondence was assem-
bled and published immediately. It revealed how profoundly she had
been affected by the literature on female emancipation in the years
1918-19 and how as a result she became totally antagonistic to the
family system and to her parents' attempts to marry her off in the
conventional fashion. She chose to live alone and pursue a modern
education. While she was in schools in Ningpo and Shanghai she
fell under the influence of several teachers who were Buddhists.
Her correspondence showed that the hallucinations she suffered a
few days before she attempted suicide had Buddhist content. Thus,
despite the modernity of her schools and her own intellectual orientation, the religious or symbolic justification of her suicide appears
to have been the timeless Buddhist one. However, the conditions

physically in campaigns to boycott Japanese imports and spiritually
in the struggle to define his own identity.   On November 17, 1919
he committed suicide.   Lin's suicide spawned numerous articles,
replies and rebuttals in several journals.   Most of these maintained
that suicide was symptomatic of a whole spectrum of social ills
which could be cured by various degrees of reform and revolution.
At this juncture Dewey predicted to Chiang Mon-lin that what he
termed the "intellectual revolution" would bring about the suicides
of a great many Chinese young people. [38]

   Dewey was right.   The several hundreds of articles in the May
Fourth literature on suicide and related topics showed that the ava-
tars of the New Thought had developed a nose for youthful suicides
for modern causes and a fascination for dissecting the morbid sui-
cidal streak in the old thought and disintegrating culture.   Other
studies of suicide took shape as fiction.   Many sketches and short
stories in this vein were part of the May Fourth-inspired movement
to establish "vernacular literature. "[39]   Four cases taken from contemporary journals and based on actual events not only help to put
Mao's writings on suicide in perspective, but also provide internal
evidence for the validity of his writings to which we have access
only through secondary sources.   The first three, Miss Chao Ying,
Miss Li Chao and Miss Yüan Shung-ying, died.   The fourth, Miss
Li Chi-ts'un, represents the revolutionary and modern alternative
for she rejected suicide and resolved to lead her own life in defiance of social convention.

   At two a. m. on the morning of September 18, 1919 Miss Chao
Ying jumped from the upper-storey of her Shanghai home, suffered
multiple fractures and died in the hospital three weeks later.   Because of tremendous public concern her correspondence was assem-
bled and published immediately.   It revealed how profoundly she had
been affected by the literature on female emancipation in the years
1918-19 and how as a result she became totally antagonistic to the
family system and to her parents' attempts to marry her off in the
conventional fashion.   She chose to live alone and pursue a modern
education.   While she was in schools in Ningpo and Shanghai she
fell under the influence of several teachers who were Buddhists.
Her correspondence showed that the hallucinations she suffered a
few days before she attempted suicide had Buddhist content.   Thus,
despite the modernity of her schools and her own intellectual orientation, the religious or symbolic justification of her suicide appears
to have been the timeless Buddhist one.   However, the conditions

which drove her to suicide had a specifically modern cast.

The nearly identical polemical style of a passage from Mao and another from the writer on Miss Chao Ying's suicide, who signs himself Hsüan Lu, suggests strongly that they both were writing at about the same time. Miss Chao Ying's death occurred on October 10, 1919. Judging from other cases of reportage on suicide and from the immediacy and freshness of Hsüan Lu's treatment, one might assume that his article was produced within a week or so after the event. Miss Chao's suicide occurred on November 14, 1919, and Mao began to publish his series of articles on it two days later. Thus it is most likely that Mao read Hsüan Lu and imitated him. However, if Hsüan Lu lagged somewhat in reporting the event, it is possible that he copied Mao, though this seems less likely. Or perhaps the striking similarity was purely fortuitous.

Hsüan wrote of Miss Chao Ying:

She is dead! If she had never lived with her family, she would not have died. Yet living with this family, if her sister had not persecuted her, she would not have died. . . . Had she been educated, yet not besieged by the noxious influences of false forms of new thought, she would not have died. Had she not been enticed by Buddhism, she perhaps would not have died. [40]

Compare this polemical treatment of conditions of inevitability with the passage in Mao's "A Critique of Miss Chao's Suicide" which begins: "If one of these three factors had not been an iron cable, or if she had been set free from the cables, then Miss Chao surely would not have died. . . ."

The resemblance between Mao and Hsüan Lu does not stop at rhetoric, but is evident in the conceptual basis as well. Like Mao, Hsüan Lu traces all noxious influences to a concept of "environment" which is coeval with "society." Both use the epithet "ten-thousand evil society." Parents, teachers and friends, who are manifestly the sources of traditional social customs and beliefs, are in fact no more than agents for the overwhelming forces of society. So, members of the older generation cannot logically be regarded as being ultimately responsible for their actions; however, both Mao and Hsüan Lu were nonetheless bitterly critical of them. What was fundamentally wrong with the older generation was that it was fatalistic.

Rather than assume responsibility for its own actions and for society as a whole, it shifted the onus of responsibility for human error and suffering onto fate. In the view of Mao, Hsüan Lu and other members of the May Fourth generation who strove to defy fate and to change the world, fatalism explained China's disastrous state of collapse in the early republican era.

In December 1919, one month after the suicide of Miss Chao in Changsha, the death in Peking of Miss Li Chao became a cause célèbre in Hsin Ch'ao (New Tide). Like the other young women who died tragic deaths, Miss Li was not a particularly distinguished person; her case is important just because it was typical rather than rare. Miss Li's mother died when she was very young and she was raised by her father's concubine. Because no son had been born either to the first wife or to the concubine, Miss Li's father adopted a son. Upon the death of the father, the adoptive son, as was customary, became the sole heir to the estate, which was considerable. When Miss Li reached her late teens the adoptive son, in loco parentis, arranged a marriage for her. However, Miss Li, who was maturing in an age when alternatives to arranged matches and to the family system in general were beginning to emerge, found family life tedious and her proposed husband odious. She abandoned her home in Kwangsi and made her way first to Kwangchow where she studied and later, in September 1918, to the National Higher Normal School for Girls in Peking. Once Miss Li ran away from home her adoptive brother's only remaining means of controlling her was the purse. He refused to send her any money for living expenses or school fees. Although girl friends gave her money from time to time, she was scarcely able to make ends meet. Prolonged hardship had so weakened her that by the winter of 1918 she was stricken with tuberculosis, hospitalised, and died in August 1919. [41]

Hu Shih, Ch'en Tu-hsiu, Ts'ai Yüen-p'ei and others wrote lengthy articles analysing the social conditions which could allow a tragedy like Miss Li's to occur. In Hu Shih's estimation the roots of the problem lay in the autocratic manner of the family head, in this case the adoptive son; the need for girls to have access to education without having to risk their lives; the need to reform inheritance laws so that female as well as male children could become heirs or share the inheritance; and the injustice of the daughters not being able to carry on the family line. [42] In his article "Patriarchalism and the System of Inheritance" Ch'en Tu-hsiu was more

ruthless and to the point.   He argued that in so far as Miss Li was
legally unable to inherit property, she was in effect merely an ac-
cessory of the household, a portion of the property to which the
adoptive son fell heir.   Ch'en claimed that this sort of patriarchal
system, like a matriarchal system, was anachronistic in the modern
age.   Like Mao he regarded individuals who collaborated with this
"ten-thousand evil society" as evil, and individuals who were weak,
persecuted and struggling against it as essentially good. [43]   In 1920
Ts'ai Yüan-p'ei declared that the problems could be reduced to a
question of economy; if the state provided equal education opportunities for all children to eliminate discrimination on financial grounds,
these problems would be solved. [44]

     In October 1920, 11 months after the suicide of Miss Chao of
Changsha, the suicide of Miss Yüan Shun-ying was hailed by contemporary writers as one of the sensational cases of the time. [45]   Miss
Yüan's suicide was handled like a case study but differed from Mao's
treatment of Miss Chao in its more psychological approach.   It focused upon conflicts within individuals between the values of the old
and new societies.   The case involved a man, Li Ch'en-p'eng, who
had both a classical education and some mastery of English, and
his wife, Yüan Shun-ying, a simple country girl whom he had married by arrangement at an early age.   Once his own horizons began
to broaden he wanted to transform his wife into a modern woman
with a city education.   The conflicts which resulted in the wife's
suicide arose from two areas of misunderstanding.   First, the wife
was evidently not clever enough to keep up with the course of study
at the illustrious Chou-nan Girls' Middle School in Changsha.   The
second grew out of the husband's notion of "face."   Although he
wanted to force his wife through sophisticated levels of education,
he was afraid of humiliation because of her humble origins and uncertain abilities.   So at Chou-nan where he taught English and she
studied, he pretended that she was his cousin, not his wife.   Moreover, he refused to live with her and accepted communications from
her only by mail.   After an incredible series of deceptions on the
part of the husband, the wife sank into nervous collapse and finally
drowned herself in the pond at the Chou-nan school.   Two days later
her body was discovered and fished out by a fellow student, and the
school was thrown into a crisis.   When the alleged cousin, now revealed as the husband was summoned to identify her, his first remark was: "It was inevitable that she should die, but she should
have died in the country . . . for by dying in the city she has
caused me to lose face!"   He swiftly destroyed her suicide note

and personal papers before the arrival of the police.

These were the bare essentials of the case. Writers for Chueh-wu (Awakening), the influential journal of the May Fourth era published by Min-kuo jih-pao (Republican Daily) of Shanghai, mined Miss Yüan's suicide for illustrations of the most compelling contemporary issues: the tyranny of the marriage system, inadequacies of the educational system, lack of freedom of divorce, the double standard of morality for men and women, and selfishness and vanity in the old-school Chinese husband.[46]

The case of Miss Li Chi-ts'un, which might have resulted in suicide but did not, serves as contrast to the rest. Her story was publicised in February 1920, three months after the case of Miss Chao. Because Miss Li was intensely opposed to the match arranged by her parents, she ran away from her home in Changsha to Peking where she joined the Work-Study Programme. Her father, who subscribed to the traditional formula regarding women, "stupidity is the only virtue," was furious that he had ever let his wife have her own way in sending their daughter to a local girls' school some years earlier. His outrage at his daugher's revolt and flight to Peking was so notorious that it became a public issue. The student press argued that Miss Li exemplified the spirit of "struggle" (shih-hsing tou-cheng): too many girls and boys merely talk about struggle and in the end are crushed by their social environment; Miss Li had shown how to struggle to the utmost against the social environment.[47]

Miss Li Chi-ts'un's case became a public issue three months too late for Mao to comment on it in his articles on Miss Chao's suicide. Nevertheless, in the terms set up by Mao, Miss Chao is vindicated by Miss Li. Whereas Miss Chao, faced with an odious marriage, gave up the ghost in the traditional manner by cutting her throat, Miss Li threw herself into relentless struggle against all opposition. Miss Li's total rejection of the family principle by running away from home and joining a school in the capital city was the activist, life-oriented and modern resolution to the same problem from which the weaker, tradition-bound girl could retreat only by self-annihilation. The same contempt for all forms of subjugation and the same involvement in struggle, have, of course, characterised Mao's own life.

NOTES

1. Chou Shih-chao, "My Recollections of Chairman Mao in Chang-
    sha before and after the May Fourth Movement," Kung-jen jih-
    pao [Workers' Daily], 20 April 1959, translated in Survey of
    China Mainland Press (hereafter SCMP) (Hong Kong: U. S.
    Consulate-General), No. 2011 (12 May 1959).

2. Hunan li-shih tz'u-liao [Hunan Historical Materials] (hereafter
    HNLSTL), No. 4 (1959); Wu-ssu shih-ch'i shih-k'an chieh-shao
    [An Introduction to the Periodicals of the May Fourth Era]
    (hereafter WSSC), 2 vols. (Peking: 1958-59).   Chou Shih-
    chao, op. cit., also contains passages from Mao's writings
    on Miss Chao.

3. Edgar Snow, Journey to the Beginning (New York: Random
    House, 1958), p. 165.

4. Yang Ch'ang-chi, "Notes on Reforming the Family Institution,"
    Chia-yin tsa-chih [The Tiger Magazine], I, June 1915, p. 6.

5. WSSC, I: 151.   See also Stuart Schram, Mao Tse-tung (London:
    Penguin, 1966), p. 63.

6. Helen Foster Snow, Women in Modern China (The Hague:
    Mouton, 1967), p. 235.

7. Ibid., p. 236.

8. Edgar Snow, Red Star over China (New York: Random House,
    1938), pp. 144-145.

9. Chou Shih-chao, op. cit.

10. WSSC, I:155.

11. Helen Snow, op. cit., p. 236.

12. Ibid., p. 245.

13.   Collected Correspondence of the Members of the New People's
      Study Society, II, in WSSC, I:155.

14.   Collected Correspondence, III, ibid.

15.   Ta Kung Pao, 8 June 1919, in HNLSTL, No. 1 (1959):52-53.

15a. HNLSTL, No. 3 (1959):6-7. In his article "Some Basic Errors
      in my Countrymen's 'View of Life' and 'View of Death,'" first
      delivered as a lecture to the Society for Establishing Study
      (Chien hsüeh hui), then published in Ta Kung Pao (Changsha),
      24-30 June 1919, and reproduced in HNLSTL, No. 4 (1960):
      20-23, Chu Chien-fan depicted his fellow Chinese as being so
      possessed by notions of "fate" that they resisted evolution and
      progress. Because of Chu's reputation it is most likely that
      Mao was familiar with these views. Mao's own articles on
      Miss Chao's suicide take similar issue with the sort of Chi-
      nese fatalism which constrains China in the deathlike clutch of
      the past and inhibits progressive attitudes towards life and the
      future.

16.   Helen Snow, op. cit., p. 191.

17.   Ta Kung Pao, 12 June 1919, in HNLSTL, No. 1 (1959):29.

18.   Ta Kung Pao, 18 June 1919, in HNLSTL, No. 1 (1959):34-35.

19.   See Hsiang-chiang p'ing-lun, table of contents, in WSSC, I:547-
      549.

20.   Hsiang-chiang p'ing-lun, issues 2, 3, and 4. For the text of
      this article, see WSSC, I:147. See also Stuart Schram, The
      Political Thought of Mao Tse-tung (New York: Praeger, 1963),
      pp. 170-171.

21.   HNLSTL, No. 3 (1959):16. The term "man-eating feudal mor-
      ality" was originally popularised by Lu Hsun.

22.   Ibid.

23.   Ibid.

24.   Chow Tse-tsung, Research Guide to the May Fourth Movement
      (Cambridge, Mass.: Harvard University Press, 1964).

25. WSSC, II:356.

26. Chow, op. cit., p. 64.

27. Chou Shih-chao, op. cit. Another periodical source on the
     woman problem in Hunan during this period was T'i-yü chou-
     pao [Journal of Physical Education], organised by Huang Hsing,
     a physical education instructor of the Chu Chih Primary School,
     Changsha, who was broadly known for his literary and cultural
     interests. His journal, intended to introduce New Thought into
     Hunan, published 40 issues. Many of its articles argued the
     importance of physical education for women, as did other
     periodicals on the May Fourth era [HNLSTL, No. 3 (1959):6.
     See also WSSC, II:356]. In the June 1917 issue of Hsin ch'ing-
     nien [New Youth] Mao published "A Study of Physical Education"
     in which he maintained that physical education was not only a
     personal means of self-strengthening, physical and moral, but
     also a way of strengthening the nation (see Stuart Schram's
     translation, Mao Ze-dong, une étude de l'éducation physique,
     Paris: Colin, 1962). In the light of this and his concerns
     with the woman problem in general it is likely that he was a
     contributor to T'i-yü chou-pao. However, this is not presently
     ascertainable because neither its table of contents nor articles
     have been made known outside China.

28. Ta Kung Pao, 16 November 1919, in HNLSTL, No. 4 (1959):28.
     A less complete version but identical in the Chinese with the
     HNLSTL record where excerpts are extant may be found in
     Chou Shih-chao, op. cit. Stuart Schram has made a selective
     and composite translation of the series on Miss Chao using
     both the above sources in Mao Tse-tung, textes traduits et
     présentés par Stuart Schram (Paris: Mouton, 1963), pp. 287-
     290.

29. Ta Kung Pao, in HNLSTL, No. 4 (1959):28-29. A lesser por-
     tion of the same article, including the last three sentences
     which are not found in HNLSTL, appear in Chou Shih-chao,
     SCMP, op. cit., p. 6.

30. Ta Kung Pao, 19 November 1919, in HNLSTL, No. 4 (1959):29.

31. Ibid., pp. 29-30. Chou Shih-chao, op. cit., preserves part of
     this text.

32. For the figurative translation of these traditional expressions regarding marriage I am indebted to the SCMP translator of Chou Shih-chao.

33. Ta Kung Pao, in HNLSTL, No. 4 (1959):30-31.

34. Ibid., p. 31.

35. "The Public Debate of Miss Chao's Suicide," Ta Kung Pao, 20 November 1919, in HNLSTL, No. 4 (1959):32-33. See also Chou Shih-chao, op. cit.

36. HNLSTL, No. 4 (1959):31.

37. Ta Kung Pao, 30 November 1919, ibid. Chou Shih-chao, op. cit., preserves some passages of the above.

38. Ch'en Tu-hsiu, "On Suicide," 1 January 1920, in Tu-hsiu wen-ts'un [Collected Works of Ch'en Tu-hsiu] (Shanghai: 1922), I, pp. 391-416.

39. Chih Hsi, "Does Youth Commit Suicide or Does Society Murder Youth?" Hsin ch'ao [New Tide], II, December 1919, p. 2. A classic example of new fiction in the vernacular on this subject is Lu Hsun's "A New Year's Sacrifice" in Collected Stories of Lu Hsun (Peking: Foreign Languages Press, 1954), pp. 95-118. Yang Ch'en-sheng's story "The Chaste Girl," which appeared in the June 1920 issue of Hsin ch'ao (II, p. 5), is a less known but equally representative example of fiction of this type. Yang's story, an uneasy mixture of sentiment and horror, is about a "chaste girl" whose fiancé died before the wedding. Nonetheless she is forced to go through with the entire ceremony, the groom being represented by his dead body, and to spend the wedding night in the bridal chamber keeping vigil over the body. The next morning she is found dead of unspecified causes.

40. Hsüan Lu, "Chao Ying, a Girl who Died within Society," Nü-hsing wen-t'i [Problems of Women], ed. Mei Sheng (Shanghai: Hsin Wen Hua Shu She, 1934), Vol. VI, pp. 153-162.

41. Ibid., p. 160.

42.   The facts of her life history were originally compiled by Su
       Chia-ying.   They were presented by Hu Shih along with his
       own critical analysis of her suicide in his article "The Biog-
       raphy of Li Chao," Hsin ch'ao, II, December 1919, p. 2.

43.   Ch'en Tu-hsiu, "Patriarchalism and the System of Inheritance,"
       Tu-hsiu wen-ts'un, II, pp. 86-89.

44.   Ts'ai Yüan-p'ei, "A Talk in Commemoration of Miss Li Chao,"
       Ts'ai Tse-min hsien-sheng yen-hsing lu [The Collected Speeches
       of Ts'ai Tse-min (Ts'ai Yüan-p'ei)] (Peking: Peking University
       Press, 1920), pp. 465-468.

45.   [Shao] Li Tzu, "The Suicide Case of Miss Yüan Shun-ying of
       Changsha," Nü-hsing wen-t'i, Vol. VI, pp. 170-176.

46.   Hsüan Lu, op. cit.

47.   An article on Miss Li Chi-ts'un by an author who signs him-
       self merely "Je" in Ta Kung Pao, 17 February 1920, in
       HNLSTL, No. 4 (1959):33-35.

Woman as Politician in China of the 1920s

Roxane Witke

The decade of the twenties was both a peak in the development
of modern Chinese feminism, and a point of departure for wider are-
nas of women's liberation. This brief survey will track some major
currents in the whirlwind of change in the lives of women, and some
new directions taken by those who chose a political way, as opposed
to a literary, sexual or other individual way of liberation. [1] A remarkable trait of politically motivated Chinese women was that the most
avant-garde would not be arrested at the feminist stage of struggle
for suffrage and women's rights. The most radical among them were
not bound by self-consciousness or self-importance as females putting
women's issues at the forefront. They chose rather to set aside
what seemed to them to be partisan sexual issues and to devote their
lives to the various revolutionary movements which eventually would
carry China from Confucianism to Communism. Or in the language
of the victors, their struggles at a turning point in history helped to
promote China from the bourgeois to the socialist stage of the Chinese revolution.

Historical consciousness of the role of women in the Chinese
revolution has lagged in the West. Although native Chinese historians of various political persuasians have recounted some aspects
of the role of women in the making of modern China, the mainstream masculinity of Western historiography has bypassed the feminine current on China's side. Despite this neglect on the part of
foreign historians, the breakaway of radical minorities of Chinese
women from the domain of family kept inviolate by the Confucian
ethos was paralleled and supported by other phases of liberation
made more conspicuous by the dictates of historical fashion: national liberation of Han Chinese from Manchu overlords; social liberation of sons from fathers, youths from elders, and individuals
from family; and intellectual liberation of new modes of thought from
the thrall of Confucian orthodoxy.

Though required for argument, it is too obvious to mention that the political elite of old China was always male. Even within the tradition of Confucian political values, men were able to strain against orthodoxy by officially dissenting or by privately taking Taoist directions. While women vied for power and position within the family structure, their political arts were never exercised beyond domestic confines. When they first broke into the public domain and looked for political signals, they could choose only the roads to the left. In the early twentieth century the political left was an uneasy mixture of nationalism, anti-imperialism, anarchism, republicanism, democracy, and various socialisms. The women who branched out into politics in the teens and the twenties ranged from the conservative left of women's rightists whose campaigns stopped short at upgrading their legal status in the emergent Republic, to women of the radical left who exhorted the female masses to forget sex struggles and other narrowly political debates, and instead to throw themselves into the work of class struggle for socialist revolution.

The upsurge of women politicians went back to the turn of the century when women first sprang into the public arena with a totally unprecedented repertoire of social and political roles: as girl students modernly educated outside the home; as teachers in the freshly established education system; as publicists in the revolutionary press which included some ambitious journals primarily by women but for the political benefit of men and women; as anarchists and assassins; and corporately, as masculinely uniformed members of the Women's National Army, the Women's Dare-to-Die Corps, and the Women's Assassination Corps which joined forces with male troops against the dynasty in its final decade.

The delivery of the Han nation from Manchu rule in 1911 marked a formal change of political structure, but almost no immediate change of social structure. Now as freshly minted "citizens," women who had risked their lives to establish a Republic found the realities of their personal and social lives not dramatically transformed. Like the American women of the mid-nineteenth century who made their first public stance on the abolition issue, and then tackled the problem of their own political status in a suffrage movement, so also many of the Chinese women who had come into political consciousness in the revolutionary campaigns against the Manchus now turned against the Han patriarchs. and set into motion China's first women's rights movement.

The first stage of the women's rights movement began within a few months of the establishment of the Republic in 1912. At this point several of the women's armies transformed themselves directly into suffrage societies, while even more organizations were quickly composed of women who had no previous military experience. In the Chinese historical literature, this first stage of what I have called the "women's rights movement" has two designations; either nü-ch'üan yün-tung, meaning literally, "women's rights movement," or ts'an-cheng yün-tung, the "suffrage movement," though it is too imposing of our own cultural perspectives to refer to its participants by the feminizing English term, "suffragette."

Although Sun Yat-sen was not an active promoter of women's rights in his own right, during his brief tenure as President in 1912 the newly founded women's organizations devoted themselves both to supporting the Republic and to securing equal rights under the draft constitution. The names of these organizations reflect their strident seriousness of purpose: the Shanghai Society of Comrades for Woman Suffrage, the Woman Suffrage Rearguard Society, the Women's Militant Society, the Women's Alliance, the Women's Peace Society, the Society for the Support of Equal Rights for Men and Women, and the Women Citizen's Society.

On January 22, 1912, representatives of women's groups from eighteen provinces met at Nanking to establish the Woman Suffrage Alliance, an overall coordinating organization which would serve as a lobby in the national legislature slated to be convened. Among its long-range goals were equal rights for men and women, universal education for women, reform of family customs, monogamy, the prohibition of commerce in women, and freely contracted marriages as a means of averting "senseless" divorces.[2] When each of these and other related issues resurfaced among the cardinal topics of May Fourth debate some seven years later, the near impossibility of bringing about radical social and institutional change solely through legislative fiat was painfully evident.

The petition submitted by representatives of the Woman Suffrage Alliance took note of the unevenness of China's revolution to date: that the political revolution had taken precedence over social revolution, whose primary goal should be to ensure through woman suffrage the equality of men and women. But when the Legislature handed down the Provisional Constitution of May 11, 1912, it did not include a clause guaranteeing male-female equality. Eight days later the

petition was resubmitted to President Sun.   The Legislature tempo-
rized, and promised vaguely that it would look into the matter.
Thoroughly outraged, the women petitioners burst into an uproari-
ous demonstration before the legislators.   Overnight they recruited
numerous supporters who joined forces with them the next day in
storming the Legislature, smashing windows and trampling the military guard.   News of the outbreak of female violence rocked the
entire nation, to say nothing of the foreign ministries, which were
quite shaken by oriental shades of the Parliament-storming London
suffragettes. [3]

The women's outrage of March 20 flared spectacularly but fiz-
zled because in number and in public appeal they were slight.   Nevertheless, their example provoked scattered coteries of women in
the provinces to submit their demands.   Beginning in Kiangsu women's
groups in most provinces submitted comparable petitions to their provincial assemblies.   Typically in the political avant-garde, Kwangtung
was the only province where women actually secured a limited fran-
chise and began to build up a contigent of women representatives in
the legislative assembly. [4]

The failure of Republican ideals after the second revolution
of 1913 caused both a short-term revival of military action on the
part of women as well as a temporary shift of women's interests
away from the political arena.   As Yüan Shih-k'ai conspired an imperial renaissance in the wake of Sun's abdication from the presi-
dency, the democratic ideals of the fledgling Republic were quietly
crushed.   Women members of the Revolutionary Party were either
brought to submission or expelled.   Suddenly deprived of a political
foothold, the most radical women of Yüan's opposition resorted again
to military means of attaining political goals.   In the course of the
second revolution some joined the National Army and others the Assassination Corps, again outfitting and equipping themselves the same
as male soldiers.

Despite these outbreaks of political militance and military action on the part of a minority of radical women in the first Republican decade, there is little reason to believe that many were opting
for military careers.   In this respect they differed from the swell-
ing ranks of young men who were asserting anti-traditional roles by
choosing military over conventionally high-status careers in the civil
service, ancient or modern.   In the course of the Northern Expedition of the late twenties mounting frustration on the part of revolu-

tionary women and men would force this to change. The flamboyant
girl soldier Hsieh Ping-ying is a well-celebrated example of growing
ranks of Kuomintang and Communist women who would choose the
modern military or traditional guerrilla warfare now revived as a
way of life. But after both the first and the second stages of the
Republican revolution most of the women's contingents laid down
their arms and dispersed to the fields of education, journalism, and
writing, where their political voices were barely audible for several
years.

Although efforts to legislate woman suffrage and women's rights
were abortive in the opening years of the Republic, the issues resurfaced in the polemics of the May Fourth era where they were linked
to borrowed liberal values of individualism, equality, and independence. In his rousing essay of 1916, "Confucianism and Modern
Life, "[5] Ch'en Tu-hsiu argued that the Confucian codes of filial piety
and the corresponding feminine rule of "three obediences" were totally inappropriate in modern nations governed by rival political parties. Since the Confucian codes ruled out intellectual and moral independence, an independent act of political commitment in the form
of the vote was impossible. He advised women who were determined
to free themselves from the old social order to seize upon the right
to vote as the most effective means of insubordination.

Another great spokesman for May Fourth values, Li Ta-chao,
conceptualized the problem of woman suffrage within his world view
derived from historical Marxism. He acknowledged that both the
working women's movement and the women's rights movement were
slow to get under way in China, and that they were contradictory in
a Marxian sense. Nevertheless, the two should cooperate in the
short run, and men should cease to consider women as their infe-
riors. [6]

The most articulate liberal spokesman, Hu Shih, proposed a
mildly jesting solution to the women's rights problem. Employing
the Hobbesian metaphor of the body politic, he claimed that Chinese
society was semi-paralyzed: the male half robust and the female
half inoperative, a condition seriously handicapping China as a whole.
By changing only one word of the Constitution, he said, complete
equality could be brought about. If, in the passage which ran, "Fan
yu Chung-hua min-kuo kuo-chi chih nan-tzu" the character tzu (suffix
to "man") were changed to nü (woman), female equality would be assured on paper at least. [7] Of course his constitutional word games
were not spelled out into historical realities.

Other May Fourth writers espoused the cause of woman suffrage for reasons which also revealed specific Chinese cultural preoccupations. The younger brother of Mao Tse-tung, Mao Tse-min, who made the history of woman suffrage in the West his special concern, indicated that its major value would be to make women more responsible as human beings. [8] A somewhat different though equally patronizing tack was taken by the socialist critic, Yü Huan-tou, who recommended woman suffrage as an antidote to the "typical" female vices of dependency, superstition, jealousy, prejudice, and conservatism. Once given the vote, women presumably would exhibit the "masculine" virtues of independence, courage, creativity, generosity, etc. Woman suffrage would also benefit domestic politics by implementing social welfare and reform programs. And by developing sympathies among women of other nations, suffrage would promote world peace. [9]

But May Fourth rhetoric belonged more to the world of thought than of action. The women's suffrage movement, which was a matter of action, had a separate though uneven momentum. Its pacing was linked to the urban centers of political transformation. The first stage of the women's suffrage movement had flared and faded with the campaign to establish an effective national government in 1911-1912. The second and final stage of a decade hence was linked to the provincial autonomy movement. Sparked by the intellectual debate of the May Fourth Movement, the second stage of the suffrage movement began in Hunan and Kwangtung where the provincial autonomy movements were most vigorous. Founded in Hunan and Kwangtung, the Woman Suffrage Alliance spread rapidly to other capitals where provincial autonomy movements had gained momentum. Among the Alliance's first accomplishments was to send a woman delegate to the International Women's Suffrage Conference in Switzerland in 1920. Perhaps under Western influence it was assumed that politically responsible women were better geared than men to break away from national isolation and to move toward international understanding. [10]

The political tactics adopted by the Hunanese women showed that they regarded the right to vote as a means to other feminist ends. The Hunan Women's Alliance was established in February 1921 as a means of coordinating public demonstrations and of mounting demands for free marriage and other personal freedoms for women. Its so-called "five proposal movement" sought the following rights for women: equal rights of property inheritance, the right to vote and to be elected to office, equal rights to education and to work, and the right of self-determination in marriage, i.e.,

"free marriage." By December 1921 the "five proposal movement"
had secured several of these rights in Hunan's provincial constitution, including the right to vote and to be elected to the provincial
legislature, as indeed several women immediately were. The success of Hunan's women's rights movement provoked similar campaigns in Chekiang and Kwangtung, and eventually in other provinces.[11] The most ambitious of the newly elected women looked
to seats in the National Assembly as their ultimate goal.[12]

Predictably, feminine success triggered masculine cynicism.
Some wry observers of the election of Hunanese women to public
office quipped that all this proved was that women now were exhib-
iting the Confucian male's classic infatuation with "the spirit of becoming an official."[13] To be sure, the most zealous of the new
women politicians held high hopes, and fully expected theirs to be
a first step in the total reform of Chinese society and government.
However, if we compare cross-culturally, it is evident that women
politicians of all stripes in modern China have manifested much less
of the messianic feminist notion that only women can set the world
aright than have their Protestant-inspired counterparts in the West.

Attempts to secure legal guarantee of male-female equality
were made also at the capital. When Li Yüan-hung's Peking government convened the Constitution Conference in the summer of
1922, women students newly admitted to the University of Peking,
a male enclave until 1919, and students of the prestigious Women's
Higher Normal School, seized the opportunity to have a clause of
male-female equality written into the Constitution. They collaborated in establishing two organizations, the Society for the Promotion of Woman Suffrage and the Alliance for the Women's Rights
Movement. Their demands were fairly elaborate formulations of
the liberal ideals of freedom, equality, suffrage, and emancipation.
Although both Peking groups failed in their campaign to alter the
Constitution in favor of woman suffrage, as in the case of the original women's rightists of Hunan and Kwangtung, the force of the
Peking example led women of the outlying provinces to pursue their
own constitutionally established equality.[14]

Interestingly, two-thirds of the original membership of the
Peking Alliance for the Women's Rights Movement was male, a
fact which came as a surprise even to contemporary observers of
the political scene. This fits in with other evidence showing that
in the early twentieth century the issue of women's emancipation

was supported as much or more by men than by women. [15] Not until feminist ideals gained broad acceptance among the intellectual
elite of the later twenties did women take over the leadership and
full-scale management of the women's movement which then fanned
out in a complex array of organizations and alliances pursuing various purely feminist, Nationalist, anti-imperial and Communist goals.

From hindsight it is too easy to speak summarily and to say
that the ripples of a suffrage movement noted here merely marked
the beginning (and end?) of the women's side of the bourgeois revolution.   We learn more by listening to voices of the times, to those
who perceived, or indeed guided China through a pivotal point of
historical transformation.   The politics of urban/rural tensions soon
would arise.   But in the early twenties the central stress point was
between the urban intellectuals and the urban workers.   The women
suffragists were among the more articulate factions of urban intellectuals, and their public appeal was narrow if not divisive.   The
still more radical minority of women intellectuals who rejected par-
liamentarism in favor of socialism built upon an urban workers'
movement began to write in ways which sharpened perceptions of
class antagonism and of the need for a new relation between intellectual and working classes.   In the socialist literature which nee-
dled or openly attacked the woman suffrage movement little was
made of the fact that the Peking suffrage alliances actually had issued calls to working women to join their movements.   Given the
elitist scope of their concerns, this was fatuous to be sure.

Wang Hui-wu was one of the first women of the intelligentsia
to commit her energies to the cause of the proletarian women of
Shanghai's labor world.   Writing in March 1922 in the Communist
organ, Women's Voice, Wang Hui-wu warned that the provincial
autonomy movements to which the women suffragists were address-
ing themselves were falling into the hands of warlords who would
twist them into dictatorships.   She urged the women of Hunan to
take the lead in forestalling this perversion of the parliamentary
principle by gaining the right to vote and organizing the female
proletariat of their constituencies to resist the warlord enemy. [16]
Other socialists applauded all signs of women rebelling against
"feudal and patriarchal" government manned by provincial warlords.
But they were equally concerned that the women's rightists not dis-
sipate their energies in battles between the sexes when they should
be girding themselves for class warfare.   Some would mock the
notorious Miss Han Ying who promoted the "hate system" which

turned women against men on the erroneous assumption that their
enemy was the male sex rather than an oppressor class composed
of men and women.[17]   Though critiques were cast in less than orthodox Marxian language, the drift of argument was that men and
women should abstain from the politics of sexual opposition and join
forces against the class enemy.

The dim hopes held by socialist writers in the suffrage movement would soon be born out in political realities.   As warlord
power mounted relentlessly in the early twenties, constitutional government created by the provincial legislatures was undermined.   The
guarantee of woman suffrage predicated upon a democratic process
subsided.   While the ideal of equal rights for women survived among
members of the urban intelligentsia who continued to believe that China could be saved by legislative correction at the top, the most far-
seeing of the women leaders now looked toward the Kuomintang and
the Communist Party as the most effective agents of national salvation.

A swift glance at the life of Hsiang Ching-yü, regarded by her
contemporaries as perhaps the most outstanding woman revolutionary
of her time, distills and renders in personal terms the major facets
of the role of woman as politician in China of the 1920s.   Born in
1895 in Hsü-pu hsien in Hunan, in 1915 she was graduated from the
Chou-nan school, Changsha's most progressive school for women.
Returning to Hsü-pu hsien, she established its first co-educational
primary school where she first experimented in the politics of social
revolution.   The school was used as a testing grounds for her anti-
hierarchical, egalitarian ideals of "mutual love" between students
and teachers.   She also instilled in her students a sense of patriotism and of mission to awaken the masses, respect for sexual equality, and contempt for the degrading customs of earpiercing and foot-
binding.[18]

When the spirit of May Fourth caught fire in Hunan in 1919,
she was at the vanguard of Changsha's massive student movement,
which sought to persuade China's faltering warlord government to
reject the compromising terms of the Versailles Peace Treaty au-
thorizing China's sell-out to Japanese imperialism.   When her fellow revolutionaries in Changsha, Mao Tse-tung and Ts'ai Ho-sheng,
went to Peking in 1919 in connection with the Work-Study program
in France, Hsiang and Ts'ai Ho-sheng's sister, Ts'ai Ch'ang, destined for a life-long career as a leader of women in the highest

echelons of the Communist Party, organized in Changsha a Women's Work-Study Group which coordinated the Hunan contingent of students who embarked for France on the Work-Study program. Hsiang served informally as the leader of the sixteen girls sent from that province.

Chinese student life in post-war France was an experiment in the theory and practice of socialism. With no private means of support in France, Hsiang financed her school expenses by working part-time in a rubber plant and textile mill, experiences which brought her into direct contact with the French proletariat. At the same time, she and Ts'ai Ho-sheng, whom she eventually married, led the Chinese Work-Study community in the exploration of current revolutionary ideologies--anarchism and social democracy as well as Marxism.[19] By the time the Socialist Youth Corps and the Young China Communist Party were founded in France in 1921, both she and her husband had resolved to join the Communist Party.

At this juncture Hsiang's political life moved onto the double track of intellectual and proletarian class consciousness which was followed arduously by the first generation of Chinese Communist leaders. As ideologue and labor organizer Hsiang devoted herself both to feminist and to proletarian causes. Upon return to China in 1922, the Second Party Congress appointed her as the first woman member of the Central Committee, and made her the first head of the Women's Department. During the next three or four years, all decisions on women taken by the Central Committee were initiated by her. Moving on to Moscow in 1925, she studied Marxism-Lenism at the University of the Toilers of the East for two years. When she returned to China in 1927, she moved directly into the labor world. Assigned by the Central Committee to a high position in the Propaganda Department of the city of Hankow, she organized both the male and female contingents of the labor movement of the Wuhan industrial center and of Shanghai. After Chiang Kai-shek purged his party of Communist membership in April 1927, she was forced to continue her work underground. In the late spring of 1928 she was captured by the KMT at Hankow and was imprisoned in the French Concession. There on May first she defended herself before her execution in the name of the French revolutionary goals of liberty, equality, and fraternity, and against the imperialism which was enslaving the Chinese people.[20]

Though executed well before her political prime, the arc of her life and writing describes the path which radical women intel-

lectuals were beginning to take in the decade of the twenties.   Hsiang
is rumored to have been writing a history of the Chinese Revolution
at the time of her execution, though no trace of that survives.   Nevertheless, in her extant political essays she develops three themes
which trace her journey from feminism to the broader issues of social revolution. [21]   She argued first that women of the intelligentsia
should exist not only for themselves and for their immediate families, but should be trained as leaders of social revolution.   Second,
women of the intelligentsia should make their overriding project the
political awakening of the women of the working and peasant classes.
Third--and this is the most crucial point--she argued that the liberation of women was not an isolated issue; that it belonged to the
larger process of the liberation of the masses; and that women could
not hope to be liberated until all the people were liberated.   Here
she departed from the elitist ranks of zealous women's rightists who
endeavored to oppose discrimination against women by discriminating
for them.   On the contrary, she set the ultimate goal of liberating
all oppressed people, whose liberation would also accomplish the
prior goal of emancipating women.

A half century later her Party inheritors cannot quarrel with
the tasks she set for them, nor can they claim to have reached her
goals.

NOTES

1.   This article was prepared with assistance from a grant from
     the Joint Committee on Contemporary China of the Social Sci-
     ence Research Council and the American Council of Learned
     Societies.

2.   Sun T'a, "Chung-kuo fu-nü yün-tung chih chin-pu" [Progress
     in the Chinese Women's Movement], Fu-nü tsa-chih [The
     Ladies' Magazine], IX, January 1923. Special issue on the
     Women's Movement.

3.   Ch'en Tung-yüan, Chung-kuo fu-nü sheng-huo shih [History of
     the life of Chinese women] (Shanghai: 1928), p. 360. See also
     Wang Ts'ang-pao, La Femme dans la société chinoise (Paris:
     1933), pp. 204-205.

4.   Sun T'a, op. cit.

5.   Ch'en Tu-hsiu, "K'ung-tzu chih tao yu hsien-tai sheng-huo,"
     Hsin ch'ing-nien [New Youth], II, December 1916, p. 4.

6.   Shou-ch'ang [Li Ta-chao], "Hsien-tai ti nü-ch'üan yün-tung"
     [The modern women's rights movement], Fu-nü p'ing-lun
     [Woman critic], No. 25, 28 January 1922.

7.   Hu Shih, "Nü-tzu wen-t'i ti k'ai-tuan" [The source of the woman
     problem] Fu-nü tsa-chih, VIII, October 1922, p. 10. See also
     Hu Shih, "Nü-tzu wen-t'i" [The woman problem], Fu-nü tsa-chih,
     VIII, May 1922, p. 5.

8.   [Mao] Tse-min, "Shih-chieh nü-tzu ts'an-cheng yün-tung k'ao"
     [A study of the world-wide woman suffrage movement], Fu-nü
     tsa-chih, V, December 1919, p. 12.

9.   Yü Huan-tou, "Chung-kuo nü-tzu hsin-li kai-tsao chi chin-hou
     tsai she-hui shang ying-fu ti tse-jen" [The responsibility which
     should be taken by Chinese women in the reform of their minds
     and thereafter of society], Fu-nü p'ing-lun [Woman critic],
     II, 1 November 1920, p. 3.

10. Wu-ssu shih-chi chi-k'an chieh-shao [Introduction to the
     periodicals of the May Fourth Era] (Peking: 1959), II, p. 200.

11. Chow Tse-tsung, The May Fourth Movement (Cambridge,
     Mass.: 1960), pp. 258-259.

12. Content analysis of Fu-nü p'ing-lun in Wu-ssu shih-chi chi-k'an
     chieh-shao, II, p. 215.

13. Ch'en Wen-ch'ing nü-shih, "Chung-kuo cheng-chih yü nü-tzu
     ts'an-cheng" [The Chinese government and woman suffrage],
     Fu-nü chou-pao [Women's tri-monthly], No. 40, 28 May 1924.

14. Kuo Chien-i, Chung-kuo fu-nü wen-t'i [The Chinese woman
     problem] (Shanghai: 1935), pp. 206-207; Y. C. Wang, Chinese
     Intellectuals and the West, 1872-1949 (Chapel Hill, N. C.:
     1966); Wang Ts'ang-pao, op. cit., p. 208; Chow Tse-tsung,
     op. cit., p. 258n.

15. [Huang] Lu-yin nü-shih, "Chung-kuo fu-nü yün-tung wen-t'i"
     [The problem of the Chinese woman suffrage movement],
     Min-to tsa-chih [People's tocsin], V, March 1924, p. 1.

16. Wang Hui-wu, "Wei Hsiang-sheng yün-tung ts'an-cheng ti
     chieh-mei-men chin i-yen" [A comment to our sisters in the
     Hunan suffrage movement], Fu-nü sheng [Women's voice],
     No. 7, 20 March 1922.

17. Discussion of the editorial policy of Fu-nü p'ing-lun in Wu-ssu
     shih-chi chi-k'an chieh-shao, II, p. 217.

18. Lieh-shih Hsiang Ching-yü [Martyr Hsiang Ching-yü] (Peking:
     1958), p. 1.

19. Li Li-san, "Tao Hsiang Ching-yü t'ung-chih" [Mourning Comrade
     Hsiang Ching-yü], written in Moscow in 1935 and reprinted in
     Hung-ch'i p'iao-p'iao [The red flag waves] (Peking: 1957), V,
     pp. 28-32.

20. Ibid.

21. [Hsiang] Ching-yü, "Shanghai nü-ch'üan yün-tung hui chin-hou
     ying chu-i san chien shih" [Three matters which the Shanghai
     women's rights movement should attend to from now on], Fu-nü
     chou-pao, No. 11, 31 October 1923.

Chinese Women in the Early Communist Movement

Suzette Leith

It is commonly held that the women of China and the Communist Party are ideal allies. The marriage law of 1950, state sponsorship of nurseries to free women from the home, and the prominence of Chiang Ch'ing in the Cultural Revolution are often cited as examples of the improving status of women under Communism. Correspondingly, women are given credit for much of the Communist Party's success in attaining power. As Jack Belden put it:

> In the women of China the Communists possessed, almost
> ready made, one of the greatest masses of disinherited
> human beings the world has ever seen . . . and because
> they found the key to the hearts of these women, they
> also found one of the keys to victory over Chiang Kai-
> shek. [1]

There have been no comprehensive historical studies, however, of the contribution of women to the revolutionary movement. And if we are concerned with one particularly important index of status, the wielding of political power, we find that there are indeed few women in top decision making positions in China. Those with the highest rank are invariably wives of top leaders (e.g. Chiang Ch'ing, Teng Ying-ch'ao), figureheads (Soong Ching-ling) or responsible, regardless of their original interests, primarily and often solely for women's affairs. Among lower level cadres, too, there is a disproportionately high number of men. Recent visitors to China have found that even in the most progressive communes only about a third of the leadership positions were held by women, and their jobs were generally confined to women's affairs. [2]

The predominance of men as decision makers leads us to question the depth and scope of the liberation of women in China. In an effort to untangle the relationship between Chinese women and the Communist Party, then, we turn to early party history (1921-27), on the assumption that an examination of women's participation in the Communist Revolution is a necessary background to understanding their current status in China, especially in relation to political power.

Before dealing with the Communist Party, it is helpful to look briefly at the development of the Chinese women's movement, which necessarily conditioned the ideas of Communists, both men and women, in the twenties. To do so, we go back to the late Ch'ing, when the influx of Western ideas stimulated many scholars to call for women's rights. Notions of the equality of the sexes and human rights for all persons influenced such men as K'ang Yu-wei, who personally set out to eradicate foot-binding. Others promoted such causes as female education. In the early twentieth century women themselves began to agitate. They did so, however, not as an organized force but as individuals, the most famous of whom was the revolutionary martyr Ch'iu Chin.

Political mobilization of women began in earnest following the 1911 Revolution, when the Suffrage Alliance was formed. The Alliance first tried to petition parliament for guarantees of equal political rights, and when petitioning failed, a small group of members actually stormed parliament demanding women's suffrage. The demonstration was easily dispersed and was taken seriously by few. The Alliance failed to gain substantial support, and concerned women returned to such causes as obtaining a modern education and unbinding feet.

Women once more emerged as political activists during the May Fourth Period. Girl students published journals, led patriotic demonstrations and developed local organizations with such names as "Committees of Ten to Save the Nation," "Progressive Association of Girl Students" and "Girls' Patriotic Associations." One patriotic group in Hunan sponsored a movement to boycott foreign goods and encourage the purchase of Chinese products. Other women organized more specifically feminist groups such as the Association for the Collective Advancement of Women and the Association for the Promotion of Women's Education.

By 1922 the feminists had won out over the patriots and two new organizations developed, purportedly on a national scale. The Women's Suffrage Organization, composed mainly of students and

teachers, focused its demands on women's participation in government, while the Women's Rights League demanded a constitutional
guarantee of total equality between the sexes and was concerned
with the whole spectrum of women's problems, including education,
husband-wife relations, inheritance, marriage, concubines, prostitution, slave trade, foot-binding, and labor pay. The activity of
these groups was propagandistic rather than organizational; they
published, spoke to meetings, shouted slogans in the streets. Both
groups were almost entirely comprised of urban, educated, middle
or upper-class women.

The "women's movement," then, had actually been a series of
discrete phases, from revolution to feminism to patriotism and back
to feminism. Throughout the twenties, efforts of the CCP and KMT
women's departments were largely aimed at effecting yet another
turn, away from feminism and towards general political radicalism.

CCP AND KMT WOMEN'S DEPARTMENTS

The Communist Party first took public note of women in a
1922 proclamation demanding women's rights and announcing the
organization of a special bureau to incorporate women into the
party. The 1922 declaration stated that

In the third conference of the Third International it
was decided that in all countries a special committee
should be established in the Communist Party to lead
women, a women's department be elected, and a special column for women be set up in the party newspaper. The CCP decided to adopt this plan as soon
as it can.[3]

Ch'en Kung-po, a party member at the time, felt that the creation
of a women's department was simply a verbal concession to the International. "Apparently the party had not yet gotten around to organizing women," he wrote. "However, in conformity with the instructions of the Third International . . . the party decided to 'adopt
its plan as soon as it can.'"[4] Ch'en is probably correct in his assessment that the party virtually ignored women during its first year
and a half of organized existence. The defect was undoubtedly due
in large part to the lack of female participation in early Communist
councils, for the women who were to emerge as most vigorous in

the coming years were not yet available: Teng Ying-ch'ao was involved in women's rights work; Ts'ai Ch'ang and Hsiang Ching-yü
were in France; and Yang Chih-hua was apparently not yet politically
active. It is difficult to accept Ch'en's theory that the bureau was
set up solely in response to International orders, however. Surely
some credit is due Hsiang Ching-yü, who at the 1922 conference
was appointed both a Central Committee member and head of the
new women's bureau.

Hsiang was later to emerge as the leading Communist woman
of the period. She had become involved in patriotic activities as a
student in Hunan, in 1918 joining the New Students' Society, organized by Mao Tse-tung and Ts'ai Ho-sheng, whom she later married.
She then traveled to France as a worker-student and helped organize
a branch of the CCP there. Hsiang's views undoubtedly influenced
the direction women's work was to take, and it is therefore instructive to look at some of her earliest comments on the women's movement as it existed in 1922.

Hsiang was highly critical of most educated Chinese women.
She classified them as three types: family reformers, business
women, and "romantics." The former, she claimed, were mainly
Western-educated women and/or wives of rich educators or politicians. Hsiang considered their goal of a Western-type small family
too individualistic and irrelevant to the needs of the broad masses
of women. Business women deserved some credit, Hsiang felt, for
their role in changing the life style of Chinese women, i.e., in
breaking out of the home and participating in community life. In
their efforts to succeed in business, however, they often became
conservative in their thinking, too specialized and mechanical.
Hsiang's sharpest criticisms were for the "romantics," young girls
who espoused free love and placed highest emphasis on individual
liberty and happiness. Hsiang labled these girls dangerous and un-
disciplined. [5]

She was also critical of contemporary women's movements.
Again, she made three divisions: working women's groups, suffragettes, and Christian groups such as the YWCA. Passing off
the YWCA as historically important but too tied to the West to be
relevant in the 1920's, she concentrated her attack on the suffrage
groups. Her criticisms were many: such groups ignored the
masses and the idea of universal participation in politics; they were
poor organizers, feeling that "all they had to do was make a few

phone calls or write a few letters and that would be a women's
movement." Their only goal was to become legislators, that is,
to participate in the corrupt politics of the time, and they completely forgot that China was in the midst of a revolution! In contrast, much praise was given to the working women's movement, a
new development which, being separate from the "mainstream" of
women's activism, was virtually ignored by most observers, male
and female alike. Hsiang considered the labor organizations to be
the only part of the women's movement with a potential for organization and struggle, the only one whose members were willing to
make sacrifices. Highly impressed with the participation of women
in strikes, she published a detailed chart of strike activities in
1922, claiming that in that one year more than 30,000 women were
active in strikes in more than sixty factories, mostly in Shanghai.[6]
Her interest in the women's labor movement carried over into another article in which she urged women to concentrate on three
things: political questions, propaganda, and working women. Most
feminist groups paid no attention to lower class women, she claimed;
indeed, they often excluded them from their meetings.[7]

These remarks suggest the direction in which Hsiang wanted to
take the women's movement, and in the years to come she indeed
concentrated most of her energies in organizing workers and planning
strikes. Hsiang had no sympathy for a bourgeois women's movement
apart from the Communist revolution, and this sentiment possibly
influenced the CCP policy of organizing its own women rather than
seeking a united front with, say, the Women's Rights League. Going
a step farther, Hsiang seemed to have been more interested in incorporating women into the party's labor movement than in developing a separate women's bureau. As the years went by, her name
is associated less with specifically feminist organizations and more
with strikes, usually in silk or cotton factories.

In the mid-twenties as the CCP worked through the KMT in
their first united front, women's activities were incorporated into
the KMT women's department under Ho Hsiang-ning in Canton.
Raised in Hong Kong, Ho in 1905 had become the first woman to
join Sun Yat-sen's T'ung-meng Hui. She was married to Liao
Chung-k'ai, a top KMT leader, and had recruited women for the
1911 Revolution. Her main activity as KMT women's director
appears to have been the creation of various groups in the Canton
area, including an organization of female telephone workers, a
"liberation" society, and the All-Kwangtung Women's Alliance,

designed to organize and educate women of the masses and to awaken them politically. Helen Snow indicates that another function of Ho's organization was to act as a lobbying group for women's rights within the nationalist government, then based in Canton.[8] Working under Ho in Canton were two Communist women, Ts'ai Ch'ang (Hsiang Ching-yü's sister-in-law), who took over as head of the CCP department in 1924 or 1925, and Teng Ying-ch'ao, who moved from the women's rights sphere into Communist work in 1924 and a year later married Chou En-lai. Hsiang Ching-yü remained primarily in Shanghai, organizing many general women's groups but now free to concentrate on labor. By 1927 it is estimated that more than a million and a half women in ten provinces were incorporated into women's groups under Ho and the KMT, 300,000 of these also being members of Communist organizations.[9]

In Communist women's history, a most revered event is the first celebration of March 8, International Women's Day, in 1924. Rallies were sponsored by the CCP throughout China, the most prominent one being organized in Canton by Ho's All-Kwangtung Alliance. Several hundred women, a large proportion of them students, participated in the demonstration. Yang Chih-hua, then a student at Shanghai University and perhaps in Canton for the celebration, describes the event: the women met in a public park, paraded, made speeches, and shouted various slogans. Although the official slogans were to be "Liberate China from being a Semi-Colony" and "Oppose the Oppression of Women by Capitalists," the students also spontaneously shouted slogans dealing with more exclusively feminist concerns such as polygamy and equal education. Yang sees the demonstration as a turning point; afterwards, "the working women's movement moved to a new stage, women's organizations springing up throughout the country and beginning to play a big part in the anti-imperialist, anti-feudal movement."[10]

Celebrations were held in other cities, too, but they were in most cases organized underground and could not compare in scope with Canton's. An example is the Tientsin demonstration, described by Teng Ying-ch'ao. The celebration was organized by the CCP and its youth organization, Teng reports, and, as neither could operate openly in Tientsin, obstacles were almost insurmountable. No propaganda tools were available, all newspapers being controlled by the government, nor could meeting places be found. Moreover, the women of the area were unorganized and very unaware. Seventy to eighty women, all contacted by word of mouth, eventually participated--a number significant for Tientsin but far smaller than the Canton turnout. For these women, Teng asserts, the larger Canton celebration provided great encouragement.[11]

Throughout the twenties, March 8 continued to be a focal point for mobilizing women. Yang Chih-hua reports, for example, that in 1925 women in Peking celebrated March 8 by surrounding warlord Tuan Ch'i-jui's residence and shouting such slogans as "Down with Imperialism!" "Down with Warlord Government!" and "Women of the World Unite!" By 1926, the movement had grown to such proportions that 10,000 gathered together in Canton, 800 in Hunan.[12]

The March 8 celebrations undoubtedly gave great symbolic encouragement to the women of China. Furthermore, as the first mass women's demonstration sponsored by the CCP-KMT, they mark the beginning of a new stage in the Chinese women's movement, one in which women's rights were to become increasingly identified with revolutionary political movements. More and more women activists were moving towards the position held by Hsiang Ching-yü in 1922: feminist rebellion was meaningless without general political revolution.

Teng's and Yang's articles on the March 8 demonstrations are written in an enthusiastic vein and leave one with the feeling that 1924-1925 were exciting years in the movement. Other articles, many by Ts'ai Ch'ang, describe the dogged efforts of Hsiang Ching-yü, going from door to door to encourage women's attendance at meetings and then returning after each meeting to solicit comments. An effort was certainly being made. Yet just how successful were Ho and Hsiang's women's bureaus in incorporating women into the revolutionary movement? Judging from a 1926 CCP report, problems were immense.

A document entitled "Resolutions on the Women's Movement," passed by the Central Committee in Shanghai in 1926, points out glaring weaknesses: The women's movement had failed to penetrate the masses, placed too great an emphasis on bureaucratic activity, neglected the party's development (especially in Kwangtung and Peking), and produced publications which were at best monotonous. To counteract these deficiencies, the resolution listed seven areas for future action:

1. Emphasis on the masses. In the past, the resolution stated, women had been content to work merely to control organi-

zations such as the KMT women's department, women's associations, or various federations of women. They had forgotten the masses.

2. A united front with women of all classes. In Kwangtung, especially, class cliquishness had been excessive.

3. Work with female laborers.

4. Work with peasant women.

5. Popularization of publications.

6. Reform of local women's departments and committees on the women's movement.

7. Expansion of party membership and training of personnel for the women's movement.

The resolution pointed out that although membership of women was increasing, most party members were still men, and female membership was almost entirely confined to Shanghai and Hunan. Kwangtung, Hupeh, and Peking were listed as areas of especially poor recruitment. "This indeed is a very bad situation," the resolution concluded. "The training of personnel for the women's movement (especially female labor and peasant women) is the most important immediate task of the party at all levels." The party was instructed to sponsor training classes and discussions and to "gather and regularly train responsible and promising women comrades."[13]

It would be interesting to know who wrote the resolution. There are strong suggestions of Hsiang Ching-yü's influence: the emphasis on uniting with the masses and concentrating on the female laborers and peasant women, and the many expressions of dissatisfaction with the work done in Kwangtung, perhaps a veiled criticism of working through the KMT department, which concentrated on organizing groups rather than on mass action. Hsiang, however, was in the Soviet Union during most of 1926, and we cannot attribute authorship to her. Her sister-in-law and successor as chairman of the CCP women's department, Ts'ai Ch'ang, appears to have a philosophy similar to Hsiang's. She was less prominent and her views are less easily traced. Her work, however, indicates strong interest in the labor movement and, as a Central Committee member, she could have been influential in drafting the document.

What is most important is the new direction the movement was to take. The references to female worker and peasant movements are in sharp contrast to previous statements which separated the women's movement from other mass movements, both in theory and

in organization. The Central Committee was finally coming around
to Hsiang's vision of a women's movement incorporated in other
mass movements.

THE STUDENT MOVEMENT

Turning, then, to the various mass organizations, we look
first at the students, for educated youths were the backbone of the
early Communist Party. The founders of the party all were intel-
lectuals--students, teachers, writers--and until about 1925, most
party recruits were middle school or college students.[14] The
early Communist movement's four most prominent women, Hsiang
Ching-yü, Ts'ai Ch'ang, Teng Ying-ch'ao and Yang Chih-hua, all
received their first taste of politics as student activists. Given
significant student participation in May Fourth demonstrations,
women's rights activities and March 8 rallies, the student movement seemed a natural recruiting ground for Communist women's
organizations and especially for future female leaders.

Our findings on the student movement are mainly speculative.
Little has been written on youth organization in the 1921-27 period,
nor could I find statistics for female participation at any one time.
It is not even certain whether party policy encouraged mixed or
sex-separated youth cells. There are indications, however, that
female activism in the movement was not what the party women
would have hoped. One such suggestion is found in a Women of
China article dealing with women's organizations in Canton. The
article noted that one way of recruiting women was through the organization of girls' cells of the New Student Society, Canton's primary Communist youth group. It was a man, however, who organized the cells, and it was reported that "as girls' experience was
small, the cells and other activities were mainly led by men."[15]
It is no doubt significant that even in Canton, the center for KMT
women's activities and an area often frequented by CCP women,
there was a dearth of initiative among girl students.

Perhaps the primary reason for this male-domination of girl
student groups was simply the small number of girls enrolled in
higher education. In 1922 it is estimated that only 6.32% of the
students in non-missionary schools were girls; by 1931 the figure
of 11.75% is given for girls in colleges and universities.[16] As a
measure of potential participation in the student movement, then,

the figures would indicate a very low availability of girls. Girls who did participate, moreover, were in such a minority that few could be expected to hold significant power in the organizations and thereby receive training for party leadership.

A second question concerns just how potentially active these girl students were. Despite Helen Snow's assertion that girls were more oppressed and therefore more radical than men,[17] we cannot assume that girls were more likely to join the CCP youth groups than were their male classmates. First, there was the competing cause of women's rights. To the middle or upper-class girl, sexist oppression would seem far more real than capitalist. Her struggle had been with male-dominated educational institutions and families, not with landlords or managers, and radical politics was for her only one among many competing concerns such as women's suffrage, birth control, and the big family system. Moreover, the percentage of middle school or college girls coming from peasant or worker backgrounds and therefore having some sympathy for the economically oppressed was no doubt lower than that of men. Stories of the early life of Mao Tse-tung indicate how very difficult it was for a peasant youth to obtain an education; if he had been a girl, we would hypothesize his chances to have been nil. Thus the socially-inclined educated woman, with her bourgeois background, would probably identify much more closely with feminist groups than with the Communists, who argued that only by liberating the masses could women be liberated. This is the picture painted by Hsiang Ching-yü, who reported, as mentioned above, that most educated women crusaded for westernized families, participation in business or individual liberty, thus leaving little time to agitate for the revolution. Indeed, some of the girl students' demands--for example, that educated men should discard their old-style wives and marry for love-- were definitely counterproductive to cooperation between intellectual women and the wives of peasants and workers.

Hsiang's distrust of educated women no doubt influenced her recruiting methods. Especially concerned with the plight of women workers and convinced of their revolutionary potential, Hsiang concentrated on the factories, perhaps neglecting the recruitment of college girls. And because of Hsiang Ching-yü's position as a Central Committee member and her many personal connections with influential Communists (for example, marriage to Ts'ai Ho-sheng, work in France with Li Li-san and Chou En-lai), her influence on the party should not be underrated.

THE LABOR MOVEMENT

It was not the student but the working woman whom Hsiang Ching-yü sought to incorporate into the movement. Not only did she herself have great respect for the woman laborers; the party, also, was basing its general strategy on labor. And women made up a significant proportion of the labor force; in Shanghai, they comprised a majority of the proletariat.

The great numbers of women workers can be explained by the prevalence of light industry in China, the willingness of women to work for lower wages than men, and the large number of industries dealing with traditional "women's work" such as spinning and weaving. Women were especially numerous in the silk, cotton and tobacco industries. Jean Chesneaux gives the following figures for Shanghai in 1923-24: in the Chinese-owned silk factories, 74.5% of all workers were women, 15.5% were girls under 12; in the foreign factories, the figures were correspondingly 55.5% and 34.9%. Chinese-managed cotton factories employed 65.8% women and 6.4% girls; foreign factories, 65.9% and 5.2%. In the Chinese tobacco factories, 69% of all workers were women; in the foreign factories, 62.7%.[18] The percentage of women was lower in other parts of the country. Fang Fu-an reports that in 1928, 56% of all Shanghai workers were women (9.2% were children), only 6% in Tientsin but 44% in Hangchow and 51% in Hankow.[19] Chesneaux documents the center of action in the labor movement as follows: 1920-22, Canton; 1922-23, Wuhan; 1924-25, Shanghai; 1926-27, Wuhan; 1927, Shanghai.[20] Through most of the period, the center of action was in areas of high female concentration.

The Communists undoubtedly saw the female labor force as a fertile recruiting ground not only because of the numbers of women workers but also because of the oppression they suffered. They worked the same 12-hour days as did men but received much less pay--sometimes only half as much as men were given for the same jobs. Some women received no wages at all. Especially in the cotton industry, girls as young as 13 were often hired through a system by which families contracted to turn over all their daughter's wages for three to five years to a recruiter, who would in turn guarantee a job, food, clothing and shelter for the girl. "Shelter" usually meant a boarding house with 10 to 15 girls to a room, many sleeping on the floor and all made to do housework, in addition to their twelve hours a day in the mills.[21]

Yet these same conditions, so necessary to provoking the dissatisfaction that leads to political agitation, were also an obstacle
to organization. Shut up in their boarding houses and kept under
close surveillance, many girls were not even allowed to write home,
much less consort with "outside agitators." Their wages were so
low (or, in the case of the recruited cotton workers, nonexistent),
that it was difficult for their unions to maintain strike funds. Recruited straight from the countryside, most spoke only local dialects
and could barely communicate with each other, much less with union
organizers. Going on strike was risky business, too, with the countryside full of the unemployed, ready and willing to break a strike.
And as women were the most unskilled of the workers, they were
the easiest to replace.

The abstract female proletarian certainly had cause to rebel.
But the shy young girl from the country, probably still with bound
feet and afraid of looking strange men in the eye . . . how militant
a striker could she become? Looking at specific strike activity, we
cannot help but be impressed--and perhaps surprised--by the activism of the female workers.

Turning to specific strike activity, we find in the early Chinese
labor movement two peaks of action, the first in 1922 and the second
beginning with the May 30 Movement in 1925 and continuing into 1926.
Between the two was a period of retrenchment and underground activity, and afterwards a total breakdown in the labor movement, resulting from Chiang Kai-shek's brutal "white terror" of 1927.

During the first high tide of 1922, Helen Snow reports that
there were all together more than 100 strikes, in many of which
women participated. [22] Neither she nor Chesneaux mentions Hsiang's
figures of 30,000 women striking in more than sixty factories, yet
both speak of the largest of those walkouts, a strike of 20,000
women workers in twenty-four (forty-four, according to Hsiang) silk
filatures in August of 1922. Organized by the Women Worker Society for the Promotion of Virtue ("a kind of friendly society"), [23] the
strikers demanded a ten-hour day and a five-cents increase in wages.
Despite their numerical strength, the women returned to work as
soon as police arrested five of their leaders. The strike was a
failure, yet it impressed many by the sheer numbers of women involved. Nor was it the only women's strike. Hsiang Ching-yü lists
seventeen others, varying in size from seventy to 3000 workers participating. Of these, half were in cotton mills, the other half in

cigarette, silk, and lace factories, and the usual demand was for increased wages. According to Hsiang's charts, about half of the strikes were successful, the others failing for such reasons as lack of unity among strikers, arrest of leaders, or "pressures of livelihood" keeping the workers from holding out. [24] Despite the many failures, it is easy to see how Hsiang was impressed by the militancy of the female workers.

It is doubtful though possible that Hsiang herself was involved in this early strike activity. Through the Secretariat of Chinese Labor, radicals were active throughout 1922 in the organization of unions and encouragement of strikes. I could find no record, however, of Communist women carrying out such agitation. In the women's movement, at least, it was in all probability the militancy of the masses which influenced leadership policy rather than the other way around.

Encouraged by the activities of 1922, both Hsiang and Ts'ai Ch'ang plunged into the labor movement. Ts'ai is said to have organized women workers in Shanghai, Canton, and Hong Kong and in 1925 to have herself worked for a time in a cotton mill. Hsiang is given credit for leading two strikes in 1924, one in a Shanghai silk filature in which 12,000 women struck and another in the Nanyang Tobacco Plant. Both strikes failed, officially "because of lack of working class leadership." Another obstacle was certainly the general deflation of the labor movement and the necessity of organizing secretly.

By mid-1925, however, the total outlook had changed, and workers were again rising in the most spectacular labor/anti-imperialist movement so far, May Thirtieth. Stimulated by the killing of a striking worker in early May, a large demonstration was held in Shanghai on May 30, organized by the cotton workman Sun Lianghui. On that date five more demonstrators were killed by the police. The Communists were quick to take advantage of the situation and on May 31 organized the Shanghai General Labor Union, headed by Li Li-san. The Union agitated continuously during 1925, and sympathy strikes were held throughout China. Yang Chih-hua is considered to have been a leader in the activity;[25] Hsiang and Ts'ai Ch'ang also participated, although not in coordinating roles.

The May 30 movement was a stunning triumph for labor and for the CCP workers' movement, yet it was perhaps a personal

defeat for Hsiang Ching-yü, for her silk workers stayed on the job.
According to Chesneaux, local proprietors had been concerned with
the 1924 strikes and had hired a social worker, Mrs. Mu Chih-yang,
to curb the excesses of the previous year and keep conditions smooth
in the silk-reeling factories. [26] This action in itself suggests how
far the women workers' movement had come and the threat factory
owners were beginning to feel.

Mrs. Mu was a leader in the Federation of Labor Organizations,
a moderate group which was on good terms with employers and sought
to moderate the May 30 uprisings with such slogans as "Let us ask
for bread only and leave politics alone."[27] In the silk factories she
organized a "friendly society for women's emancipation" as an alternative to the more radical groups the Communist women were trying
to organize. She was somewhat successful in containing the silk
workers in 1924 and again in 1925. But a year later, thousands
struck, one of their complaints being dissatisfaction with their labor
union (presumably Mrs. Mu's group), which they accused of being in
conspiracy with factory owners.

Communist emphasis on workers continued throughout 1926 and
early 1927, the two most prominent women organizers being Ts'ai
Ch'ang and the textile worker Liu Chien-hsien, who in early 1927
succeeded in organizing the Shanghai silk workers to strike in welcome of the Northern Expedition. Women such as Liu, Hsieh Yun-
hong of Taiwan and Ch'en Hu-ch'ing of Canton, classic proletarians
who had worked in the factory even as children, were developing
into enthusiastic organizers. If the movement had continued to grow,
it probably could have been a good recruiting ground for female cadres. But just as factory women were becoming aware and gaining
respectability in labor organizations, the movement collapsed. The
success of the Northern Expedition was directly followed by Chiang
Kai shek's "white terror" in which thousands of workers were
killed--many women simply for having bobbed hair. Chiang's slaugh-
ter of women workers was a final confirmation that their organizers
had been--if not totally successful--at least very threatening.

The labor movement had been significant for the twenties. But
in the thirties and forties the party discarded its urban strategy and
moved to the villages. Action centered on the peasants and the Red
Army, and we therefore turn to the roots for that work laid among
women prior to 1927.

THE PEASANT MOVEMENT

Although outside the mainstream of party concern, efforts to organize peasants began in the early twenties. The most notable of these attempts was that of P'eng P'ai, a landlord's son, who managed to set up a prospering peasant organization in his native Hailufeng (the area around Haifeng and Lufeng), Kwangtung. Women were involved from the beginning. They were organized into a separate women's union, according to Hailufeng women's leader Ts'ai Teng-li, and often made up a quarter of the peasant organization's total membership. The women's union's two primary tasks were to develop a communications network throughout Hailunfeng and to counsel women on their marriage problems--the first task a significant contribution to the general peasant movement; the second, often a source of friction within the movement. According to Ts'ai, "Some men hated the organization because it defended the rights of women and took care of the divorce problem"[28] Building a strong women's union was from this angle actually counterproductive to achieving the general movement's goal of peasant unity.

The divorce problem was to crop up again in the peasant organizations formed in Hunan and Shenyang in 1926. By this time, the party had begun to take note of the peasants and to encourage students to go into the countryside and organize. There was also official sanction of a woman peasant movement parallel to the women workers movement. Again, unions found their members to be especially concerned with divorce, and again, the issue made for trouble within the peasants' union. As one young organizer related to Anna Louise Strong, if the women's association did not grant a divorce, the wife would be dissatisfied and the organization would lose support; if it did, there would be problems with the overall peasants' union. "It is hard for a peasant to get a wife," she added, "and he's often paid much for his present unwilling one."[29]

At the same time as girls from Changsha were penetrating the Hunan countryside, others were performing a similar function behind the lines of the Northern Expedition army. The KMT-CCP alliance, despite growing tensions, was kept alive for the Expedition. It is estimated that three to four hundred young girls were involved, their task being to propagandize among women in the newly liberated areas. Women's leader Ts'ai Ch'ang was a member of the Northern Expedition force. She, however, was assigned to the general propaganda department--the only women permitted to

propagandize among the soldiers--and probably had little contact
with the girls who were organizing peasant women. Many of these
girls had been trained at the Women's Training School, set up in
1926 by Soong Ching-ling in Hankow.   Soong had originally conceived
of the school solely as an institute to train propagandists. As the
best-known women's organization in the area, however, it became
involved in a multitude of other women's issues, many of which indicate further difficulties besetting the women's movement. One
problem was community disapproval of the school and of some of
its enthusiastic but politically naive students, who would frequently
descend on the streets of Hankow, cutting the hair of every woman
in sight. A more serious problem was money. Once they heard
of the school, runaway slave girls flocked to Hankow in search of
care and shelter. ·As its director pointed out to Anna Louise Strong,
the school sincerely wanted to help these girls, but it hesitated to
tax local factory women--its only source of revenue--in order to do
so. [30] Women simply didn't control enough wealth to successfully
support their movement.

It is uncertain how successful the girl propagandists were.
Obstacles, we know, were many. In Honan, for example, the girls
had to be removed because the sight of short-haired girls traveling
with men caused too much of a scandal in conservative districts.
Rumors of "common wives" were rampant, and villagers were too
shocked to be receptive to Nationalist propaganda.

Another obstacle was the unwillingness, particularly among
village women, to talk to strangers. P'eng P'ai supposedly spent
months in the Hailufeng villages, making no headway at all because
most of the area's adult males were overseas making money, leaving only taciturn women. [31] We would assume, then, that female
organizers were needed. Yet as the case of the Northern Expedition propaganda teams showed, the potential scandal of young girls
(especially with such short hair and such big feet) traveling in the
company of men who were not their husbands, was enough to turn
many villagers against whatever doctrine they might be propounding.

We find, then, two main problems confronting the peasant
women's movement. Upon entering a village, organizers had first
to overcome the conservatism of the women--their fear of strangers
combined with their disapproval of "liberated" girls--if they were
just to set up a women's union. It is only after this obstacle was
overcome and women's organizations formed that the second problem,

conflict between males and females within the overall peasant movement, developed. The enthusiasm with which peasant women sought
out divorces indicates that they, like the girl students, perceived
themselves as primarily sexually rather than economically oppressed,
in struggle not with the landlord but with the male. This perception
was certainly justified, for even the most politically radical of fathers
generally retained his prerogatives as head of the household and decision maker for his women. Two prominent examples are the stories
of future Communist leaders K'ang K'e-ch'ing and Li Chien-chen.
K'ang's foster father was an ardent Communist who encouraged his
daughter to organize youth bands within the immediate area. Yet
upon reaching marriageable age, K'ang discovered that even a Communist father could not conceive of his daughter's breaking an arranged marriage contract. He answered her protests by locking her
up, and she was not to escape until the Nationalist army came through.
Li, similarly, was brought up in a Communist family, yet at age 17
she was forced to marry the family's son, more than ten years her
senior. Her liberation came in 1931 when her politically radical yet
personally oppressive husband was killed.

Such stories point out the special nature of women's problems
and the consequent need for organizing semi-independent women's
unions. They also indicate the potential tensions arising between
the sexes among politically aroused peasants, tensions which could
blow a peasants' union apart.

Organization of peasant women was particularly difficult in the
twenties. The general peasant movement was just beginning, with
little party support and no Soviet advisors to point the way. Nor
was there much apparent support from the party's female leaders.
Even those conscious of the need to penetrate the masses in practice defined those masses as workers rather than the peasant wives,
daughters, and, in the South, farm laborers. Only at the Hankow
Training Center, it seems, were there women seriously concerned
with such thorny issues as the divorce problem.

CONCLUSION

In its short history the Chinese women's movement had gone
through alternating phases of feminist separatism and integration into
general radical movements. May 4 women had campaigned for patriotic causes; in 1922, they swung back towards women's rights. But

as the decade progressed, we see another turn, towards concentration on economic rather than feminist issues.   Within the CCP, it
was a two-step progression.

Stage 1 was the decision to forego alliance with women's rights
groups and instead build a women's movement within the party.   An
example of and at the same time an influence on this development
was the scorn shown by Central Committee member Hsiang Ching-
yü towards the activities of bourgeois women's rights groups.   Some
Communist leaders, to be sure, got their start in the feminist movement.   Teng Ying-ch'ao apparently worked actively in women's rights
groups in Peking and Tientsin until her entry into the Socialist Youth
in 1924, and even Hsiang appears to have participated in a Shanghai
feminist group around 1922.   I could find no evidence, however, of
plans to use such groups as an arm of the party.

Nor were the Communists sympathetic to women's demands for
the right to vote and for participation in the existing government.
As Hsiang pointed out, with government so corrupt, what was there
to participate in?   The KMT, like the CCP, set up its own women's
department, in which many Communist women participated during the
united front.   Again, the decision not to rely on women's rights
groups is no doubt related to the background of the leaders.   Ho
Hsiang-ning, like Hsiang Ching-yü, grew up politically within her
party and was married to one of its most active leaders.   Her loyalty, like Hsiang's was to the party rather than to her sex.

Within the formal party structure, however, women were still
to be organized separately.   In 1922 Hsiang Ching-yü's proposal that
women be directly incorporated into the general labor movement was
overruled.   Instead, women were confined to a special department
which Hsiang, ironically, was chosen to head.   Many factors could
account for this decision.   One is the example and direction of the
Soviet Union which, according to Ch'en Kung-po, simply informed
the CCP that it was to set up a women's movement.   Women's rights
groups had set an example (incorrectly, Hsiang would argue) of setting women apart as a separate force dealing with special problems.
Probably most important was tradition: women had participated in
the 1911 revolution--in separate women's battalions; they had led
strikes and demonstrations during the May 4 Movement--again,
through separate organizations.   The question was not one of pro-
priety but of efficiency: men and women, it was assumed, could
simply work better separately.   Still in its earliest "identity crisis"

stage, the party had given little thought to the question of women
cadres. It was simply assumed that men worked with men and
women worked with women.

Around 1926, however, party emphasis changed from the
women's department to incorporation of women into overall mass
movements, the second stage in the anti-feminist progression.
Again, the Soviet example was perhaps significant, Lenin having
declared that feminism, or the conversion of class struggle into
sex struggle, was counter-revolutionary. [32]   Tensions in the CCP-
KMT alliance and the new Communist concentration on mass movements were important, as were the actions of such leaders as
Hsiang, Ts'ai Ch'ang, and Yang Chih-hua, all class rather than
sex-oriented.

The change might be seen as important only in theory.   Women
were still organized into separate branches within peasant unions.
In the labor movement, organization was based on the factory, and
women tended to be clustered in certain light industries such as
cotton and silk.   Only the labels had changed, "women who worked"
becoming "workers who happened to be women."   Yet there were
implications for the relationship between women and political power.
From a feminist point of view, the shift was perhaps a dangerous
one, for women would no longer be able to rise within their own
power structure and, once on top, command respect within the party
as heads of their own mass base.   For individual women leaders,
on the other hand, the change meant less danger of their being
shunted off into a low priority women's department by their male
competitors for power.

Also relevant to the power issue are the differences first made
apparent in the twenties between the two mass movements women
were to participate in, peasant and labor.   From the party's standpoint, the female labor movement had many advantages over the
woman peasant movement.   The women workers were, first, easier
to organize.   They lived apart from their families and were therefore
somewhat independent of them.   Many were unmarried and thus not
yet dominated by husbands.   And as participants in the capitalist
system it was possible for women workers to see themselves as
oppressed by that system and therefore be more favorably inclined
to movements directed at its destruction, in contrast to both students
and peasant women, who perceived their oppression as sexist.

Moreover, women as workers were the more compatible with overall Communist strategy. The concerns of women workers were precisely those of men workers: more pay, better conditions, freedom to organize. They could therefore work together quite harmoniously. The peasant women, on the other hand, had a special concern: marriage and divorce. Both in the twenties and afterwards, it appeared that whenever peasant women became active, their issue was divorce. Because of these specialized concerns, women's organizations in villages would tend to be more separatist. Even the young, awakened peasant girls who believed in general liberation preceding women's liberation had their own personal problems with fathers and husbands who, however radical politically, still insisted on arranged marriage. Sexism and conservatism similarly hampered the work of girls in the army. Even when liberated from family domination, they could not escape the popular sex stereotypes of the countryside. Peasant beliefs about group marriage and consequent scorn for all revolutionary propaganda led to the girl propagandists being dropped in Honan, and perhaps in other areas as well. The concerns of women's peasant unions and the attitudes regarding girl organizers in the rural areas thus made for a situation in which women's activities were often dysfunctional to the overall rural movement and therefore received less male support than did the female labor movement.

The best road to incorporation within the Communist movement was thus labor. Yet is has been pointed out that the key to political control in China was not labor but the students and peasants.[33] Even within the party, student and peasant organizers were to emerge as the most powerful: Li Li-san was to lose out to Mao Tse-tung. Here was an implication for woman leadership. Women had a power base, yet their base was not where the party needed it. Women students could be lured by women's rights organization; women peasants were preoccupied with divorce. It was the women workers who had the potential for becoming ardent Communists. Yet workers were but a minimal part of the general Communist thrust.

And even in a time when labor was important, few women leaders emerged. Martin Wilbur's listing of over 100 top party leaders in 1928, for example, names only four women--Hsiang Ching-yü, Ts'ai Ch'ang, Teng Ying-ch'ao, and Yang Chih-hua.[34] From other sources I could find only about twenty names of women influential in the Communist movement at the time. Two of these, Soong Ching-ling and Ho Hsiang-ning, were not even Communists but are included because of their presence on the left-fringe of the KMT and their participation in the Communist government after 1949. Other women among the twenty would be considered martyrs or heroines rather than possessors of political power. Part of this trend is due to the Communist historiographical tendency to praise "working heroes" rather than leaders. But at the same time there were apparently few power-holders who could have been lauded if party historians had chosen to do so.

There appear to be two main reasons for this lack of power. First is the high percentage of the educated in top roles. Robert North has pointed out how even in the CCP, proletarians enjoyed only limited access to the elite. [35] As mentioned above, the politically aware girl students had many competing areas of activism and probably saw themselves as sexually rather than economically oppressed. More important was the sheer preponderance of men in the educated elite. The second reason is the tendency of CCP leaders, who were almost all men, to confine party women to the women's movement. There were exceptions, such as Ts'ai Ch'ang's role in propagandizing in the army. Still, the case of Hsiang Ching-yü is instructive. Her early support for the labor movement rather than a separate women's movement would indicate a desire to play a leading role in that movement. Instead, she was made chief of women. In the long run, the development of a forceful women's department or women's unions could perhaps have propelled Communist women into positions of general party leadership. In the twenties, however, the women's department was given such low priority that power in it meant little. De-emphasis on the women's department in 1926-27 perhaps meant short-run power gains for various women cadres, yet the trend was a brief one, as the party was soon to concentrate almost exclusively on the countryside, where, again, the special concerns of peasant women once more fostered separatism. Jumping ahead three decades, we note the case of K'ang K'e-ch'ing. K'ang's interest was the military, she told Helen Snow in Yenan, not women's problems or activities, and she had decided not to have children, for they interfered with her work. Yet her first post-1949 assignment dealt exclusively with children, and her work was destined to be not in the PLA but in the All-China Federation of Women.

From the standpoint of 1927, then, the potential for female leadership was extremely low. There continued to be few educated women, and those who did enter the party were given responsibility

primarily within the women's movement--a movement which, given
the coming concentration on the peasantry and women peasants' insistence on marriage and divorce rights, was perhaps a hindrance
to the general goal of peasant unity and to the overall Communist
movement.

Our study of the twenties has pointed out the multitude of problems women had in attaining power, even within the progressive Communist movement.   The problems of women students and peasants,
in contrast somewhat with the workers, put into focus the pressing
need for a feminist movement.   Although all Chinese women were
sexually oppressed, the workers had attained a degree of self-suf-
ficiency.   Less dependent on fathers and husbands, they could more
fully participate in class movements.   The resulting view is a twist
of Hsiang Ching-yü's doctrine of the twenties.   Hsiang's view was
that only after there was political revolution could women be liberated.   Yet within that political revolution, it was only after being
liberated from psychic and economic dependence on husbands and
fathers that Communist women could hope to truly share in political power.

NOTES

1. Jack Belden quoted in William Hinton, <u>Fanshen</u> (N.Y.: Vintage Books, 1966), p. 396.

2. Committee of Concerned Asian Scholars, <u>China! Inside the People's Republic</u> (N.Y.: Bantam Books, 1972), p. 275.

3. Ch'en Kung-po, <u>The Communist Movement in China</u> (N.Y.: Columbia University Press, 1960), p. 28.

4. <u>Ibid.</u>, p. 38.

5. Hsiang Ching-yü, "Chung-kuo chih-shih fu-nü ti san-p'ai" [Three Groups of Educated Women], originally published in <u>Fu-nü chou-pao</u> [Women's Magazine] (n.d.), reprinted in <u>Fu-nü nien-chien</u> [Women's Yearbook] (Hsin-wen hua-shu she, 1924), pp. 30-35.

6. Hsiang Ching-yü, "Chung-kuo tsui-chin fu-nü yun-tung" [The Contemporary Women's Movement in China], originally published in <u>Ch'ien-feng</u> [Pioneer] (n.d.), reprinted in <u>Fu-nü nien-chien</u>, <u>op. cit.</u>, pp. 77-87.

7. Hsiang Ching-yü, "Shanghai nü-ch'üan yun-tung chin-hou ying chu-ti san chien-shih" [Three Things the Shanghai Women's Rights Movement Should Concentrate On], originally published in <u>Fu-nü chou-pao</u>, reprinted in <u>Fu-nü nien-chien</u>, <u>op. cit.</u>, pp. 104-107.

8. Helen Foster Snow, <u>Women in Modern China</u> (The Hague: Mouton & Co., 1967), p. 107.

9. <u>Ibid.</u>

10. Yang Chih-hua, "Pu neng wang-chi ti jih-tzu" [Days I Can't Forget] in <u>Chung-kuo fu-nü</u> [Women of China], March 1956, p. 7.

11. Teng Ying-ch'ao, "San-shih nien ch'ien ti-i-tz'u san-ba
     chieh" [Thirty Years Ago: The First March 8], Chung-kuo
     fu-nü, March 1956, p. 6.

12. Yang Chih-hua, op. cit.

13. "Resolution on the Women's Movement," in C. Martin Wilbur
     and Julie How, Documents on Communism, Nationalism and
     Soviet Advisors in China 1918-1927 (N.Y.: Columbia Univer-
     sity Press, 1956), p. 120.

14. C. Martin Wilbur, "The Influence of the Past: How the Early
     Years Helped to Shape the Future of the Chinese Communist
     Party," in John Wilson Lewis, ed., Party Leadership and Rev-
     olutionary Power in China (Cambridge: Cambridge University
     Press, 1970), p. 37.

15. "Ta ke-ming shih-ch'i Kuang-tung fu-nü yun-tung" [The
     Women's Movement in Kwangtung], Chung-kuo fu-nü, Septem-
     ber 1967, p. 22.

16. Florence Ayscough, Chinese Women Yesterday and Today
     (Boston: Houghton Mifflin Co., 1957), p. 84. Similar figures
     are given by John Israel in Student Nationalism in China 1927-
     37 (Stanford: Stanford University Press, 1966), p. 5, and
     Snow, op. cit, pp. 16, 176.

17. Snow, op. cit., p. 16.

18. Jean Chesneaux, The Chinese Labor Movement, 1919-1927
     (Stanford: Stanford University Press, 1968), pp. 74-75.

19. Fang Fu-an, Chinese Labor (London: P. S. King & Son Ltd.,
     1931), p. 31.

20. Chesneaux, op. cit., p. 345.

21. Dorothy J. Orchard, "Manpower in China II," Political Science
     Quarterly, March 1936, pp. 3-4.

22. Nym Wales [Helen Foster Snow], The Chinese Labor Movement
     (N.Y.: John Day Co., 1945), p. 31.

23. Chesneaux, op. cit., p. 195.

24. Hsiang Ching-yü, "Chung-kuo tsui-chin fu-nü yung-tung," op. cit., pp. 78-79.

25. See Chesneaux, op. cit., pp. 254-264, and entry for "Li Li-san" in Donald W. Klein and Anne B. Clark, Biographic Dictionary of Chinese Communism 1921-65 (Cambridge, Mass.: Harvard University Press, 1971).

26. Chesneaux, op. cit., p. 282.

27. Ibid., p. 225.

28. Nym Wales [Helen Foster Snow], Red Dust (Stanford: Stanford University Press, 1952), pp. 199-202.

29. Anna Louise Strong, China's Millions (Peking: New World Press, 1965), p. 115.

30. Ibid., p. 111.

31. Ibid., p. 133.

32. Janet Salaff and Judith Merkel, "Women in Revolution," reprinted in this volume, pp. 145-177.

33. Conrad Brandt, Benjamin Schwartz and John Fairbank, A Documentary History of Chinese Communism (Cambridge, Mass.: Harvard University Press, 1959), p. 16.

34. Wilbur, op. cit., pp. 63-68.

35. Robert North, KMT and Chinese Communist Elites (Stanford: Stanford University Press, 1952), p. 47.

Women in the Liberated Areas

Delia Davin

On women, Mao Tse-tung wrote, "A man in China is usually subjected to three systems of authority (political authority, clan authority and religious authority). As for women, in addition to being dominated by these three systems they are also dominated by men (the authority of the husband). "[1] The women's movement in twentieth century China can broadly be divided into those of the socialist tendency who considered socialism to be a prerequisite for women's liberation and who therefore engaged in general political struggle against all four authorities, and those of the feminist tendency who concentrated on the struggle for equal rights, in the belief that true equality could be achieved through reforms without a revolution in the whole organization of society. The feminist tendency drew great support from college-educated women, often Christian or Christian-influenced, who were struggling to make their way in the professions or to be allowed a modern western-style courtship and marriage. Socialist revolutionaries attracted a lot of student support, but they also successfully mobilized peasants and women workers in the struggle for a revolution to alter the economic basis of society, which they held ultimately responsible for women's oppressive condition.

The period of the Kiangsi Soviet, during which Communists governed a population of millions for several years, was important for the testing and development of practical policies. Among them were social and economic measures designed to alter the whole status of women. A brief description of these measures seems essential to this study.

The equality of men and women, which was of course taken as a principle and also laid down in law in the Soviet Republic, was given more chance to become a reality by the creation of women's organizations to fight for it. The picture is confused and in this as in other matters, it is hard to judge the degree of success achieved

73

in Kiangsi.   Agnes Smedley, using eyewitness accounts by participants, says that the Army and the Party were often too busy to
assist the local Soviets much even with agrarian policy.[2] This was
probably the case generally with social and economic policy.   Moreover, it was as we now know, a time of serious tension and dis-
agreement amongst the leadership, so that even had trained or experienced cadres existed to carry it out, policy on women might
well have lacked consistency.

From Agnes Smedley we hear of Women's Unions formed in
some villages,[3] and in his report on the Chang-kang district in
Kiangsi, Mao tells us about the district women's congresses and
women's representatives who were elected in each village to defend
women's interests.   However he is critical of the way that work
was performed in the district, saying that too little was done to explain the point of it all to ordinary women.[4]

The laws of the Kiangsi Soviet of most concern to women were
the two marriage laws promulgated by the Central Executive Committee: the first (Chung-hua Su-wei-ai kung-he-kuo hun-yin t'iao-li) in
late 1931, and the second (Chung-hua Su-wei-ai hun-yin-fa) in April
1934.[5] Both follow marriage law in the Soviet Union in dealing not
only with marriage, but also with divorce, and the subsequent disposal of property and children.   Although very similar in tone and
content, a few significant changes contained in the second probably
reflect the experience during the two and a half years when the law
was in force.   For example, clause ten in the second law favors
the Red Army soldier by making his consent to divorce indispensable
in any action brought by his wife.   Clause fourteen decrees that if
after divorce the women moves to another area, she has a right to
land there under the local land reform.   In general, however, both
laws define marriage as a free association between a man and a
woman to be entered into without interference from other parties
and ended at the wish of either.   For the first time in China the
state became involved in the marriage system by requiring that marriage and divorce be registered with the local government.   Although
the parties were held to have equal responsibilities towards each
other, in the event of divorce it was declared necessary to protect
women because they were still economically dependent.   Women were
favored in the custody of children, but the man was given the heavier
financial responsibility after divorce.   Later communist marriage law
follows similar lines.   Judging by the great efforts and the length of
time which were later found necessary to change ideas on marriage

elsewhere in China, it seems unlikely that the law was very thoroughly implemented in those early years.

The greatest stress in woman policy, since the Soviet Republic was constantly at war, was on aid to the army. A few exceptional women like K'ang K'e-ch'ing (wife of General Chu Teh) and Li Chien-chen served with the combat troops. [6] Thousands of others belonged to defense forces like the Women Guards which accepted girls over sixteen of hired-hand, poor or middle peasant origin. A larger organization than this was the Women's Aid Corps which was responsible for rescuing and nursing the wounded and for carrying supplies to the fighters. Women were also used extensively for intelligence work and even for sabotage.

Soviet directives give the impression that the appeal to women to engage in productive labor was made in terms of their replacing soldier-husbands, as well as for the sake of gaining independence or improving their status. Since it was less unusual in southern China for women to work in the fields, and the custom of foot-binding was less tenacious than in the conservative north, this task may not have been too hard. In his investigation of Ts'ai-hsi, Mao reported that about 30% of the representatives in the lower district congress were women in 1931, and that this rose to 62% in 1932 and 64% in 1933. [7] This impressive rise appears partly due to the absence of men in the army, but even the first figure is surprisingly high, which seems to indicate that women's right to participate in public affairs was comparatively easily accepted in Kiangsi.

Very few of these women would have been able to continue their activities. Only thirty women left the Kiangsi Soviet on the Long March to the north (though many more left Szechwan) and of those left behind, many activists were killed. [8] Others must simply have resumed their former lives.

During the early years in the northwest, official policy on women showed no change from the days of the Kiangsi Soviet. The Soviet Marriage law which was reprinted in Pao-an in 1936, remained in force. [9] But women were more difficult to mobilize in the conservative north. Foot-binding, for example, was still the rule in rural Shensi and the peasant women found their big-footed sisters from Kiangsi very odd. [10]

Westernized women intellectuals from urban areas like Shanghai who came to Yenan in the early years of the united front brought

with them ideas of women's emancipation influenced by feminist tendencies developed since the May Fourth era. They seem to have
favored an all-out attack on the feudal marriage system. The great
clash between them and the Party came in 1942, when Ting Ling
published an essay in the <u>Liberation Daily</u> attacking policy towards
women, saying that they were being overworked, expected to play a
dual role, and subjected to criticism if they failed in either. [11] The
Party counterattacked and, as Ting Ling told the journalist Gunther
Stein, she and some others were severely criticized in that year.
They were told that "full sex equality had already been established"
and that their feminism was outdated and harmful. [12]

The resolution on women issued by the Central Committee in
February 1943, [13] follows up this attack: "Women cadres must stop
looking on economic work as unimportant. " Its sole reference to
the "feudal oppression of women" lies in the assertion that women
can escape it through production. Male dominance, purchase marriage and other such problems are not mentioned. Foot-binding is
brought up as a practice which is harmful both to health and production and in which reform is therefore desirable. In a speech
welcoming this resolution, the woman leader Ts'ai Ch'ang attacked
"intellectuals isolated from the masses who are always talking about
women's emancipation. "[14] Although insisting on the need for a
democratic, harmonious family, she also said "our slogans are
no longer 'free choice marriage' and 'equality of the sexes, ' but
'save the children, ' 'a flourishing family' and 'nurture health and
prosperity. '"[15]

Isabel and David Crook have said that in the mountain village
of Ten Mile Inn in Hopei, after the resolution of the Central Committee was received, it was realized that women's general emancipation depended on their role in production. Woman-work* no longer
involved launching campaigns on so many fronts simultaneously, and
other objectives were given attention only when they could be tied in
with production. Thus by the end of the war the position of women
in this village was greatly improved economically, but other advances
still had to be made. [16]

---

*I use the term "woman-work" for the Chinese, <u>fu-nü kung-tso</u>.
This made-up word seems preferable to the usual misleading translation "women's work. " The term covers all sorts of activities
among women, including mobilizing them for production, literacy
and hygiene campaigns, social reform and so on.

Many reports of production heroines were published in this period, but there were very few models of the type later to become so common, in which peasant women fought back against ill-treatment by husbands or mothers-in-law. Each of the border regions replaced the Soviet marriage law with its own regulations, of which the first were those of the Shensi-Kansu-Ninghsia region, promulgated in 1939. But at this stage there seems to have been little work done to enforce them.

What was the reason for this soft-pedalling? That "full sex equality" had already been established in the border regions is hardly consistent with later statements about the very long period of education and propaganda needed before it could be achieved. But Ting Ling was also told that for the sake of victory both men and women should get on with the political problem of improving cooperation among all groups.[17] This was a very difficult period of the war for the Communists, in which they had to unite against the national enemy with as many classes and groups as possible. In agrarian policy the militant class struggle of land reform had been replaced by a more conciliatory campaign to reduce rents and interest. Similarly, militancy in the women's movement had for the moment to be given up in the long-term interests of socialism (and therefore of the women themselves). Failure to recognize this was regarded as feminism in a pejorative sense.

In the 1943 resolution the main criticism of earlier approaches to woman-work was, "We have not regarded economic work as the most suitable for women, nor grasped that the mobilization of women for production is the most vital factor in safeguarding their special interests."[18] The resolution continues this strong emphasis on production throughout, stating, for example, that work amongst women should be judged by how well women do in production, and that only through economic prosperity and independence can women start to gain liberation. The tactics of the women's movement changed and developed considerably during the Civil War, and it is only in the late 1940s that we have a sort of miniature preview of the social struggles which were to erupt all over China after 1949. But since economic independence arising from involvement in production was seen throughout as the key to women's equality and social independence, it is important to examine this aspect of woman-work more closely and to consider the attempt to establish women as a productive labor force.

The daily routine of the northern peasant woman was hard.
Before she could cook she first had to husk and grind the grain.
Water had to be fetched, possibly from a distance, and she usually
made both clothes and shoes for her family. However she rarely
undertook remunerative work and her domestic tasks lacked status
compared with the more obviously productive jobs done by men.
Only exceptionally, if her family were both short of manpower and
too poor to hire help, would a northern woman work in the fields,
and then it was felt to be a cause for shame. This was particularly so in the heartland of the liberated areas. J. L. Buck's surveys
showed that nowhere in China did women do less farm work (they
were responsible for only 5% of all farm work) than in this, the
winter-wheat millet region.[19] Apart from the desirability of increased production for its own sake, the Communists argued that
if women could make a significant contribution to family income
their status would rise in consequence. But although there are
many reports of women learning to plough and to hoe, clearing
new land and raising record crops in the early years of the production campaign, they are comparatively few, and it seems that it was
still unusual for them to work on the land on any scale until the
time of land reform.

This is confirmed by a 1948 report which says that during the
anti-Japanese war only in families or areas where manpower was
short did women frequently go to the fields. The main effort of
the campaign went into getting women to spin and weave because,
cut off from the centers of textile production by the Japanese occupation and the Kuomintang blockade, the liberated areas were very
short of cloth.[20] Inflation resulted and was aggravated by the increased demand for cloth created by growing numbers of men in
uniform.

When the problem was first faced in 1939 the solution attempted
was that of joint state-private factories. But large-scale enterprises
turned out to be difficult to organize in the primitive countryside,
and it was not easy to find the amount of capital and the numbers
of full-time workers which were required. Production did increase
in the next few years, but not enough to satisfy demand.[21]

In 1942 Mao set the target of making the industry supply the
needs of the people, the army, and the cadres by reliance not only
on factories but on cottage and cooperative handicrafts.

Reviving the handicraft industry required considerable effort. The village of Chehu in Hsing-t'ai county, Hopei, was thriving by 1948 with 196 spinning wheels and 61 looms in its 220 odd households; but in 1942, its few spinning-wheels had been out of use for years. Only three women knew how to weave in 1942, at least one of whom had married into the village from another county. When she started weaving early in 1942 she had to make a long journey to buy a loom. At the start she had five companions but was quickly joined by so many others that in 1943 they were already able to tide the village through a year of drought with their earnings. This achievement gained added respect for them. By then a co-op had taken over the purchase of cotton and the sale of cloth and organized a training class in weaving. Women were better clothed and could afford to buy draught animals so that they no longer had to push the heavy grindstones themselves. A beneficial side-effect of this was a fall in the number of miscarriages and births of deformed children. Such obvious advantages were vital to the success of the campaign as they induced women, already heavily burdened with domestic work which could not be greatly reduced, to take on extra jobs. Older women had to help younger ones in order to get everything done. This was hard on the older women who had formerly been able to sit back a bit and supervise the household. Now they were often left with both the cooking and the children while their sons' wives went off to spin or weave. In Chehu some of them became very annoyed. When their daughters-in-law returned from work they dished up only cold food, and grumbled, "Everything is upside down since the Communist Party came. Mothers-in-law have become daughters-in-law." They were somewhat mollified however when the young women brought back their earnings in the form of grain from the co-op. [22]

It was common for women to group together to spin, reel and wind the yarn, and set up warps. Even when the task did not actually require more than one pair of hands, they tended to work together, sharing heating and lighting expenses. So much contact with others must have had a profound effect on people who had always led rather enclosed and solitary lives. As they worked in groups and arranged to care for each other's children they learned to organize themselves and their time. So much was the textile industry the concern of women, that at the village level, it was frequently managed by the Women's Association.

By 1947, the liberated areas of Shansi-Chahar-Hopei and Shantung were self-sufficient in cloth, and those of Shansi-Suiyüan

and Shensi-Kansu-Ninghsia partially so. In the T'ai-hang mountains
about 74 of the women could spin or weave, and income from supplementary occupations, of which textile production was the most
important, had risen to approximately 30% of total household income. [23] (However this was probably exceptional since T'ai-hang
is a very poor agricultural area.) It was estimated that production
of cloth increased eight-fold in the liberated areas between 1942 and
1944.

Other supplementary occupations in which women began to play
an important part included the production of vegetable oil, cured
leather, and paper. Even more important were the sewing workshops
which served the army. Besides cloth uniforms for the summer and
quilted cotton ones for the winter, the soldiers had to be provided
with Chinese cloth shoes, which take a whole day to stitch but can
be worn through in only two weeks of marching or a few months of
ordinary wear. Bonus schemes were operated, with competitions
and ever-rising production targets in attempts to boost production. [24]

During the anti-Japanese war, woman-work was directed by the
Women's Committee of the Central Committee (Chung-yang Fu-wei).
In 1945 the Preparatory Committee of the Women's Association of
all the liberated areas was set up in Yenan with thirteen members. [25]
At the village level the mass organization was usually known as the
Women's National Salvation Association until the Japanese surrender,
and afterwards more simply as the Women's Association or the
Peasant Women's Association. By 1945 it is claimed that these
associations in Shensi-Kansu-Ninghsia and seven other liberated
areas had 7,100,000 members. Great stress was laid on the importance of these associations as a way of mobilizing women, and
women cadres who were said to have underestimated the importance
of such work were criticized. [26]

In 1948 a report was published to show the usefulness of special organizations for women. [27] It said that in the winter of 1947,
several defunct organizations for women had been abolished in Ling-
ch'iu county, Shansi, and at the beginning of mobilization for land
reform no distinction had been made between men and women who
all joined the New Peasants' Association and the Poor Peasants'
League. Few women spoke at meetings and they complained that
it was not natural for them to hold meetings with men. They themselves admitted: "If we're speaking with men present, those who
ought to say a lot say very little." The county leaders chose two

villages in which to experiment with separate organizations for women.
These were a great success; women attended meetings enthusiastically and lost their reserve in talking, so the experiment was extended
to cover the whole county.   Women's Congresses were set up in
every district and through these 90% of the women were organized
to play an active part in land reform.   It was concluded that the
preliminary work of mobilization was best done through two organizations, one for both men and women, the other exclusively for
women.   The latter could hold small meetings where women would
gain confidence in speaking.   Such meetings should not last too long
so that they would not inconvenience women with small children, and
should be timed so that they would not interfere with household rou-
tines. [28]

     In spite of the existence of their regional and central head-
quarters, the village Women's Associations were subordinate to the
local Peasants' Association. [29]   This made them vulnerable to local
cadres who might consider themselves as good revolutionaries and
yet have very backward attitudes to women.   In Ten Mile Inn village in Hopei, middle peasant cadres forbade their wives to attend
meetings of the Women's Association which they called "prostitutes'
meetings." [30]   In Long Bow village in Shansi Province when Wang
Yü-lai, vice-chairman of the Peasants' Association forced an under-
age girl to marry his son because he had already "bought and paid"
for her, the Women's Association was afraid to interfere. [31]

     In spite of such setbacks, the importance of the Women's As-
sociation in village life continued to grow.   In areas near the front
it organized its members to sabotage and repair bridges and roads,
to prepare food for the soldiers and carry it to them, to rescue
and nurse the wounded, and to carry messages and gather intelligence under the cover of going to market or visiting relatives.   The
importance of such support activities in mobile guerrilla warfare can
hardly be exaggerated; they should certainly not be despised as a
mere secondary role.   Information about enemy movements was vital to the survival of the resistance.   The army needed not only
friendly villages which would extend help when needed, but the underground had to be organized so that even a small village could
feed a hundred soldiers who might have to leave after only an hour.
Even the collection of this amount of food presented formidable
problems in mountain villages where most of the inhabitants grew
little food for the market and were themselves living close to the
subsistence level.   Women were found to be better at this work

than men because they knew how much grain their neighbors had in
store and who might be persuaded to sell some, and because they
had more gift for talking people round. Communications were difficult and much of the fighting was in remote areas, so that several
food carriers might be needed to supply one fighting man. "Hospital"
administration, also often in the hands of women, could be very com-
plicated. In guerrilla areas, which were free territory by night but
all too often penetrated by the enemy by day, a "hospital" had no
centralized existence. Stretcher bearers carried wounded men to
peasant homes, gave brief instructions on dressing wounds and on
sterilization by boiling, and then disappeared, leaving the family
to care for the patient as their own. Medical workers might come
if they could, but most of the care devolved on the women of the
family. If the Japanese came to search they would claim the patient was a sick son of the house, usually naming some highly in-
fectious illness so that the search might not be too close. These
activities increased women's commitment to the new society by
giving them a sense of participation, and brought them experience
and self-confidence which they then drew upon in land reform.

Agrarian policy underwent a radical change with the end of
the anti-Japanese war and the outbreak of the Liberation war. It
was no longer necessary to avoid alienating the landlords. The peasant had to be given a stake in New Democracy, to be shown what
it could mean to him; and so, after the implementation of "double
reduction," or in some places even omitting this stage, came land
reform. The change in policy on women was less sharp. Too
sudden and strong a campaign for women's rights would have alien-
ated many peasants, including even many of the women themselves.
In the words of the Central Committee's 1948 resolution on woman-
work: "It must be recognized that this is work to change the peasants' ideas and is a long and demanding job which cannot be hur-
ried. "[32]

Nevertheless, profoundly important changes occurred in the
course of land reform as the first paragraph of the resolution acknowledged: "Women have become much more aware and enthusiastic, and consequently there has been a fundamental change in their
political and economic status, and in their position in the family and
in society. "

Under land reform, not only did men and women get equal
rights to the land, but separate land deeds were sometimes issued.

To quote again from the resolution: "When the family is taken as
the unit for issuing land deeds, a note must be made upon them to
the effect that men and women have equal rights to the land.   Every
member of the family has democratic rights in the disposal of the
property.   When necessary, land deeds for women can be issued
separately. "

Women were quick to realize the significance of this development.   In Chao Chen village in Shansi, many said, "When I get my
share I'll separate from my husband, then he won't be able to oppress me any more. "[33]   Mass meetings to determine the division
of land, the disposal of confiscated landlord property and the treatment that the individual landlords should receive were an important
part of land reform.   Women took an active part in all of them.
In some villages where all the able-bodied men were away in the
army, women were even the main force in land reform. [34]   As the
textile movement had encouraged women to come out of their homes
and group together, so land reform led them to assume a bigger
role in general village affairs.   It is significant that a dispropor-
tionate number of women activists in land reform seem to have been
widows forced by their atypical situations to represent their family's
interests.   Married women must have left this important affair to
their husbands in accordance with custom.

At the same time the transition from scattered guerrilla
fighting to large-scale positional warfare brought many more men
under arms, causing a shortage of agricultural labor which could
only be relieved by women.   At the end of the anti-Japanese war
it was still unusual for women to do fieldwork, yet Teng Ying-
ch'ao claimed that by 1949, 50-70% of the women in the older liberated areas were working on the land, and as many as 80% in the
best organized places. [35]

Often it was not possible to find substitutes for the absent
soldiers within their own families, and though it had been the responsibility of the village cadres or the Peasants' Association to
help them and see that their land was tilled, it was now more
often members of the Women's Association which undertook the
work.   Mutual-aid teams and agricultural cooperatives were more
commonly set up in areas relying heavily on women in order to
overcome the shortage of really strong workers.

Both the morale and the consciousness of women had been
raised by the production movement and by land reform, and women

increasingly came to reject their old subordinate role in the family
and in society. The 1948 resolution encouraged them to do so actively and warned them against just letting things take their course:
"It should not be thought that once women take part in production
all the remnants of feudalism which still constrain them will just
naturally disappear and there will be no need to do anything more."

The resolution asserts that: "The basic policies laid down by
the Central Committee Resolutions of 1943 are still completely appropriate," and that, "after rent and interest reduction or land reform has been carried out, productive labor remains the pivot of
the women's movement." However, production is no longer advocated
as a panacea. The need for laws against foot-binding, infanticide,
purchase marriage and adopted daughters-in-law, followed by education on the equality of the sexes, is acknowledged. On the means
to be employed in emancipating women, it states:

> The small number of backward elements who want
> to preserve old feudal customs and who constantly oppress
> women must be suitably struggled against where necessary.
> But it must be understood that this sort of struggle is an
> ideological struggle amongst the peasants, and should be
> radically different from the class struggle against the
> feudal landlords. [36]

Propaganda and persuasion are advocated, and violence is by
implication rejected. But as in land reform, furious peasants sometimes took things into their own hands and beat their landlords,
so women in their struggle for emancipation sometimes resorted to
violence. Jack Belden recounts how the members of one village
women's association beat a man to try to stop him from ill-treating
his wife, and when he escaped several women told her they would
bite him to death if they caught him again. [37] Reports of such incidents of collective struggle are quite common but they appear to
have been allowed to pass without action by the higher authorities.
When women as individuals used violence it was a different matter.
There were only four women in the prison in Yenan in 1946 and
they were all in for the murder or attempted murder of their husbands. [38] Violence sometimes made it easier for the women's association to rely on persuasion alone in subsequent cases. For instance in Long Bow village after one man had been beaten for pun-
ishing his wife for going to meetings, the others all became more
careful. [39] Violence posed too great a threat to family and class

solidarity to be condoned. The Long Bow Women's Association
acted in a more acceptable fashion when it persuaded a poor peasant to stop beating his wife by reminding him that it was hard
enough for a poor man to find a wife at all, so he had better not
drive her to demanding a divorce. [40]

These sorts of quarrels sometimes split Women's Associations.
Hinton says that though women were united in support of their right
to own land, they did not agree on free-choice marriage, which the
older women saw as a threat to their authority over their daughters
and daughters-in-law. [41] One of the tragedies of the traditional family system was that it set women against each other. The mother-
in-law was jealous of her daughter-in-law, whom she regarded as a
threat to her own position. In her efforts to establish her authority over her son's wife she was at best hard; in many cases her
fears and resentments poured out and she was cruel. In the course
of changing this situation, contradictions between the aspirations of
the older and younger women inevitably emerged and could also
easily manifest themselves in hostility. Jack Belden met one young
woman who, in her zeal for catching "bad mothers-in-law" used to
eavesdrop on family quarrels and, at the sound of blows, drag the
offender off to appear before a reform meeting. [42] In Chao Shu-li's
story The Heirloom[43] the mother is gradually won over to her efficient modern-minded daughter-in-law's way of doing things, but
it is easy to imagine that the frustrations of older women, who had
reached a position of dominance within the family only after many
years of subordination, must have been harder to resolve.

In this transitional period when tradition was crumbling but
had by no means collapsed, odd situations arose. A couple in
their early twenties who lived in Tung-nan county, Kiangsu, had
been betrothed since childhood. Both were Party members and she
was head of her village Women's Association, so they would presumably have been considered as amongst the most modern young
people in their area. Yet though they had seen each other by
chance sometimes, and had once even attended the same peasants'
conference, they had never spoken to each other. A recruitment
campaign finally induced her to communicate with him because she
wanted to urge him to join the army. She got the village political
worker to help her write a letter, in which she promised to wait
for him and marry him when he came back. In the meantime, she

pledged herself to care for his family as though it were her own.
Her letter ended with a shy suggestion that they should "meet for a
chat when you have time." No doubt if the boy returned, the marriage was recorded statistically as a free-choice marriage, one of
a percentage used to prove the successful implementation of the new
law. But this story probably tells us more than statistics-about the
way things changed. [44]

In the liberated areas of north China between January and June
1948, 64% of all civil cases were petitions for divorce, of which the
great majority were brought by women. Yet the new ideas were still
far from being generally accepted. The other side of the picture was
brought out in figures collected by the Women's Federation, which
showed that of 464 cases where a woman's death had been investigated 40% had involved women who had wanted divorces, but had
been unable to get them. [45] (There were both murders and suicides
amongst these.) In 1950, Chang Chih-jang, a vice-president of
the Supreme Court admitted: ". . . Because the feudal marriage
system is so deeply rooted, it is still no easy thing, even in the
old liberated areas, to carry through the new policy regarding marriage." [46]

But at least the basis for change had been laid. Cases of
young women who set themselves against tradition by insisting on
choosing their own partners and who won their battle, occurred
more and more frequently. They set an example in new-style family relationships. Through handicrafts, co-ops and work on the land
women played a greater role in the family and village economy. The
impact of such widened horizons on the individual and her conception
of herself could be revolutionary.

Many might cling to the old idea of women's subservience and
dependence, but nowhere was it unchallenged. Women were to be
found in the army as doctors and nurses, and even more important,
in the political and propaganda departments. They worked in the
new territories taken by the army as front-line representatives of
the new order. They worked in government administration, land
reform and cadre training programs. By 1949 30% of the elected
village representatives were women. In government they numbered
20% of the cadres at district level and 10% at the county level. [47]

In China women struggled against a cruder oppression than
women in the West have faced at least in this century. The Com-

munist Party leadership encouraged them to struggle for their emancipation in the context of a peasant society in revolution. It held
that the underlying cause of women's social inferiority was her economic weakness and that the solution to the problem should be an
economic one. However in a backward, agricultural economy where
physical strength is a major factor in prosperity it is extremely difficult to make women, especially women whose energies are taken
up with frequent child-bearing, economically equal with men. Not
surprisingly, the attempt was only a partial success. Even those
who are themselves caught up in women's movements in the West
may find certain aspects of the movement in liberated areas very
alien. From our perspective, the right to work in the fields and
a strict monogamous marriage system may not seem desirable privileges. To understand the success of the movement we must drop
this perspective or we repeat the mistakes of some earlier Chinese
feminists who, as products of an urban, bourgeois and rather westernized society, also failed to take account of peasant realities, and
in consequence had little impact on Chinese society as a whole.

Even judged by its own criteria, the women's movement in the
liberated areas was not completely successful during the hectic years
of the liberation war, but a great deal was accomplished. Women
organized to fight for their rights on a larger scale than ever before.
In April 1949 the All-China Democratic Women's Federation was
formed to give unified direction to the thousands of Women's Associations in the old liberated areas and to the new ones organized in
village after village as the People's Liberation Army swept south.
Millions of women learned to stand on their own feet economically,
freeing themselves at least partially from their dependence on men.
As they broke through the bonds which had tied them to their homes
for centuries, their social and economic status began to change.
Traditional attitudes toward women were crumbling. In the words
of the 1948 Resolution they had "started on the road to complete
liberation."

NOTES

1.   Mao Tse-tung, Report on an Investigation of the Peasant Move-
      ment in Hunan (1927).

2.   Agnes Smedley, China's Red Army Marches (New York: 1934),
      p. 57.

3.   Ibid., p. 55.

4.   Mao Tse-tung, Chang-kang hsiang tiao-ch'a [Investigation of
      Chang-kang district]. Included in the edition of Mao's col-
      lected works published in the Shansi-Chahar-Hopei liberated
      areas in 1947.

5.   See Chung-hua Su-wei-ai kung-he-kuo hun-yin t'iao-li, pub-
      lished in Hung-se Chung-hua, 18 December 1931. Also
      Chung-hua Su-wei-ai kung-he-kuo hun-yin-fa published in
      Su-wei-ai fa-tien (Jui-chin: 1934).

6.   For brief biographies see Chung-kuo fu-nü yün-tüng te chung-
      yao wen-chien [Important documents of the Chinese women's
      movement] (Peking: 1954). Women were active politically
      rather than militarily in Kiangsi, whereas in Szechwan and
      Hainan Island they bore arms on quite a large scale.

7.   Mao Tse-tung, Ts'ai-hsi hsiang tiao-ch'a [Investigation of
      Ts'ai-hsi district] in the collection cited in note 4.

8.   Helen Snow, Women of Modern China (The Hague: 1969), p. 225.

9.   Edgar Snow, Red Star over China (London: 1939), p. 230.

10.   Helen Snow, op. cit., p. 224.

11.   Ting Ling, San-pa-chieh yu-kan [Feelings on women's day],
      Chieh-fang Jih-pao, 9 March 1942. See also Merle Goldman,
      Literary Dissent in Communist China.

12.   Gunther Stein, The Challenge of Red China (London: 1945),
      p. 206.

13. "Mu-ch'ien fu-nü kung-tso fang-chen-te chüeh-ting" [Decisions
     on the present direction of women's work] in Documents of
     the Women's Movement in the Liberated Areas of China
     (Shanghai: 1949).

14. Ts'ai Ch'ang, Ying-chieh fu-nü kung-tso te hsin fang-chen
     [Greeting the new direction of women's work]. Included in
     the collection cited in note 13.

15. Quoted in Chung-kuo fu-nü ta fan-shen [Chinese women stand
     up] (Hong Kong: 1949).

16. Isabel and David Crook, Revolution in a Chinese Village
     (London: 1959), p. 69. See also pp. 100-108.

17. Stein, op. cit., p. 206.

18. See note 13.

19. See J. L. Buck, Land Utilization in China (Nanking: 1937),
     p. 293; and The Chinese Farm Economy (Nanking: 1930),
     p. 235.

20. Lo Ch'iung, "Chin-nien lai chieh-fang-ch'ü nung-ts'un fu-nü
     sheng-ch'an shih-yeh" [Production by village women in the
     liberated areas in the past year] in The Village Women's
     Production Movement in the Liberated Areas of China (1949).

21. Lo Ch'iung, Shen-Kan-Ning pien-ch'ü min-chien fang-chih-yeh
     [The cottage textile industry in the Shen-Kan-Ning border re-
     gion] (Nym Wales Collection. Hoover Library, Stanford, Ca.).

22. Liu Heng, Chia chia fang-chih-te Chehu ts'un in the collection
     cited in note 20.

23. See note 21.

24. See note 15.

25. Chung-kuo chieh-fang-ch'ü fu-nü fan-shen yün-tung [The move-
     ment in which the women of the liberated areas of China are
     standing up] in the collection cited in note 13.

26. Teng Ying-ch'ao, T'u-ti kai-ke yü fu-nü kung-tso te hsin jen-wu [Land reform and the new tasks of women's work] in the collection cited in note 13.

27. T'u-kai chung ch'u-hsien-le hsin-lieh-te fu-nü tsu-chih hsing-shih [New forms of women's organizations emerge in land reform] in The Movement in Which the Village Women of the Liberated Areas of China are Standing Up (1949).

28. Pei-yüeh-ch'ü t'u-ti kai-ke yün-tung-chung fa-tung fu-nü te ching-yen [Experience of mobilizing women during the land reform movement in Pei-yüeh district] in the collection cited in note 27.

29. Decisions of the Land Reform Conference (1947), quoted in the book cited in note 15.

30. Isabel and David Crook, Revolution in a Chinese Village (London: 1959), p. 107.

31. William Hinton, Fanshen (New York: 1966), p. 465.

32. Chung-kuo kung-ch'an-tang chung-yang-wei-yüan-hui kuan-yü mu-ch'ien chieh-fang-ch'ü nong-ts'un fu-nü kung-tso te chüeh-ting [Decisions of the Central Committee of the Chinese Communist Party on the present direction of women's work in the countryside of the liberated areas] (1948) in the collection cited in note 13.

33. Hinton, op. cit., p. 397.

34. Erh Tung, Fu-nü erh-t'ung ting-le ta shih [Women and children do important work] in the collection cited in note 20.

35. Teng Ying-ch'ao, "Chinese Women Help to Build a New China," People's China, No. 6, 1950.

36. 1948 Central Committee Resolution on women. See note 32.

37. Jack Belden, China Shakes the World (New York: 1949), pp. 304-7.

38. Robert Payne, Journey to Red China (London: 1947), p. 104.

39. Hinton, op. cit., p. 158.

40. Ibid., p. 159.

41. Ibid., p. 396.

42. Belden, op. cit., p. 294.

43. Chao Shu-li, Rhymes of Li Yu-ts'ai and Other Stories (Peking:
     1955), pp. 69-89.

44. Ch'ien Hsiu-ch'ing yü Chiang Chin-chai [The story of Ch'ien
     Hsiu-ch'ing and Chiang Chin-chai] included in the Enlistment
     Campaign of Women in the Liberated Areas (1948).

45. Hsin Chung-kuo hun-yin wen-t'i [Marriage problems in new
     China] (1949).

46. Chang Chih-jang, A Much-Needed Marriage Law (Peking:
     1950).   Published with the English edition of the marriage
     law.

47. Teng Ying-ch'ao, Chung-kuo fu-nü yün-tung tang-ch'ien te
     fang-chen jen-wu pao-kao [Report on the present direction
     and tasks of the Chinese women's movement] in the collection
     entitled The First National Representative Congress of Chinese
     Women.

Institutionalized Motivation for Fertility Limitation

Janet W. Salaff

THE PROBLEM AND THE MODEL

After initial misgivings based on orthodox Marxist ideology regarding population control, the People's Republic of China officially came out in favour of population limitation. The government denies the dire Malthusian prophecy that population will outstrip China's supply of food and natural resources.[1] Instead it supports population limitation to ease the costs of economic growth, which under Chinese conditions requires a strong labour force and a concentration of capital in productive enterprises rather than a high rate of consumption.[2] By applying the experience of the developed nations, China has reduced pre-industrial levels of mortality and morbidity.[3] This has decreased the expense to society of a non-productive populace which dies before it repays the costs of its upbringing and training.[4] As a result, China undoubtedly has a high rate of population growth.[5] Lower fertility will lessen the proportion of children to adult workers and will release females for employment; for these reasons the government advocates fertility control. Observers lack data from the two national censuses (1953-54 and 1964)[6] and registration system to assess China's success in fertility reduction. Instead the patterns of social mobility and social control which shape reproductive motivation must be evaluated. In so doing I address myself to one main question: how has China's approach to economic development in the past five years affected the motivation of her youth to reduce fertility?

The experience of the now developed nations may not prove useful in charting the direction of China's fertility levels. When

Reprinted with permission from Population Studies, Vol. XXVI, No. 2, July 1972.

West European population growth was checked during periods of initial industrialization and urbanization, fertility reduction was most marked in the urban middle strata. The costs of bearing numerous offspring exceeded their utility in the parents' drive for social mobility.[7] If the Chinese were to imitate this experience they would plan for more urbanization, greater opportunities for mobility for the bureaucratic and professional strata, and an increase in consumer goods for the entire population. However, the Chinese developmental model has shifted from this strategy to one that is historically unique. The government has experimented with three approaches to modernization. The earliest "Soviet" model (1952-57) featured investment in urban-based heavy industry; rapid social mobility for the middle strata was stressed. In the second, a transitional approach (1960-65), China's "New Economic Plan" allowed greater freedom to market forces, encouraging profit from agricultural investment and trade. During these years Chinese citizens were encouraged to reduce fertility to gain economic rewards, to win higher social positions, and to avoid political pressure. This was preceded and succeeded by a third, so-called "Maoist" economic plan in late 1957-59 and again from 1966 to the present. The Maoist approach aims at halting the urbanization process and the partial industrialization of rural areas.[8] Income differentials by geographical location, occupation and social rank are narrowed. The political values for leaders stress "service" to the community without material incentives. The schools and mass media curb competition for individual achievement and upward mobility. Young people should postpone marriage and limit fertility without the promise of higher social position. At first glance this approach to development appears to have pro-natalist implications. Can the norm of "service to the people" really motivate young parents to reduce their family size?

Answers to this question will have far-reaching implications. Failure to reduce population growth will jeopardize any plan for future economic advancement. Furthermore, observers from less developed nations with low capital resources and outside international aid networks look to China's latest modernization strategy as an alternative model for their own development. The demographic consequences of China's developmental policies thus figure in any evaluation of alternative models of socio-economic change in the Third World.

In a systematic attempt to put and answer this question, I employ a model of the utilities and costs of children.[9] This model assumes that people's fertility responses are rational, because most people act in their own perceived interests. The inability to plan is a social fact to be explained, not an irrational response. I intend to detail the reasons for persistent high fertility and the social groups among which fertility can be expected to decline.

THE ECONOMIC UTILITIES OF CHILDREN

The Child as Productive Agent in Rural China

In the People's Republic of China the peasantry is being transformed into a rural labour force organized without regard to kinship. In the process the productive utilities of children are decreasing.

Evidence of fertility differentials, 1900-1930

Under the system of private ownership of agricultural property and family businesses, children contributed to family income. The following tables show that in the rural hinterland and urban centres throughout the 1930's fertility was related directly to economic status.

TABLE I. *Relation of crop area of farm to fertility of married women, rural China (women 45 years or over, 1929–31)*

Size of farm	Average number of children per wife	Number of wives
Very large	5·51	2,946
Large	5·35	2,284
Medium large	5·28	1,845
Medium	5·06	1,697
Small	5·03	1,514
Total	5·29	10,286

Social class and fertility of married women, urban China (women aged 40 years and over, 1923–31)

Class	Total number of children born per 1,000 mothers			Number of mothers
	Total	Living	Dead	
Upper class	6,250	4,570	1,680	438
Lower class	4,700	2,300	2,400	1,000

SOURCES Herbert D. Lamson, 'Differential reproduction in China', *The Quarterly Review of Biology*, **10**, 3 (September 1935), pp. 308–321; John L. Buck, *Land Utilization in China* (New York, 1968), p. 385.

TABLE 2. *Average number of births for ever-married women, with at least one pregnancy, by age and rural–urban status, Hupeh Province, 1959*

| | Average number of births | |
Age	Urban	Rural
15–19	1·60	1·40
20–24	1·70	1·76
25–29	2·98	2·93
30–34	4·33	4·56
35–39	4·93	6·19
40–44	5·34	7·25
45–49	5·74	7·30
50+	5·79	7·25
Total, average	4·04	5·74
Number	11,881	5,478

SOURCE: 'Hu-pei sheng 22,251 ch'eng-hsiang fu-nu yueh-ching chi sheng-yu ch'ing-kuang t'iao-ch'a fen-hsi' (Investigation and analysis of the childbirth and menstruation conditions of 22,251 rural and urban Hupeh women), *Chung-hua fu-ch'an-k'o tsa-chih* (Chinese Journal of Obstetrics and Gynaecology). 1, January 1960 pp. 5–11. The total number of women surveyed in the table is only 17,359; no reason is given for the lack of data on the 4,892 women who make up the figure of 22,251.

It may be argued that the causal relationship was not that many children contributed to the family's wealth but that after the family became wealthy it raised more children. This direct relationship between fertility and wealth may be explained by the fact that high economic status led to earlier marriages.[10] According to Gamble's surveys in Ting Hsien, one-quarter of the women of the poorer families married at ages above 20, in contrast to 8.5% of the women of wealthier families. However, fertility by duration of marriage might not show differentials between social strata. If mortality were higher among lower-class adults, there may have been more years in which these women were not exposed to risk of conception. This could account for much of the differential by social class.

Francis Hsü has argued that in the past richer families conformed to the values of the community which demanded many more children as a sign of status.[11] Children not only lacked productive utilities, he claimed, but they conspicuously consumed more than they contributed. In fact, if the mechanisms by which children contributed to the family income are examined, we can see how the upwardly mobile family in the late nineteenth-century agrarian setting employed numerous sons to raise the family position. First, the nature of property relations and inheritance patterns required that mobility be accomplished simultaneously inside and outside agriculture. Since all sons held equal claim to the father's property, land fragmented easily. Wealth was obtained more readily through commerce, trade, usury, army service and banditry than through land. Commercial wealth was legally insecure, and wealth was re-invested

in land.[12] The structure of the family was suited to mobility
through the division of functions among sons. Following Myron
Cohen, I focus on the chia or the "economic family,"[13] which had
a common budget, property, and family head (chia chang).[14] Family members held kinship ties and economic claims to one another.
The chia was not necessarily a single productive unit; family members were often physically dispersed, the offspring being sent by
the household head, as manager, to different parts of the economy.
If the offspring were successful, they would remit their earnings,
which he would invest. An able household head thus cornered resources he could use to raise the economic level of the entire
household.

Post-1949 fertility differentials

In Republican China the economic mix was changing. Children
lost some of their economic usefulness, as commerce became legally secure. In the cities one well-trained son became more profitable than numerous uneducated ones. Parents lost some control
over their offspring. The 1931 Nationalist family code, which diminished the power of the chia head over the income and property
of the adult members, reflected and furthered this change.[15] However, rural property concepts were still fundamentally unchanged.[16]
Land continued to fragment under the impact of multigeniture, which
limited social mobility in rural areas. Furthermore, offspring were
necessary for survival, since mortality was still high (see Table I).

In the People's Republic of China the nature of property ownership and organization was altered, facilitating centralized economic
planning and control. Familial control over children was attenuated
even before the economy was industrialized. The rural inhabitants
were to be organized into a factory-like labour force, and whereever possible they would work in rural industry on the basis of
skills rather than kinship connections. Urban culture was gradually
introduced into the village. Has this approach to rural development
reduced the productive utilities of children in rural and urban China?

I can establish benchmarks regarding differences in rural and
urban fertility in the late 1950's. One survey, conducted in north
China in 1959, demonstrates that for a long time rural women had
borne more children than urban women. The differentials appear
among women aged 30 and over, and among those who have been
married eight or more years.[17]

According to this survey, younger married women in urban and rural areas had similar numbers of children. Urban women over 30 years of age had somewhat fewer children than their rural counterparts. Table 3, in which the duration of marriage is held constant, shows that higher rural fertility was not caused by women marrying at a younger age. The table does not rule out higher mortality among spouses of rural women. For women with the same marriage duration, the average number of children ever born is still greater at older ages; however, the length of cohabitation with a spouse is not available. At that time the higher rates of rural infant and neo-natal mortality may have amounted to as much as 50% of total births.

In the following pages I present some reasons for believing that the second decade of Communist power saw a drop in fertility among women in urban and rural China as a result of changing norms, values, and sanctions motivating childbirth.

TABLE 3. *Average number of births for ever-married women, with at least one birth by marriage cohort and rural–urban status, Hupeh Province, 1959*

Years married	Average number of births		Average years between births		Number of women	
	Urban	Rural	Urban	Rural	Urban	Rural
1	1·01	1·00	0·99	1·00	156	42
2	1·11	1·17	1·80	1·71	391	72
3	1·37	1·28	2·19	2·34	407	95
4	1·93	1·66	2·07	2·41	397	114
5	2·04	2·02	2·45	2·48	342	122
6	2·34	2·27	2·99	2·64	548	166
7	2·61	2·59	2·68	2·70	477	162
8	2·72	2·73	2·94	2·93	545	154
9	3·17	3·21	2·84	2·80	488	163
10	3·36	3·59	2·98	2·79	560	165
11	3·92	4·11	2·81	2·68	400	138
12	4·19	4·28	2·86	2·80	379	113
13	4·30	4·68	3·02	2·78	327	122
14	4·48	5·03	3·12	2·78	329	71
15	4·65	4·83	3·44	3·11	327	103
16	4·88	6·15	3·69	2·93	1,340	586
21	5·82	7·16	3·95	3·21	1,141	634
26	5·81	7·70	4·82	3·64	813	521
30	5·81	7·34	5·16	4·09	2,105	1,798
N.A.	5·01	5·83			349	137

SOURCE: *Ibid.*

Rural Social Reorganization after 1949

Land reform by itself (1951-52) fundamentally reduced the utilities of numerous children. Political struggle sessions accompanying land division led poorer families to believe they would have the opportunity to own their own land. Large, wealthy households of several related nuclear units were divided, but land reform brought little increase of cultivable land into production. The land was parcelled out to even more households and individuals than before. [18] As a consequence of the new regime's promise of increased wealth, but its inability to fulfil the promise, competition for land must have increased. When these competitive demands could not be met, pressures must have welled up for sons to seek roads to wealth, other than through investment in land. Although information on the impact of land reform on fertility levels is not available, mainland Chinese families probably responded by migrating to nearby cities and elsewhere, by delaying marriage, or by limiting fertility where competition for land had intensified as a result of the deep-seated reform. These were the responses in Ireland after the Great Famine and in Japan and Taiwan where landholdings were consolidated after World War II. [19]

With collectivization of land and industry in China in 1956, private capital could not be invested for public profit. Family income derived largely from individual members' labour in the collective. Remuneration was tied to the output of the collective's harvest and therefore was less predictable than factory wages. During 1955-57 and again from 1960-66, each person's income was differentiated by skill and hours worked, with the more skilled performance earning a higher income. During the "Maoist" economic reforms agricultural wage levels were equalized. Skill counts less than willingness to work, political conformity and social-class background. [20]

Does the upwardly striving family head now use numerous children to improve family income? Children still have some productive functions in the commune. (1) To begin with, the household operates as a unit of consumption. The household purse is managed by the patriarch himself, or in younger homes by the couple sharing decision-making about household expenditures. [21] Each family member contributes his or her income from the collective to the household. Family members keep a part of their income only if there is a surplus remaining after household expenses have been met. [22]

(2) The division of labour in the family corresponds in some ways to the traditional division of labour before collectivization. [23] Peter Schran has noted that when household members earned wages according to their strength and skill (i.e. under the wage system

in force before 1966), the family operated as a unit of production,
as in the past. Children and the elderly contributed the fewest labour points: they helped around the house, cared for younger siblings, and tended livestock or poultry. Adolescent youths and women
earned second-class labour points, while the father and adult sons
earned the most, as before collectivization. One survey in the early
fifties showed that before collectivization families with the most "labour power," i.e. with adult workers and few dependants, had the
highest income.[24] Schran also argues that before collectivization
such families generally obtained larger family holdings and that even
after collectivization they continued to hold the edge in earnings.[25]
Do parents even now bear many children in anticipation of their becoming productive utilities in the communes?

(3) Labour production teams apparently organize kinsmen to
work together. The unit of day-to-day labour is often the commune
sub-unit corresponding to the village. Does not this mean that the
family operates as a productive unit, as it did before collectivization? Despite similarities to the pre-land reform organization of
the family as a consumption and production unit, great changes in
property relations in fact have rendered children less valuable.
For one, the chia no longer operates as a legally based economic
unit and family members do not hold claim to the father's property.
The house and its furnishings cannot be sold or transferred outside
the family. In addition, the family head cannot legally control the
adult offspring's income. He must depend on customary family
norms, which have been weakening. Next, while children are useful workers, a family can no longer derive gain from the offspring's
surplus income because it cannot be re-invested. The sale of private plot produce in the market place does not greatly enrich the
family because others cannot be hired to transform the surplus into
capital. Hence, although family income improves after all young
children have matured, but before sons marry and themselves father
children, the family head cannot organize his sons' labour in order
decisively to alter his economic status. Further, the quasi-religious
link to the ancestral tomb has been broken and there is little impetus for children to work the ancestral land. Therefore, when parents do plan to improve their economic status they take the children
out of family production and send them into the school system, thereby hoping to steer them toward salaried income.

Finally, opportunities outside agriculture no longer depend on
nepotism or connections through the family line.[26] Land reform and

collectivization have increased the number of political positions in
the village, as well as the non-agricultural opportunities outside it.
Adolescents enter the Young Communist League, or the local militia;
they lead production teams and other political units, migrate to urban areas or join the army. As industrial opportunities decline in
urban centres and an emphasis on semi-industrial workshops in rural
collectives promises to absorb excess labour power, young people
may seek local work. Again, they are placed in a job more through
political participation than through old family connections. In sum,
peasants no longer regard numerous sons and daughters as productive
utilities.

Two responses to the changed social structure have emerged.
A Chinese peasant whose sons remained in agricultural-related work
described the shifting economic contributions of children in this way:

> "You need two sons because you have to make sure at least
> one has ability. He must be good at agricultural work and
> clever so he can contribute to the family income. If you
> have only one son you can never tell whether he will be
> clever when he grows up. But, if you bear a second one,
> you have a better chance."[27]

In this view, the sons would remain in agriculture, engaging in petty
trade and marketing of surplus from the private plot. Children remained useful in the economy, but two sons were considered the maximum that could be used.

The two sons means an average of four offspring, which still
implies a high rate of population growth. The ideal family size of
those wishing to rise in the political hierarchy, on the other hand,
is lower by one or more children. The politically mobile rural
cadre explained that village youths like himself felt great pressure
on their standard of living and possible access to political opportunities because of village population growth and job scarcity.

> "It is wrong for the family to feel that if it has two grown
> sons and two daughters its income will be greater than if
> it had only one son and one daughter. In the latter case,
> one daughter is married outside the village, a daughter-in-
> law will be brought in for the son, and the collective in-
> come and the number of people there to share it stays the
> same. Each one's share is bigger than if there were two

sons and two daughters, because fewer people would split
the same income. So only the older generation would think
that the larger the household, the better the income. The
young understand that it is not necessary to have so many
children in order to contribute to the family income. Children belong to the nation, not to the family."[28]

This and numerous other accounts show that the productive utilties
of large families among the rural elite, and to a lesser extent among
citizens at large, have been reduced.

Productive Utilities of Children in Urban China

        The value of children has declined drastically in urban China.
Evidence is plentiful. Family firms were eliminated by 1956, for
example, and there are few jobs to which child labour can be applied. Children are more likely to attend primary and lower-middle
school in urban areas.[29] The desire to rear few children is shaped
by the relatively clear delineation of career paths in the urban setting. In the fifties those who planned to raise their family status in
the Communist hierarchy would best have done so by putting their
children through school and obtaining civil service positions for them.
But this path has become clogged since the early sixties. As will be
seen, alternative paths to mobility had to be created by the regime.

        The opportunities of the urban labour force have been charac-
terized by a rapid expansion through the fifties followed by a rapid
contraction. This has been true for both blue-collar and white-collar
occupations. The early pattern of investment in heavy industry absorbed a great deal of capital and the modern non-agricultural work
force increased by more than 200% between 1949 and 1957. The total non-agricultural work force (modern and traditional) increased by
only 51% over that period. (Part of this increase, from 1949 to
1952 especially, may have been the result of improved statistical
reporting.) If we look at the period of highest investment in heavy
industry, from 1953 to 1957, we find that non-agricultural employment did not increase.[30] The development of the modern sector
thus merely changed the mix of the labour force without apprecia-
bly adding to the non-agricultural work force. As a result of such
economic problems, 25% of the urban labour force in the sixties
may have been unemployed.[31] In response to this dilemma, government plans switched to stress the rural development of small-
scale industry. In 1958-59 experimental, jerry-built industrial

enterprises in urban and rural areas doubled non-agricultural employment and halved unemployment.[32] This has been tried on a somewhat smaller scale since the Cultural Revolution. Rural young people
are not only discouraged from migration to urban centres in search
of jobs, but urban young are sent to rural centres to work.

Families in urban China have experienced a sudden increase
and then a sudden scaling down of white-collar opportunities for themselves and their offspring. Urban children found the channels of mobility predictable for the first post-revolutionary decade,[33] but after
this period few new positions opened because of the youthfulness of
the bureaucracy and the labour force (half the professionals were
under age 26 in 1957). Thus, even urban-educated young could not
obtain the jobs for which they had trained. The government's response to this politically explosive situation has been to send school-
leavers to rural jobs or urban factories. The urban school system
has been reorganized to train students for the technical jobs they are
likely to hold. At the same time the school socializes its pupils to
serve the nation and to accept less desirable manual jobs.

What has this clampdown on aspirations to mobility done for
the family-building desires of urban youth? Will family members
continue to find new values in numerous children if the possibilities
of their extra-familial mobility are slim? The answer would seem
to depend on the satisfactions, roles and statuses alternative to economic mobility that exist and which will be discussed below.

The Utility of Children in Providing Old-Age Security

In the past parents who bore numerous sons were confident
their children would care for them in their old age. The Chinese
Communists have not been able to substitute adequate welfare for
that provided by offspring. At present the agricultural collectives
provide two sorts of funds to support the elderly--welfare pensions
and old people's homes. Urban parents depend on labour union insurance. None of these offers an adequate substitute for the status
and mutual help provided by offspring. Do offspring, therefore,
give so much assistance that parents will have many children for
this purpose?

Rural welfare funds are extremely limited. In 1960 only 1%
of the commune surplus was invested in such funds.[34] Only those
applicants of approved political background and experience qualify

for support, e.g. widows of soldiers and martyrs. Those whose
need is caused in part by bearing numerous children, despite commune advice, may have difficulty in getting support. Elderly peasants with dependants expect to rely on their offspring for support in
their old age. Children, too, gain prestige from caring for their
parents. Thus, some parents may still desire to bear sons, for
fear they will be abandoned in their old age. The story told by a
woman interviewed in 1962 by the Myrdals in northern Yenan illus-
trates the continuing mutual obligation of children to support their
parents.

> "There were six of us children, three sons and three daugh-
> ters. Mother is still alive. She is 72. I send mother
> money. In 1961 I gave her 20 yuan. All six children send
> her the same amount, and this means that she has proper
> pocket money. She lives alone, but her daughters-in-law
> go and cook for her. She still makes quilt jackets for the
> family. "[35]

Another kind of community social assistance was introduced in
1958 when the Communists tried to counter such parental desire for
large families by establishing "happy homes for the aged." Their
slogan was: "You don't need sons for support in your old age, go
to the old folks' home instead." These homes cannot substitute for
the status that parents and children gain through caring for the older
generations. [36] Furthermore, old people's homes have to be self-
supporting; the elderly inmates do handicraft work and gardening.
Since the elderly must work anyway, if they have children they might
just as well help around their own homes, as with child care, instead of going to the old people's home. In most cases homes are
used by those old people who have no adult sons or daughters willing to support them. Such services do have an impact on rural
social structure. Widows who might have been forced to re-marry
to obtain personal care may now be able to avoid it if assured community assistance. In sum, the elderly expect to be supported by
their offspring. Those parents who expect that their sons will be
relatively successful will be prepared to have few children. The
rest may opt for a greater number.

In urban China workers and employees are entitled to retire-
ment insurance, the amount depending on the specific conditions of
the union where they work. Generally, the worker's status and
length of employment are taken into account. [37] Parents who are

supported by a working son or daughter will receive pensions if their offspring is disabled or dies. The pensions are generally adequate to live on, but even so, many would wish their youngsters to help.

RELIGIOUS AND CEREMONIAL
UTILITIES OF CHILDREN

The religious norms of the traditional Chinese community accorded high status to those families with numerous sons who would worship their ancestors in the lineage temple. Three religious units are relevant to an assessment of the current ceremonial utilities of children: the lineage hall, the household domestic shrine, and the wu fu--or five mourning relations which provide support in life crises.

Daniel Kulp described the "religious" family as one that was wider than the chia: it included several family units[38] which formed lineage branches, tracing their ancestry from a common grandparent. Lineage branches were solidary if formed around a hall with property.[39] After land reform the Communists took away the land and removed family ancestor plaques from the halls. Since the halls could no longer support their community functions, they were easily taken over for meeting places and schools.[40] At present, peasant families still observe spring and autumn festival sacrifices to ancestors, although they are requested to turn such festivals into days of production and frugality. Large gatherings of lineage members are rarer, for they are politically dangerous and the community can no longer afford them without land. Thus, the status formerly obtained through extravagant displays of ritual can no longer be publicly accorded. One peasant commented:

"We still meet together at festivals to worship our ancestral graves, but it is no longer necessary for everyone to gather as before. We ourselves--the older generations--think that when we die it will be enough if three generations worship us: our own, our sons, and our grandsons. That is enough."[41]

Occasionally, expensive funerals are held by those without suspect political backgrounds.

Families still surreptitiously pay respects to their ancestors in domestic shrines. During the Cultural Revolution many homes tossed away their ancestral plaques as "feudal superstitions"; some of them

turned up as blackboards in schools.[42] Informants anticipated that
these plaques would find their way back into homes after political
pressures ceased.   The wu fu is not a structure, but is defined
vis-à-vis ego and is relative to each male.   The wu fu did not
fully function in the early part of the twentieth century.   Instead
a smaller core of patrilineal kinsmen participated in mourning and
marriage ceremonies.   The same core apparently continues to support its relatives at such occasions today, as suggested by the peasant quoted above.

Thus, the main ceremonial unit--the lineage branch, which
traces its origin to the ancestor who founded the hall and incorporated property--has lost its solidarity.   It was primarily at this
level that numerous sons earned community prestige.   Since sons
cannot now be utilized for ceremonial purposes, most of the religious incentives for desiring sons have been removed.   Elders still
are respected by their offspring in the family, but this worship is
no longer integrated into the social structure.   These religious values by themselves probably do not have pro-natalist results.   Political values supporting devotion to the community and service without
remuneration have replaced religion in the mass media and educational system.   The main thrust of changes in values has not necessarily been to replace the desire for large families with the desire
for small ones, but to alter the reasons for bearing small families.
The ability of families to aggrandize themselves and to use their
numerous sons to earn money or to gain power in the community
was transformed by some into the ability to use fewer sons to gain
family power.   Political values have been introduced in recent years
to counter the latter motivation for small or medium-sized families.

THE ECONOMIC COSTS OF CHILDREN

During the Republican era the costs of maintaining and raising
children increased for the emergent urban bourgeoisie.   In the Communist period those who sought to put their children through school,
and who competed with their reference groups to improve their life
style within the regime's tolerated limits, found numerous children
expensive to rear.

From 1949 to 1966 education comprised the largest cost of
children as perceived by parents.   The middle groups sought to put
their children through selected urban schools with good reputations.[43]

The cost of schooling was lower than in the Republican era, but less money was available. Costs were greatest for boarding schools. They ranged from a kindergarten in which fees were $30 per month[44] in 1965 to $3 per term in another.[45] Fees rose to $15 monthly in middle school. Recently a rural brigade in Szechuan complained that board and pocket money alone for a child in lower-middle school cost parents $100 to $200 per year.[46] There were no tuition fees at college level, but scholarships were not generous. At Tsinghua University the largest scholarships were $19.50 per month; many students did not receive full scholarships and relied on siblings for monthly subsidies.

Where both parents worked as cadres, each earning $100 per month, such fees would not be excessive but would require budgeting. Such parents would limit childbearing to provide opportunities for all their children. Factory workers and peasants would have to save a much larger proportion of their income, for factory workers earned less than $50 a month and peasants earned from $12 to $400 a year, depending on the wealth of the commune. Peasants also had to do without the labour of their children for the interim, which raised the costs of their schooling.[47] In fact, schools did contain high proportions of workers and peasants who must have saved considerable amounts to afford costs. Enrolment of working-class youth in the school system may disguise the fact that many had parents who were cadres with working-class backgrounds. The main problem that the school reforms sought to overcome was the small proportion of the cohort attending lower-middle school. Students of worker and peasant background comprised 19% of college enrolment in 1950 and 67% in 1962, at which time only 1.4% of their cohort attended college. They accounted for half the enrolment of middle school students in 1950 and three-quarters in 1964. Varying estimates noted that from 50 to 80% of the cohort were enrolled in 1957-58, but middle-school enrolment dropped to 20% of the cohort in 1966.[48] The small number of school places available meant that parents with high aspirations for their offspring would push their children to succeed. This kind of planning was likely to involve reducing the number of children as well.

Parents also saved to purchase consumer goods. This was an established pattern for the Chinese bourgeoisie of the early twentieth century. Now workers' life styles became almost as costly, as middle-class values and standards were disseminated by means of the press.[49] The limited production of consumer goods meant that many

goods were sought after at high prices, e.g. saccharin, cigarette
lighters, foreign fountain pens, most of which were available only
on the black market. The cadres differentiated their life style by
consuming goods and services available by virtue of rank, such as
housing, private medical services, cadres' and army officers' dependants' schools, and cars. Differentiated cadres' reference
groups became institutionalized; they were patterned after the civil
service scale. Cadres competed with those at the same level and
those below for higher status. For example, whenever two cadres
met, each immediately would determine the other's rank in order
to place him in the social system. [50]

Factory workers in the sixties demonstrated their relatively
high status in the new regime by the amount of money they spent
on consumer goods. Families of skilled workers had greatly improved their social position since 1949 and were relatively better
off than the unskilled workers and peasantry. Workers' parents
and neighbours, as well as co-workers, urged them to spend their
wages on celebrations, such as weddings or funerals. They saved
for such occasions over long periods. As expenditures to keep up
one's social position increased for the workers, presumably more
of them delayed marriage in order to marry "well."

The income of the peasantry could not be saved easily, for it
was not as predictable as that of urban cadres and workers. The
peasants' income varies with the wealth of the locale and the pro-
ductivity of the harvest. In less prosperous areas expenditures
equal income. In Liu Ling, for example, a woman spent from $4
to $5 for food for her family (two adults and three children) fort-
nightly. Villagers accorded her great respect because she succeeded in remaining in the labour force while managing her household so efficiently that she purchased a bicycle at the end of the
year. Only one village woman had a sewing machine. [51] The difficulties in predicting their wages and in saving for consumer goods
in such poor rural areas suggest that most families did not plan consumption to obtain such goods. Accordingly, most extra money would
be spent on dining out. [52] In wealthier areas more money was available, and peasants would compete to improve their housing and more
of them would purchase bicycles.

The Cultural Revolution introduced reforms to the school system and political pressures against the consumption of goods which
have reduced the direct economic costs of children. In contrast to

the one-fifth of school-age children enrolled in middle school on the
eve of the Cultural Revolution, all children now are to graduate from
lower-middle school.   Parents pay little for school because children
earn money through manual labour.   School hours have become flexible so that rural children can perform their homemaking and productive chores.   Education will not promise a payoff in the form of
passage to white-collar or technical status.   Schools in rural areas
train pupils for agrarian-related activities rather than for college
entry.   Urban schools channel more young people from lower-middle
schools to factory labour.   Students in upper-middle schools in urban areas learn technical skills for the factory, rather than take
college preparatory courses.   College entrance is reserved for workers and peasants who have been at work and who have demonstrated
political loyalty, leadership talents, and technical abilities. [53]

The downgrading of consumer goods as a sign of status has
recently been accompanied by emphasis on improving the standard
of the entire productive unit.   Each family is urged to contribute
its extra labour and time to the collective without thought of individual remuneration.   In sum, recent policies have culminated in an
across-the-board reduction of such economic incentives for reducing
family size.   These changes in the structure of the school system
and the down-playing of competition for status and social mobility,
if taken by themselves, would appear to be pro-natalist.   However,
other social reforms have accompanied the reorganization of channels to mobility.   In particular, for women in the villages there
has been an increase in alternative opportunities to childbearing.
As the direct costs of children have decreased, opportunity costs
have risen.

SOCIAL OPPORTUNITIES AVAILABLE
THROUGH CHILDREN

The Status of Women in the Rural Family

Marion Levy has described how the statuses attached to the
women's role in the Chinese family determined her desire to bear
many children. [54]   The main stages in her life cycle related to childbearing activities, and these have changed little.   The first stage
was marriage into another lineage, which meant that all were tied
to the community as members of families of procreation and families of orientation.   In other words, women related to the community

through their children.   There still is no social position in the natal
community for the celibate.   Ultimately, the woman must marry into
another lineage.   As one informant remarked:

> "It's the custom for people to marry, even if they are over
> 40.   As soon as the husband or wife has died, the survivor
> tries to re-marry.   People should not live all alone, and if
> a woman can re-marry she should do so.   After all, who is
> going to carry water for her otherwise?   Someone has to
> cook food for him."[55]

Only older women with children can refrain from remarrying.

After marriage the bride is expected to bear a child immediately.   Marrying patrilocally, the woman is still estranged from her
spouse.   In the past the strong filial bond meant that the son would
align himself with his parents in decision-making rather than with
the young bride.   He did not publicly display affection toward her,
although he was affectionate in private.   Marjorie Wolf has observed
on Taiwan, that this continued open aloofness and public estrangement
means that the bride finds her closest support in a child.   The child
fills important emotional needs, and the young woman will try to have
one soon after marriage.[56]   In China, where the majority of marriages are arranged and the filial tie remains strong, children continue to meet this need.   The hierarchy of relationships in the rural
family is shifting slowly as the emphasis on the conjugal bond
strengthens.   Where this occurs the bride is more prepared to postpone childbearing, because her husband will satisfy more of her emotional needs.   Family members provide warmth that non-kinsmen do
not provide, but this function could be performed by a small family
as well.   As in the past, the Chinese bride becomes fully accepted
into the household by the mother-in-law and often by her husband
when she bears a son.   Most rural respondents report that it still
is considered important for a woman to bear a son to continue the
family line, whereas in urban China such pressures have abated.

In addition to her role in reproduction, the woman has to socialize her children and perform housework to keep the family in the
labour force.   One of the themes of the Myrdal interviews is that the
highest praise is accorded those who manage their homes well, and
purchase consumer goods from their earnings.[57]   They probably
would not praise a woman who turned her back on housework solely
to earn money.   Housework remains a heavy job, but several children

lighten the work as they grow up; older children care for younger ones, and each has a household task.   There is a conflict between the contribution young children make in running the home and the extra costs they require, but this is not always apparent to the woman.   If she must bear children to prove her worth, then she can have several, for they will help each other.

It is thus necessary for the regime to alter the image the women defined by their contribution to "expert" household management.   There are several ways to do so.   In an effort to bring women into the community,. the authorities have tried first to collectivize housework (1958-60)[58] and later to distribute household tasks more equally in the family (1963-64[59] and 1965 to the present).   One article written in 1964 argued that housework should be shared:

> The rural areas have overcome the old mores according
> to which women cannot do any other work but housework.
> [Sic!   Actually, we will see women were allowed to work
> in agricultural production.]   Now, women and men alike
> go to work in the fields.   If the housework is all left to
> the women, they will be more than busy.   Every day af-
> ter they finish work in the fields and return home, they
> have to build the fire, cook rice, wash dishes, feed the
> pigs, draw water, and grind flour, and still do the sewing
> and even feed their babies.[60]

Equal participation in housework is not a popular solution to the problems of women's double work obligation.   The older mother-in-law feels she has earned the right to retire from active homemaking; she looks forward throughout her married years to having daughters-in-law serve her.   The men will participate in an occasional task at their own discretion; they do not accept the obligation to share the housework.   If successful, such efforts would release women from their chief roles as producers and socializers of family members.   This would have an anti-natalist impact because when custom no longer demanded that women alone do housework, women would become more aware of the existing costs of rearing numerous children while performing heavy household tasks.

The third major stage in the life cycle comes when a woman's own sons have children.   She socializes her offspring to marry and have children so that she may have daughters-in-law to do the housekeeping and bear grandchildren to complete the family cycle. Many respondents note that their own mother or mother-in-law pressed them to marry and have children before they grew too old. Since most children born in China are likely to survive, numerous children may not be necessary for a woman to perform the tasks expected of her in the family.

We have seen that many statuses can be attained only through children. Only if alternative expectations of women increase will they decide that fewer children will enable them to perform the traditional roles in the family while meeting the other demands on them as well.

Rural Women's Status in the Community and the Importance of Children

Numerous obligations, expectations and responsibilities link women to the community; many of them are related to women's childbearing activities. Non-familial roles are becoming more numerous for women in rural China than in the past. But at present only a minority of women, generally the younger ones, relate to the community in a capacity other than as a family member.

In traditional China the bride was integrated into productive activities gradually. Even in the southern rice culture where women performed field work, they did so only after months of marriage. Since collectivization, increased demands have brought the new bride into village production a few days after marriage. However, she is still isolated from other non-familial relationships. The intense proprietary jealousy of husbands and face-saving concerns of parents-in-law mean that brides may be excluded from co-educational peer-group activities. Agnates proscribe organized sports, recreation and political activities which bring them into contact with young village men. As non-kinship community activities attenuate, childbearing assumes importance.

The older woman associates with other women of her age and relates to them mainly through her kinship and childbearing experiences. In winter the women look forward to sitting on their doorsteps, doing housework and gossiping about family affairs.[61] Even when seasonal work in the fields assumes priority, the division of labour by age and sex means that women associate together. Older women fulfil a community expectation when they marry off their

children. Traditionally, if the mother could marry several offspring
well, she demonstrated both her good planning and family status.[62]
At present, women still assert family status through arranging good
matches for their offspring.[63] Women without children cannot obtain this satisfaction. Finally, numerous children often are valuable
because families and lineage branches vie for scarce political positions in the community.[64] Many parents feel more satisfied with
several children to represent the family. "Many sons mean that my
family is well protected," said one old grandmother. But two sons,
she claimed, might suffice. Integration and solidarity in the village
depend less on kinship lines than before.

In contrast to their urban counterparts, the bulk of middle-aged
and younger married women in the village still define their main social roles as tied to childbearing and housekeeping. The creation of
non-familial opportunities for them is of crucial importance to altering these pro-natalist institutional determinants of fertility.

THE OPPORTUNITY COSTS OF CHILDBEARING

The Chinese Communists have attempted to bring all adults into the active labour force. According to the Marriage Law of 1950,
married women do not become economic dependants of their husbands.
The reorganization of labour in the collective rationalized the labour
force, increasing the number of opportunities for women to work outside the family.

Rural Women in the Labour Force

Proportion of women in the agricultural labour force

One study describes the increase in the average number of
days worked by each female labourer in collective projects from
1955 (lower-stage collectives) to 1957 (higher-stage collectives).
This survey shows that the proportion of women in the total labour
force declined slightly after higher co-operativization. There may
have been an actual increase in female participation which is disguised by the simultaneous increase in male labour participation in
collective work (see Table 4).

It can be seen that although women did not join the collective
labour force in the same proportions as men, they did increase

TABLE 4. *Proportion of male and female labour units and average numbers of labour days per male and female labour unit, 1955, 1957*

	Total		Male		Female	
	1955	1957	1955	1957	1955	1957
Share of labour units	100·0	100·0	54·8	56·7	45·2	43·3
Share of labour days	100·0	100·0	75·6	71·7	23·5	28·5
Average number of labour days per labour unit	96	175	134	204	50	105

SOURCE: Adapted from Schran, *op. cit.*, p. 195.

their share of work days during the year. In examining the increase in average number of labour days for women, one should compare within male and within female labour categories, not between the columns of male and female labour units. A "labour day" does not equal a full day's work; it is a conceptual tool based on a day's labour by a skilled man. This artifact of computing labour days means that women might work a full day and earn only three-fifths of a labour day.

Nonetheless, it is likely that women work fewer actual days than men. The following data from 1957 show that women are concentrated in those classes of workers who work fewer work days. One-third of the women worked for less than 50 days, and almost two-thirds worked less than 100 days during that year.

TABLE 5. *Days worked by male and female workers in 228 agricultural producers co-operatives, 1957*

Number of days worked per year	All labour units	Male labour units	Female labour units
0–50	17·6	6·5	32·2
51–100	19·6	11·9	29·7
101–150	18·6	18·3	19·0
151–200	18·3	24·0	10·9
201–365	25·9	9·3	8·2
Total	100·0%	100·0%	100·0%

SOURCE: Adapted from Schran, *op. cit.*, p. 196.

The same survey revealed regional differences in female labour force participation. Women work almost twice the number of labour days in the southern rice culture as in other regions (Table 5). Weather and cropping patterns also account for some of these differences, for both men and women work more days in the south where there are two major crops per year than in the north where there is only one. The regional differences in labour days worked are greater for women than for men, so it is clear that cultural definitions of the proper agricultural work for women assume a great role. That is, where simple agricultural tools are used, such as in the rice paddies, women do much of the transplanting. Few women till the soil where ploughs are used, as in the wheat areas of the north. [65]

TABLE 6. *Proportion of days spent in productive labour by women in the main geographical areas, 1957*

Area	Percentage of total labour force		Average labour days worked		Percentage of total working days	
	Males	Females	Males	Females	Male	Female
North-west and Inner Mongolia District	60·1	39·9	170	88	74·5	25·5
North-east District	65·3	34·7	185	60	85·5	14·5
Central District	55·8	44·2	195	84	74·6	25·4
Southern District	54·3	45·7	226	133	66·8	33·2

SOURCES: *Hsin-hua Pan-Yueh-K'an*, **18** (September 1958), pp. 94–98; *JPRS*, 41, 914, p. 5.

It appears that collectivization resulted in more labour days worked by women; there is no evidence that it resulted in a larger proportion of women entering the work force than before.

The 1956–57 National Programme for Agricultural Development, drafted in January 1956, but never implemented, set a goal of raising the labour days worked by women. In ten years men were to work for an average of 250 labour days and women 120 labour days per year. This goal envisaged a great increase by women, who in 1957 were working 105 days (Table 4). [66] The Ta-chai Production Brigade set an even higher goal for labour participation. Men were to work 330 labour days, "ironside girls" 320, and other females from 180 to 260 labour days per year. [67]

Women perform heavy labour in the communes; however, much of it is sporadic. In one commune in Kwangtung Province 25,000 women formed 45% of the total labour force working on water conservancy projects. [68] Women also contributed 30% of the labour force collecting natural fertilizer. Such work does not redefine the woman's primary task to that of a labour force participant. She is expected to perform household tasks first.

In sum, although women comprise about 40% of the labour brigades they do not work as many days as do the men. Women drop out of the labour force at will to fit farming in with household demands and the family cycle. Given the heavy household duties they perform, and the fact that their families do not expect them to till the land as their primary duty, this is inevitable. Women perform

more labour in the Ta-chai Brigade, an exception that proves the
rule.   There, women are expected to contribute to labour to the
same degree as men.   Ta-chai women thus cut down on domestic
chores and probably on childbearing as well.

Several kinds of conflict arise between childbearing and work.
First, work opportunities may be physically distant from the home;
women may delay marriage to pursue jobs in other places, or they
may marry and leave their homes for the jobs.   This has been true
for urban China, but not for rural China generally.   Women are less
likely than men to leave the home for non-agricultural labour.
Women enter into local productive work in their natal or affinal village; they need not delay marriage or childbearing to work.   Secondly, agricultural labour conflicts with childbearing in that it demands
much time and energy.   The undercapitalized labour and homemaking
tasks make it difficult for women to pursue both simultaneously.   Rural work organization is therefore adjusted to fit the childbearing and
housekeeping cycle.   Women are trained by their families from an
early age to assume different production roles from men. [69]   When
they are pregnant or lactating they are transferred to light work
near home, such as seed selection, at less pay.   Later, women can
resume only women's work without penalty; it is difficult to return
to the time-consuming heavy agricultural work performed by men.
So long as women accept the traditional "women's work," they enter
and leave the labour force in sequence with their family formation.
In such cases work participation by itself does not have anti-natalist
implications.

In other words, whereas Chinese women have long worked in
the economy, in the past their agricultural participation was not defined as socially contradictory to their holding family roles.   Any
conflict that arose was in terms of the time and energy available
for both jobs, and usually such a conflict was resolved in favour of
familism.   In the north and central areas of China, women performed handicraft work at home with remuneration equal to agricultural labour.   Handicraft work, which kept the women isolated in
individual families, has been a conservative influence.   Home-based
handicraft work also removes a large sector of women from production for the community which can be collectively organized, directed,
and from which income for the collective can be extracted.   It makes
economies of scale difficult to create.   For these reasons the regime
has tried to organize collective handicraft work in rural areas.

In the mid-sixties the political organization of women agricultural workers was intensified in an effort to keep them on the job. As they enter employment in the fields, women are organized into political study groups; they are thereby deterred from coming under the influence of the more traditionalist older women working alongside them. Rest hours are spent in political study. As a result, agricultural participation presently brings women into situations where family norms are criticized. Women are urged to redefine themselves as workers rather than as family members. In recent years the regime has also tried to redefine the social meaning of work. The transfer of agricultural training to the rural school system has altered the strict segregation of tasks by age and sex. Boys and girls in lower-middle school learn equal agricultural skills. Educated girls also learn that heavy labour has the highest status in the community. As young mothers who do not wish to perform "women's work" and who learn in school that political activism is measured by endurance in labour, they will have to reduce their family size to stay in the labour force. This role conflict has been discussed frequently since 1963 when many urban young people settled in the countryside. "How can a woman continue to make progress when she has children?" was one recurrent question.[70] In this view young women who drop out of the labour force to care for their families are considered faitures.[71] The extension of education to larger numbers of women means that more women will define childbearing as a cost, if it requires renouncing production in heavy labour, alone imbued with honour in the community.

Non-agricultural jobs for peasant women

Agricultural jobs are acceptable tasks for young women, married or single. The unmarried village girl can also seek the small number of jobs in town. Once married, however, she is pressed to renounce positions away from home. A consequence of the social definition of rural-centred, non-agricultural labour is to remove married rural women as an eligible labour force. An important source of anti-natalist pressure is thereby closed to them.

According to my interviews, only the most determined women delay marriage to follow such non-agricultural occupations. The most common response that I have encountered is for women to opt for marrying and dropping out of the labour force. Family norms are too strong for many to resist. For example, one young former peasant girl from Kwangtung Province married a fellow worker from an urban factory, whereupon she renounced the job and returned to live in her affinal village. She noted that such jobs are much sought after as opportunities to escape the agricultural routine, and also a means of locating an urban spouse.

> "My husband would not allow me to continue. He thought his income of $40 a month was adequate to support the family and that I did not need to work."
> "Did you feel unhappy about this?"
> "Of course, I was unhappy! On the other hand, people would say good things about me. You know, like, 'This is a good daughter-in-law; she is kind to her mother-in-law. She goes out to cut wood every day, and goes to the market. When she works in the fields she gets the money and contributes it to the family purse. How lovely and good a daughter-in-law she is.'"[72]

Political leadership roles for women

The top leadership generally has favoured the inclusion of women in leadership positions. Since the egalitarian ideology adopted by female political leaders has anti-natalist consequences, the wholesale according of political positions to women might have important results. However, there appears to be resistance to this development among those holding power in society. Both men and older women in the family oppose the assumption of leadership positions by married women. Despite the "party line" that women are liberated, the problem of women in political positions has been long standing. As early as the Yenan period (1935-49) this problem had attracted the concern of the female leadership. Ting Ling, a well-known woman novelist, noted that women were still subjected to contradictory expectations. If these women did not marry, she wrote, they were ridiculed; if they did marry and had children they were chastised for holding political posts rather than remaining at home with their families. If they remained at home for a number of years, they were called backward. In the new society they were condemned for a predicament not of their own making.[73] Contradictory expectations continue regarding the political role of women. Women are eligible for top leadership positions in China, but they rarely attain them. They do attain jobs which relate to women's work and which are committed to carrying out party policy regarding women. They cannot easily oppose their unequal treatment as women in the labour force and at home when it counters the current party policy decisions of the period.

Rumours have also served to keep women in their place:

"There are many rumours invented when you go out to
work as a cadre.   There are many occasions when a
female cadre has to discuss certain matters with a male
cadre.   Others will then say that they have illicit relations.   Who likes to hear such rumours?   And parents,
of course, think that such rumours affect their reputa-
tion, and so prevent their daughters from working in the
commune or brigade. "[74]

The force of parental reaction is also a result of their ignorance of
the goals and operation of the political system.   For instance, do
cadres get paid as much for their work as do agricultural workers?
Some parents wanted their daughters to contribute to the family income and believed that work in political positions was not manual
labour and could not possibly lead to such contributions.   Thus, the
issue of prejudice against women's political participation had not been
discussed until the Cultural Revolution required that women be
brought into the political arena to support approved candidates.

The proportion of posts allocated to women in the political hierarchy varies according to the level of power.   In 1956 women
were only 10% of the party membership. [75]   Recent data are not
available, but there is no reason to assume this proportion has increased greatly.   I will now estimate the political job attainment
by women of marriageable age in 1960.   Their representation in
the political hierarchy in the wake of the Cultural Revolution will
be described below.   A 1965 news release figure noted that one-
quarter of the production team positions in Kwangtung were held
be women;[76]   it is assumed here that this same proportion of
women held positions in 1960.   The proportions of women in brigade and commune level jobs were probably substantially lower.
I will estimate the proportion of women holding commune posts as
5% of all posts, and that holding brigade posts as 10% of these
posts.   It will be assumed that women were more likely than men
to be between the ages of 15 and 25 when they held such jobs.
The taboos and pressures against women continuing in these positions after they marry meant that they were more likely to drop
out, opening the way for other young women.   Thus, I assume
that 70% of the women in leadership positions were less than 25

years old. Women probably comprise half their age cohort. Based
on these assumptions, I calculated that 4.2% of the women aged 15
to 25 in 1960 held high-status political jobs in their villages.

More women were brought into higher levels of rural political
leadership under the impulse of the Cultural Revolution, which increased their participation in the new revolutionary committees.
Heilungkiang Radio met International Women's Day in 1968 with the
caustic comment that "among some of our comrades, tendencies to
belittle and discriminate against women still persist."[77] It was suggested that revolutionary committees gradually allot 20% of their
seats to women. This goal has not been reached. Subsequent to
this announcement, the Chao-tung county revolutionary committee of
Heilungkiang was commended for implementing the proposal, having
placed women in 16.4% of the membership of the revolutionary committee of the county. With one or two women on every committee,
2,939 women members served at all county levels. In the Chao-
tung county revolutionary committee itself there were seven women
members out of 35, three on the 13-member standing committee.[78]
Women do not appear to figure prominently in the leadership, even
where special efforts are made to include them. The number of
participants is smaller elsewhere. In one special district of An-
hwei Province, which was singled out for praise for the number of
women appointed, only 10% of the membership of the revolutionary
committees were women.[79]

Many of these were token appointments. The women were not
expected to rise in the political hierarchies. Shanghai's Wen Hui
Pao commented that people who urged that "we should show concern
for women" by including some women in revolutionary committees
often engaged in tokenism. Their basic attitude, the paper continued, was that women should take the "lighter load of the revolution"
since they were heavily burdened with household chores.[80] As a result, women were elected to revolutionary committees as "decorative
fixtures," expected to return to home and hearth after marrying.
They were young at the time of their appointment. Female members of the Chao-tung commune of Heilungkiang averaged 20 years
of age. While it was the intention of some committee members
that women should remain on the committees for such short periods,
the women themselves may not hold such expectations. Those women
who do enter political leadership positions will be most likely to reduce their family size in order to keep their jobs. They stand to
lose the jobs when they marry early and bear children. The holders

of these positions are probably selected for their prior attitudes.
They also are socialized outside the family and have had their commitment to the job reinforced. Participation in political jobs brings
young women into contact with other leaders who are committed to
the goals of the collective. The women learn new self-definitions
which contrast with the definitions of themselves as mothers, often
held by their mothers-in-law. Women political leaders are an elite
likely to remain committed to the goals of the collective when they
run counter to those of their families. These women will alter their
family-building behaviour to retain their jobs.

Agro-technical rural jobs for women

The economic policies of the Cultural Revolution stressed the
creation of self-sufficient local plants to manufacture products, such
as small tools, useful for agricultural production. Communities also
are to become self-sufficient in social welfare and services. These
policies have gradually created a corps of rural-based non-agricultural workers. These new rural occupational positions expand the
involvement of women in non-familistic jobs and environments, and
alter the traditional sexual division of labour in agriculture. The
new skills related to agricultural mechanization and the application
of education to farming may lack sex labelling. Women are eligible
to operate light agricultural machinery, to work in village experimental agricultural stations, and to act as semi-skilled "barefoot"
doctors and veterinarians. The reorganization of rural education to
reach school-age youth and orient them to such jobs equalizes opportunities by sex.

Do these agro-technical jobs in the village differ from handicraft work in respect of their anti-natalist implications? Jaffe and
Azumi noted that cottage industries employed women in Japan and
elsewhere, but employment experience did not greatly reduce their
fertility. They argued that developing nations should turn their resources to urban-located jobs in industry for women to remove the
employed women from family settings.[81] I have claimed similarly
that traditional agricultural pursuits in Chinese villages probably did
not reduce women's motivations for having many children. In what
ways do the new rural, semi-industrial jobs establish alternatives
to childbearing? The jobs remain in the village, but in theory they
are not controlled by kinsmen. (In practice it would be hard to eliminate the control of jobs by certain families who dole them out to
their kinsmen.) The time required by the jobs competes with the

time available for family work.   Whereas in agricultural pursuits
the women drop out of the labour force to do housework or work
part-time in the labour force, the new semi-industrial rural jobs
stress continued commitment.   They socialize the job-holders to
place community interests before family interests.   Peer-group
pressure is exerted on new workers to stay on the job.   Agro-
technicians are imbued with the spirit of their mission in contrast
to the general female agricultural labour force.   Thus, women who
drop out of their jobs to bear children will lose the high-status positions for which they have been selected and trained.   Finally, some
of these workers, such as barefoot doctors, are expected to educate
the women around them in family limitation.   As propagandists, they
must abide by the message they convey to others.

Although the locally based, semi-industrial jobs do not remove
women from the influence of their parents in the community, they
do involve them in peer groups which are co-educational and based
on an egalitarian ethos.   These positions do not satisfy the drive
for social mobility to the same extent as do jobs through the educational system.   Nevertheless, women who have adopted an egalitarian ideology and have entered these jobs lose much by giving
them up for childbearing.   Most important for the anti-natalist aims
of the government are the increased number of women who enter the
local elite.   However, a small proportion of women enter local leadership positions.   Therefore, the main anti-natalist efforts are bringing the masses into the school system where they learn the ideology
of equality through their manual labour for the collective; this education is followed up by pressure for their continued participation
in the labour force to attain local status.

Recent changes in the nature of local-level jobs reveal a trend
altering the nature of status.   Authority in recent years has been
earned by those who became leaders and were respected by those
around them.   Proper attitudes and behaviour were to be displayed
continually by the leadership.   Recently it has been stressed that
those in leading posts not only do not have a monopoly of prestige,
but that they must share it with non-leaders.   The concept of activists is a long standing one in China, referring to political participation by participants without formal leadership posts.   This has been
given more weight in the guise of setting up new agro-technical and
political propagandist jobs.   The power of local leaders is reduced.
Leaders are to mingle with the led; they are to work alongside them,
earning little more than the villagers.   The emphasis on proper at-

titudes stresses that jobs must be earned repeatedly or the leaders
can be removed.   Finally, the jobs are not narrowly defined, specialized positions, but are of a general nature and require little advanced training.   The job-holders are to earn status not only through
knowledge but through their abilities to help.   As a result of de-em-
phasizing the division between leadership and led, authority is available to many.   This should spread more widely the desire for women
to continue in the labour force to achieve recognition from their peers
and from the community.   Childbearing will deny them this opportunity.

*Proportion of women aged 15 to 25 in rural leadership
positions in the wake of the Cultural Revolution*

The institutional reforms of the Cultural Revolution increased
the agro-technical positions available for women in the villages.
Women were also appointed to positions of generalized power, such
as membership of revolutionary committees.   Have the purges and
institutional reforms increased the proportionate representation of
women in such non-familial posts?   First, I estimate that one-quarter of the newly created agro-technical positions in the production
team (barefoot doctors, technicians, veterinarians) went to young
women.   Further, in Kwangtung Province 3,500 women joined the
armed forces in 1968; I assume that the same number were recruited in 1970.   Finally, an estimated one-quarter of the turnover
in lower-level cadre positions was accorded to young women, and
the proportion of positions allocated to them at the brigade and commune levels increased to 15 and 10% respectively.   I make no assumptions as to the numbers of women who participate in the new
semi-industrial rural factories; it is not clear that they are numerous.   I again assume that women comprise half the population between the ages of 15 and 25.

Based on these assumptions I find that the proportion of rural
women in this age group who have entered the village elite increased
from 4.2 to 7.5%.   The regime still has far to go in extending positions to young women to reward them for compliance to leadership
policies, or to set up alternative opportunities for childbearing.   This
7.5% may be increased further if substantial numbers become semi-
industrial workers in the commune; however, there may be prejudice
against bringing young women into the factories and workshops.   Alternatively, the regime must increase political socialization among
non-leadership women to an even greater extent than among the men,

since the men already have a better chance to become leaders.

Major Non-familial Roles for Urban Women

Urban women are involved more directly and intensely in community activities than are rural women. Their greater participation
in non-kinship institutions weakens the urban women's ties to the pa-
triliny in comparison with rural women. Because of their greater
involvement outside the home, the conflicting expectations of urban
women's proper place make the role conflicts they experience even
more acute.

Urban women are more likely than rural women to live neo-
locally. Consequently, their relations with parents and in-laws are
not structured by means of obligations arising from living under a
common roof. Housing in urban China, which is smaller and more
cramped than in rural areas, can accommodate fewer children. This
shortage of space is an incentive for women to work. The statistical data of the fifties show the numbers and proportion of women
employed in non-agricultural labour to have increased since 1949.
Nevertheless, the pre-industrial nature of much of China's economy
cannot bring the bulk of urban women workers and employees into
industrial work. The numbers and proportions of women employed
as "workers and employees" has increased more rapidly than women
in all non-agricultural employment. In 1949 the proportion of women
among workers and employees was only 7.5%. Women constituted
14% of the total non-agricultural labour force at that time. In 1957,
the end of the first five-year plan, the proportion of women among
workers and employees had risen to 13%; 18% of the non-agricultural
labour force were women. The opening of small-scale workshops
between mid-1958 and 1960 did bring more women into the labour
force. However, women comprised only 20% of the total increase
in non-agricultural workers in that period. This was close to their
existing proportion in non-agricultural labour; hence, the proportion
of women in the non-agricultural labour force remained at 18%.[82]
In 1960 many of these enterprises consolidated or closed their doors.
The workers returned to agriculture or handicrafts. Consequently,
I suppose that the proportion of women among workers and employees has declined since 1960. The current drive to re-open many of
the small-scale workshops may again increase the numbers of women
in non-industrial employment.

The proportion of women working in industry is somewhat higher in the larger cities than in the nation as a whole. Their concen-

tration in light industries in the coastal cities gives rise to the common notion by visitors that all Chinese women work. Barry Richman estimated that 25% of the workers and employees in China's "major cities" were women.[83] He arrived at this figure from his survey of 35 enterprises in urban centres. I have estimated the proportion of urban women aged 15 to 25 working for wages. Although women comprised less than one-fifth of the agricultural labour force by the end of the first five-year plan, according to my estimates, only 16% of urban women aged 15 to 59 were working for wages. Approximately one-third of these were employed in handicraft work. The proportion of women aged 15 to 25 inclusive who were employed as workers and employees in modern industry in 1956 can be estimated. I assume that women in this age group comprise 10% of the urban population. Based on these assumptions I find that 24% of the urban women in this age bracket were employed as workers and employees in 1956.

The low proportion of women in non-agricultural work and as workers and employees is the result of norms regarding woman's place. The rapid expansion of the industrial labour force in the first five-year plan was concentrated in heavy industry, which was thought inappropriate for women. Light industries were de-emphasized. High levels of unemployment among the male labour force and the continual stream of rural migrants to the cities in search of work put women at a disadvantage when competing for jobs.

Chinese authorities claim that women were laid off in large numbers in the sixties when investment in industry declined. They have not commented on the ease with which women could obtain employment in 1970, in the aftermath of the Cultural Revolution. With much of the investment turned towards improving agricultural production, it is clear that the rate of growth of workers and employees in the cities is much lower than it was in the fifties. The emphasis on heavy industry in the first five-year plan meant that women were not hired at the rates of male workers; it is possible that a relatively greater number of women will be hired in an investment programme that emphasizes small-scale industry. However, since the overall rate of increase of non-agricultural employment is much lower than in the fifties, absolute numbers of women newly employed each year should decrease. I would expect that the figure of 24% of women aged 15 to 25 employed in Chinese cities will decline somewhat.

At the higher levels of managerial and white-collar work women were also at a disadvantage because fewer of them had received the

necessary training and education in the pre-Communist period. Most
of the half-million junior-level women cadres added from 1953 to
1955 had come through the educational system during the Communist
period. Most had received only lower-middle school training at best.
Approximately 10% of them had graduated from higher-level educational institutions, since not many more than this proportion were attending schools in the forties. [84] Consequently, women cadres generally
were considered to be less well-educated and less effective on the
job than their male counterparts. Women comprised the same proportion of white-collar, professional employees as they did of the
non-agricultural labour force. The percentage of women in the total
group of cadres increased in the fifties. [85] In 1951 women were 8%
of all cadres; by 1955 they were 14.6%. [86] At the same time their
proportional representation declined at the highest levels of senior
county and provincial administrative positions. The proportion of
positions held by women dropped from 6 to under 3% from 1951 to
1955. Women apparently were laid off in larger numbers than were
their male counterparts in 1958 when there was a retrenchment in
the ranks of urban cadres. [87] Their relative position did not improve
again until after the Cultural Revolution.

At higher levels of the factory managerial leadership, women
hold still fewer posts. Richman met no women directors of industry in his trip through China. Seven of the 90 assistant directors
of 35 industrial plants were women. Roughly 15% of the department
heads and 10% of the workshop directors he met were women. The
proportion of females was greater at the lower levels of management.
Up to 50% of the floor foremen or group leaders were women in some
enterprises. [88] Richman does not specify whether these enterprises
were the light industries that hired only women. At the lowest levels of leadership women held still more positions. In Peking in 1963
one-third of the city's cadres were women. This probably included
unpaid cadres and those hired by the neighbourhood stations (i.e. residential cadres), not career women.

Of the 24% of urban women likely to adhere to government policy regarding family formation, a smaller core are most committed
by virtue of their being in leadership positions. In 1955 there were
764,000 female cadres in China. To this number female students,
who comprised one-quarter of all students, must be added. Based
on these assumptions, I estimate that 12% of all urban women in
this age group were "leaders" in 1956. Women from the ages of
15 to 25 had a 0.12 probability of entering into leadership positions

in the 1950's, but women in the 1960's did not. The government's
concern to curtail the size of the bureaucratic leadership must have
resulted in a slower expansion of the elite than during the first five-
year plan. The reforms in higher education meant that students
would be drawn largely from factory workers. Since I estimated
that women still form one-fifth of all workers and employees, they
would comprise a similar proportion of the new student bodies, unless special efforts were made to over-select female students. Finally, women who entered government posts in the fifties would still
be employed. The proportion of women aged 15 to 25 who can enter the urban leadership in 1970 must have decreased. It would be
necessary to increase ideological pressure through the schools or
through political associations to counteract the lack of leadership
positions for these young urban women.

The existence of some opportunities to work, and the concomitant double standard that persisted regarding the expense of hiring
women, meant that women were attracted to the labour force but
compelled to reduce their family tasks to stay in it. In contrast to
rural women, urban workers do not attempt to fit production activities into homemaking schedules. The demand for their jobs is such
that they cannot afford to lose their positions. Employment for urban women has anti-natalist consequences absent for rural workers.
First, the desire to obtain positions may lead many to postpone marriage. Secondly, once in the labour force they are under pressure
from their bosses and co-workers to reduce fertility. Although
women are covered by trade union regulations and therefore have
maternity leave and hospitalization paid by the union, they are considered unpatriotic if they have large families; they should not waste
state money on childbearing, they are told. Co-workers, in particular white-collar workers, are likely to define work as more interesting than childbearing. They thus encourage women to consider
themselves workers first, and mothers second. Factory workers
are more likely to reduce fertility than are women who remain at
home. Thirdly, women learn about family limitation during work
hours in meetings and in conversations. Labour force participation
has influenced Chinese urban women to reduce their fertility.

Women who cannot get employment in factories or offices may
obtain handicraft work in the neighbourhood "service stations." The
urban handicraft workers are in a position most similar to rural
productive workers in terms of the familist environment surrounding
them. However, even the housewives who manufacture handicrafts

do so in putting-out stations. They are likely to interact to a greater extent with women who are not kinswomen than do rural women
who work in the fields. Also there are more opportunities for handicraft workers to come into contact with political norms regarding
proper family size than is true for their rural counterparts.

Other non-family opportunities such as political positions exist
in urban areas. The street association offices are staffed by housewives, providing them with opportunities to assume political leadership. Political leadership positions exist for rural women, but they
are given to the woman worker, not the housewife. Unemployed
housewives form the main pool of political leaders for the urban
neighbourhood associations. Most of their activities involve volun-
teer labour and community service. This work has high status in
the community and should provide some alternative to childbearing
in terms of community recognition. The shortcomings of such work
are that they do not commit women to long-term leadership positions.
After some years at these jobs, many women turn to their homes to
care for their children. The urban leadership attempts to revitalize
the neighbourhood associations, trying to infuse more enthusiasm into the local political leadership.[89] Residential association leaders
remain more familistic than other urban workers and leaders. During the Cultural Revolution urban residents were put in close contact
with politically conforming students. The residential association
small groups expanded to include student and worker participants.
Neighborhood associations now help run the urban schools and other
social services, such as public health clinics. As a result, urban
women political leaders have been more closely linked with non-familistic organizations than before.

It is easier for married urban women than for married rural
women to enter into political leadership positions. These posts are
more numerous and more psychologically accessible. Family members do not resist women's acceptance of these jobs for the same
reasons as in the rural areas. In the urban centres the greatest
complaint is that such jobs do not pay anything, and families prefer
women to earn money. As a result, urban political leaders and
handicraft workers do not necessarily retain their commitment to
the organization, for they lack channels of mobility available to
working women.

THE DIVISION OF TASKS IN THE URBAN HOME

The social organization of urban housework is less strictly divided along the lines of traditional sex roles and tasks. Women do spend more time than men in raising and socializing children, but housework is often performed by husbands. The jobs that women fill and their remaining housework tasks deter them from participating in political activities unless they reduce family size.

Services that lighten housework are more readily available in urban China. It is easier to purchase pre-packed foods. Child care centres are available in factories and in some neighborhood residential offices. The latter are ill-equipped, but they provide rudimentary services for women working part-time. Finally, residential centres may provide collective housekeeping services, such as clothes washing and mending. Women are encouraged by local party units to aid one another in their housework; however, they generally help one another only when one of them is ill.

Urban women have been in closer contact with egalitarian ideology through collective service. Their duties of housework and child care are heavy enough to deter them from participation in work. They are therefore highly motivated to reduce family size.

CONCLUSION

In the first decade of Communist power the government of the People's Republic of China introduced social reforms of the marriage system, land tenure and organization, and Chinese religion that reduced the productive and ceremonial utilities of children. It became less easy for parents to control their children's future jobs or income. Achievement-oriented families in rural and urban areas found that numerous children were an economic drain. In urban centres families organized their resources to train their children for high-status jobs; they saved for consumer goods. Rural families in the environs of urban centres sent their children to the cities in search of jobs. Some of them began to limit their fertility, having experienced population pressure and increased competition for slowly expanding job opporutnities.

Some data demonstrate the interest in limiting fertility in rural China without providing information on how widespread this interest is. The first survey is that of IUD insertions in a Chinese commune in 1965. This study shows that women opted for the IUD when they already had borne several children. Rural women did not appear to be using the IUD to postpone the first child or to space children, but rather to terminate childbearing (Tables 7 and 8). There is no indication as to whether these women already had been limiting their fertility by some other method. I tend to believe they were not doing so successfully, if at all. Consequently, their adoption of IUD's would reduce fertility in the rural areas rather than act as a substitute for other methods already in use. I cannot extrapolate from these data the proportion of all rural women who were using methods to limit fertility, since the size of the population at risk in this commune is not given. I must turn instead to data gained from interviews with refugees from the mainland.

TABLE 7. *Insertions of IUD in 1,528 rural women, 1963–65, Shantung Province, by parity*

Parity	Percentage of women
1	5·2
2	10·6
3	19·4
4	25·6
5+	39·1
Total	99·9

SOURCE: Calculated from 'Kuan-yu tsai nung-ts'un fang-chih chieh-yu-huan- sui fang ch'ing-kuang chi kai-chin i-chien' (Conditions and suggestions for improvement of insertion of IUD in the village), *Shantung I-k'an*, 2 (1966), pp. 13–15.

TABLE 8. *Insertions of IUD in 2,170 rural women, by age*

Age	Percentage of women
21–25	8·5
26–30	18·4
31–35	31·1
36–40	28·6
40+	13·2
Total	99·8

SOURCE: *Ibid.* The data were gathered by mobile medical teams responsible for inserting IUD's in rural areas from 1963 to 1965. One might question the reliability of these statistics. Clearly the Chinese medical world was motivated to prove that the mobile medical teams were the best method of providing for mass contraception. The statistics given may have been distorted and exaggerated to prove that women were accepting IUD's from the teams. However, in examining internally the spread of these data, I find the demographic characteristics of the IUD acceptance, i.e. the parity and age of the acceptors, similar to IUD acceptance in Taiwan. This somewhat strengthens my confidence in the figures.

In evaluating the responses to questionnaires regarding their fertility behaviour, we must keep in mind the special nature of Chinese refugees in Hong Kong and Macao. Those who fled China since the early sixties do not represent a cross section of the southern

rural population.   They are highly selected in terms of their ability
to plan; they also tend to have more education than those they leave
behind.   Their social class origins are often politically stigmatized
on the mainland.   Generally, they are peasants who want to get
ahead, but who leave China when they find their paths to mobility
blocked.   Hong Kong and Macao represent an opportunity for social
mobility.   Since before 1949 the areas were contiguous with the
mainland and migration to and fro was patterned.   In sum, the refugees represent a highly mobile population in geographical and social terms.   Although I do not know how representative the refugees
are of the mainland population, I would argue that their fertility behaviour most closely follows that of the socially mobile rural population.

   In Figure I and Table 9 are reproduced the results of two efforts at evaluating the fertility responses of the refugees.   The first
survey was carried out in 1965 on rural refugees into Macao.   It
shows that relatively young rural women had lower ideal family sizes
than older women.   For those aged 18 to 44 modal preferences were
four children as first choice and two as second choice.   In contrast,

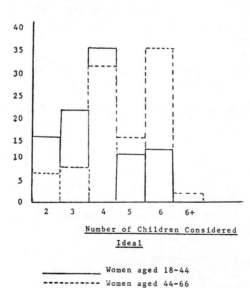

SOURCE: Adapted from Robert Worth, *Current Demographic Patterns among Kwangtung Chinese* (Honolulu:
University of Hawaii, Department of Public Health, n.d.), mimeographed, p. 6.

FIGURE I. *Ideal family size desires of 456 rural migrants*

the bimodal distribution for women older than 44 was six and four children. A second survey that I carried out on rural migrants suggests that they had limited their fertility after they had borne the desired number of children. This was a sample of convenience, including only those women and men introduced to me, without any attempt at representativeness of the migrant population. Although only a minority had ever limited fertility, those aged between 31 and 40 had tried to limit their fertility more than those too old or those considerably younger. I would argue that those couples aged under 30 were unlikely to limit their fertility until they had borne the desired number of children, especially sons. They would be more likely to try to limit fertility when they moved into the age range 31 to 40.

My interpretation of these data is that those who were mobile and able to do something about their future (like migrating) and their counterparts in China were controlling fertility when they had borne the number of children desired. The anti-natalist motivation in China would then be limited by the slow expansion of opportunities throughout the nation. As I have suggested, opportunities had declined by the second decade of Communist power, it would be critical for the regime to expand alternative leadership positions. Further, the village women who had not completed lower-middle school had few real alternatives to familism. The majority of the population consequently was unable to anticipate with the certainty of educated women that fertility limitation would aid them in becoming mobile. It would be they who sought to bear four or more children

TABLE 9. *Contraceptive usage and intention to limit fertility among married Chinese refugees, 1967–69, by urban and rural origin*

	Number of respondents
Urban origin	
Ever-used form of mechanical or surgical fertility limitation	11
Used *coitus interruptus*	3
Intend to limit fertility after bearing more children	4
Considers self infertile (no need to limit fertility)	1
Rural origin	
Ever-used form of mechanical or surgical fertility limitation	6
Used *coitus interruptus*	2
Intend to limit fertility after bearing more children	10
Have no plans to limit fertility at time of interview	21
No information	2
Total	60

SOURCE: Refugee interviewing in Hong Kong from 1967 to 1969. The interviews on which these tables are based are in the form of coded face sheets in my possession.

and who looked for traditional status through their familial roles.

TABLE 10. *Fertility limitation among married Chinese of rural origin by age, Chinese refugees, 1967–69, number of respondents*

	Age	
20–30	31–40	41+
Ever used some form of mechanical, surgical or other fertility limitation:		
0	8	0
Never used any form of mechanical, surgical or other fertility limitation:		
13	6	12
Total		(N=39)

SOURCE: *Ibid.*

As opportunities contracted for young, educated graduates to serve the country in urban jobs discontent intensified. It was difficult to reward the majority of youth with mobility opportunities. The anti-natalist policy in the first decade depended essentially on such rewards for gaining compliance. Consequently, in the mid-sixties, in particular in the wake of the Cultural Revolution, social-structural changes in career lines and alternative socialization practices and values were introduced through the school system. Some observers have assumed that the anti-natalist efforts of the late sixties were directed at attitudes alone.[90] In fact, although attitudes undoubtedly were affected by the ideology of service to the nation without thought of reward, with a concomitant anti-natalist result, the structure of opportunities also changed. The majority of young people now enter lower-middle school. Others, chosen on the basis of evaluations and technical promise, will continue to upper-middle school. Despite a de-emphasis on personal achievement through education, the school experience will encourage young people to plan their future. Further, more young people now come into contact with organized peer groups which oppose familism. These new social institutions will therefore have an anti-natalist impact despite the down-playing of individual achievement as a reward for deferred marriage and reduced family size.

The ideological emphasis on equality through work that accompanies these institutional reforms also requires women to reduce fertility. The communes have expanded alternative opportunities to childbearing for more women. Younger women who have been through the new lower-middle schools are likely to want to compete for the new status positions in the community and to sacrifice the bearing of large families. Deep-seated social reforms when introduced in a large and complex society will not be introduced uniformly.

Many young people are likely to become demoralized; finding their rural work experience unsatisfying and unappreciated by the peasantry, they will attempt to return to urban centres. Many communities also have probably decided not to push local small-scale industries. Still others are reluctant to implement new opportunities and to recruit women for them. It can be hypothesized that where the new structural and ideological changes have been implemented, anti-natalist behaviour is supported by rural community institutions. Competition for individual achievement in rural and urban areas may not have achieved even this result since opportunities were non-existent.

NOTES

1. A neo-Malthusian perspective held by Ma Yin-ch'u was sub-
    jected to considerable criticism. ["A New Theory of Popu-
    lation," translated in Current Background (hereafter CB), 469
    (25 July 1957), p. 8.]   See an alternative view, Wang Ya-nan,
    Ma-k'e-szu-chu-i ti jen-k'ou li-lun yu chung-kuo jen-k'ou wen-
    t'i [Marxist population theory and the problem of the Chinese
    population] (Peking: K'o hsueh ch'u-pan she, 1956).

2. One of the major deleterious impacts of high population growth
    on economic development is that the large number of depen-
    dents requires expenditures on consumption. In the short run,
    rapid population growth eats up savings. Joseph Spengler es-
    timates that a population growth of 1% absorbs 4 to 5% of the
    national income. J. J. Spengler, "Demographic Factors and
    Early Modern Economic Development," Daedalus, 97 (Spring,
    1968), p. 435. This hinders capital accumulation for develop-
    ment.

3. There were both similarities and differences in the patterns of
    mortality decline in the developed and less developed nations.
    The nature of the diseases that were first eliminated were
    similar, but the timing of disease reduction has been more
    rapid in the underdeveloped nations; the methods of reducing
    mortality and morbidity levels also are somewhat different.
    Kingsley Davis, "The Amazing Decline of Mortality in Under-
    developed Areas," American Economic Review, 46 (1956), pp.
    305-318; George Stolnitz, "A Century of International Mortality
    Trends, I," Population Studies, 9 (1955), pp. 24-55.

4. Demographers have estimated the levels of fertility, mortality
    and population growth in China prior to 1949. John Aird ar-
    gues that a growth ratio of 1.25-1.35 is the most reasonable
    for the period of 1851 to 1953. This slow growth rate results
    from applying high birth rates (45) and a high and fluctuating
    crude death rate (about 35). He uses a modification of the
    stable population model, based on the United Nations level-20
    life table, for these estimates. John Aird, "Population Growth,"
    in Alexander Eckstein et al., ed., Economic Trends in Com-
    munist China (Chicago: 1968), pp. 261-277.

5. Aird uses four models to estimate China's population growth from 1953 to 1965. The highest natural increase is 22.5, his "Model I" (c.b.r. of 45.0 combined with c.d.r. of 22.5). The resulting natural increase of 22.5 would double the population in 31.4 years.

6. John Aird listed six major efforts at collecting demographic data since the Communists came to power. These were: (1) the land reform population investigations which began before 1949 and ended in 1953; (2) urban population registers set up in major cities from 1949 to 1953; (3) experimental vital registration carried out by the Ministry of Health between 1950 and 1954; (4) a national population census taken during 1953 and 1954; (5) rural population registers set up 1954-56; (6) a "field count of some kind" undertaken during the summer of 1964 by the Ministry of Public Security. John Aird, "Population Growth and Distribution in Mainland China," in Joint Economic Committee of the U. S. Congress, An Economic Profile of Mainland China (New York: 1968), pp. 344-352. The Chinese government never officially announced a 1964 Census. Information about this count came from travellers to China and from refugees who were living in China at the time. Aird called it a police check, suggesting that it was an effort to restore the defunct population registers and to derive from them at the same time a current total population figure. Aird, ibid., p. 351. Edgar Snow heard about the "census" from officials with whom he talked in 1965. He called it a "spot census." Edgar Snow, "Too Many Chinese? The Chinese Agree!" (N.p.: number 3 of series, mimeographed, n.d.), p. 2. South Chinese cadres I interviewed had participated in this population investigation. See the report by one participant in a work group that registered households, Hsueh Feng, "Chungkung ti i-chiu-liu-ssu-nien jen-k'ou pu-ch'a" [Communist China's General Census in 1964], Tsu kuo [China Monthly], 56, I (1968), pp. 17-19, 52. On the other hand, many refugees could not recall such a registration. This indicates that it may have been an updating of household registers: in some areas the census work group interviewing each household, in others collecting information directly from the brigade leadership.

7. This is the argument made for the rising age of marriage of the British middle classes in the nineteenth century. J. A. Banks, Prosperity and Parenthood (London: 1954). See the

discussion on this issue in David V. Glass, "Population Growth and Population Policy," in Mindel Sheps and J. C. Ridley, ed., Public Health and Population Change (Pittsburgh: 1965), pp. 13-20. J. Berent finds similar social causes have precipitated a fertility decline in certain socialist countries, "Causes of Fertility Decline in Eastern Europe and the Soviet Union, II," Population Studies, 24 (July 1970), pp. 242-292.

8. There have been numerous recent discussions of the so-called Maoist plans for economic development. One of the most extended is E. L. Wheelwright and Bruce McFarlane, The Chinese Road to Socialism (New York: 1970). See also John G. Gurley, "Capitalist and Maoist Economic Development," Monthly Review, 17 (February 1971), pp. 15-35.

9. Harvey Leibenstein, Economic Backwardness and Economic Growth (New York: 1957), p. 161.

10. Sidney Gamble, Ting Hsien (Stanford: 1968), p. 44. Gamble's data show that of 766 couples investigated in this north China rural community, those women whose agnates owned less than 50 mou of land married considerably later than those owning more than 100 mou. In 23% of the cases of the poorer stratum, and in only 8.5% of the cases in the richer stratum, the brides were over 20 years of age.

11. Francis Hsü makes a somewhat circular agrument that the gentry conformed more closely to the ideal village virtues regarding household composition (the ideal is held to be that which is characteristic of the gentry). "The Myth of the Chinese Family Size," American Journal of Sociology, 48 (May 1943), pp. 555-562.

12. Marion J. Levy and Shih Kuo-heng, "The Rise of the Modern Chinese Business Class" (New York: mimeographed, 1949), pp. 5, 12.

13. Myron L. Cohen, "Developmental Process in the Chinese Domestic Group," in Maurice Freedman, ed., Family and Kinship in Chinese Society (Stanford: 1970), pp. 32-33.

14. Olga Lang, Chinese Family and Society (New Haven: 1946), p. 13.

15. M. H. Van der Valk, Conservatism in Modern Chinese Family Law (Leiden: 1956).

16. H. Franz Schurmann, "Traditional property concepts in China," Journal of Asian Studies, 15 (August 1956), p. 508.

17. One brief comment is in order regarding the methodology of the survey. The purpose of the survey was to determine the impact of participation in heavy agricultural labour on the health of the women. In the process of gathering these data, information was also obtained on fertility levels. There is no evidence that the data were falsified; the political future of the cadres does not seem to have been at stake. The data also appear internally consistent. The sampling procedure was not discussed, and the sample may not have been a probability sample. Most critical is the fact that the survey was conducted in 1959, a time of widespread social and political change; perhaps the statistics were not reliably recorded. Finally, we cannot determine the representativeness of this sample for other areas of China.

18. Buck estimated that land reform would bring into cultivation at most 5% more cultivable land; this 5% would come from gravesites! Choh-ming Li estimated that cultivable area was increased in China by the extension of irrigation networks and multiple cropping, not by bringing much new land into cultivation. Economic Development of Communist China: An Appraisal of the First Five Years of Industrialization (Berkeley and Los Angeles: 1959), pp. 66-67.

19. Glass, op. cit., argues that land reform in Japan and Ireland consolidated the peasants' holdings; they were encouraged to hold on to their land and they sent their sons off in search of employment. In Japan, land reform encouraged the peasants to reduce fertility as well.

20. Chen Mae-fun, "Paying the Peasants," Far Eastern Economic Review, 54 (3 November 1966), pp. 263-264.

21. Jan Myrdal, Report from a Chinese Village (New York: 1965), p. 237.

22. Ibid.

23.   Peter Schran, "The Structure of Income in Chinese Agriculture" (Berkeley: University of California, Department of Economics, unpublished Ph.D. dissertation, 1961), pp. 171, 176, 204, 206.

24.   T'ung-chi kung-tso [Statistical Work] (29 May 1957), cited by Schran, p. 206, Table 4.45. The survey was of 16,000 peasant households in 1954.

Stratum	Members of household	Labour units per household member if the poor peasant = 1·00
Poor peasants	4·2	1·00
Co-operators	5·1	1·07
Middle peasants	5·0	1·05
Rich peasants	6·2	1·02
Former landlords	4·2	1·10
All strata	4·8	1·05

The differences in family structure and size are not very great between strata, however.

25.   Schran, op. cit., pp. 171-206.

26.   Levy, op. cit.

27.   Interview, 1968: I.   This is one of a series of interviews conducted with Chinese refugees from the Mainland in Hong Kong, 1967-69.

28.   Interview, 1967: I.

29.   Some 50% of middle-school students and 75% of college students were urban in 1955, according to Feng Chi-Hsi, "Growth of China's Economy as Viewed from the State Budget," T'ung-chi kung-tso, 2 (June 1957), p. 30.

30.   Calculated from Chi-ming Hou, "Manpower, Employment and Unemployment," in Eckstein, et al., op. cit., pp. 366-367.

31.   Ibid., p. 369.

32.   Ibid.

33.   John W. Lewis, "Political Aspects of Mobility in China's Urban Development," American Political Science Review, 60 (December 1966), pp. 899-912.

34.   Chin Ming, "The Way in Which Financial Work in People's

Communes Serves Distribution, Hung-ch'i [Red Flag], 22 (16 November 1960), p. 38. This was a period of cutback in welfare, and the sum may have increased since that time.

35.   Myrdal, op. cit., p. 206.

36.   Robert Marsh, "The Taiwanese of Taipei: Some Major Aspects of their Social Structure and Attitudes," Journal of Asian Studies 27 (May 1968), pp. 571-584. Marsh notes that urban Taipei families gain much prestige from the help that their children provide them.

37.   Joyce K. Kallgren, "Social Welfare and China's Industrial Workers," in A. Doak Barnett, ed., Chinese Communist Politics in Action (Seattle: 1968), p. 553.

38.   Daniel Kulp, Phenix Village Kwangtung, China, Vol. I of Country Life in South China, The Sociology of Familism (New York: 1925), pp. 145ff.

39.   Maurice Freedman, Lineage Organization in Southeastern China (London: 1958), Chaps. viii-x.

40.   C. K. Yang, A Chinese Village in Early Communist Transition (Cambridge, Mass.: 1959), pp. 191-194.

41.   Interview, 1968: I.

42.   Jen-min jih-pao [People's Daily], 11 February 1969.

43.   Donald J. Munro, "Egalitarian Ideal and Educational Fact in Communist China" in John Lindbeck, ed., China: Management of a Revolutionary Society (Seattle: 1971), pp. 256-301. Munro describes the emergence of tracking in China and the special party and army officers' offspring in the fifties.

44.   All dollars henceforth refer to the Chinese jmp; one jmp equals 42c U.S.

45.   Marianne Bastid, "Economic Necessity and Political Ideals in Educational Reform During the Cultural Revolution," China Quarterly, 42 (April-June 1970), pp. 18-19, provides figures on the costs of schooling gathered during her sojourn in China as a teacher in 1965 and 1966.

46.   Jen-min jih-pao, 31 October 1968, p. 2.

47.   Myrdal, op. cit., pp. 214-215.   Li Shang-wa, one of the two
      primary school graduates of Liu Ling village, could not con-
      tinue to middle school because her mother was dead and she
      was needed at home to care for her siblings and to do the
      household work.

48.   Cheng Chu-yuan, Scientific and Engineering Manpower in Com-
      munist China, 1949-1963 (Washington, D. C.: National Science
      Foundation, 1965), p. 88, Table 12, "Kung-fei ti hsueh-hsiao
      chiao-yu" (Taipei, n.p., mimeographed), p. 4; Stewart Fraser,
      Chinese Communist Education (Nashville: Vanderbilt University
      Press, 1965), p. 17.

49.   The press of 1963-64 carried a correspondence regarding wheth-
      er working people should lead a life of austerity or should they
      "honourably enjoy" the wages they earn.   See especially Kung-
      jen jih-pao [Workers' Daily], April 1964.

50.   Interview data.

51.   Myrdal, op. cit., p. 237.

52.   Stanley Karnow, "Why They Fled: Refugee Accounts," Current
      Scene, 2, No. 22 (15 October 1963): "Paradoxically, many
      villagers splurge their market earnings on fancy meals in ex-
      pensive city restaurants instead of taking the money home.
      'Ostentation in your own village,' explained a Canton doctor,
      'may irritate the local party official, and you may be branded
      as 'bourgeois.' It can also irk your less fortunate neighbours.
      And perhaps a big dinner in a city restaurant gives them a
      feeling of wealth.'"   Although Karnow cites this information to
      the effect that the villagers do not rationally plan their incomes
      and expenditures, the extent to which villagers do plan must be
      established empirically.   Thus, Marjorie Topley notes that Hong
      Kong workers also spend their excess income on banquets, but
      they, too, are beginning to save for education for their off-
      spring.   "The Role of Savings and Wealth among Hong Kong
      Chinese," in I. D. Jarvie and J. Agassi, ed., Hong Kong: A
      Society in Transition (London: 1969), pp. 167-224 passim.

53.   "Peasant and Soldier Students Entering Institutes of Higher Learn-
      ing in Shanghai," Peking Review, 10 (5 March 1971), pp. 21-22.

54. Marion Levy, The Family Revolution in Modern China (New York: 1968).

55. Myrdal, op. cit., p. 210.

56. Marjorie Wolf, "Child Training and the Chinese Family," in Freedman, ed., op. cit., pp. 37-62.

57. Myrdal, op. cit., p. 237.

58. Liu Sung, "Kuan-yu chia-wu lao-tung ti chi-t'i-hua, she-hui-hua" [On the collectivization and socialization of household labour], Hsueh-hsi [Study], 10 September 1958, pp. 492-97.

59. "All Women in Our Village Emulate Ta-chai," China's Women, II (1 November 1965).

60. "Liberation from the Burden of Home Chores," Yang-ch'eng wan-pao [Canton Evening Post], 1 March 1965, p. 3.

61. Myrdal, op. cit., p. 332.

62. Martin Yang, A Chinese Village, Taitou, Shantung Province (New York: 1965), pp. 107ff.

63. Yang Ta-wen, Liu Su-p'ing, "On the Function and Task of Our Nation's Marriage Law," Cheng-fa yen-chiu [Political and Legal Studies], 2 (5 May 1963), translated in Joint Publications Research Service (hereafter JPRS) 22983, pp. 92-93; and interviews.

64. John W. Lewis, Leadership in Communist China (Ithaca: Cornell University Press, 1963), pp. 235, 237, 238, cites several examples of villages in which members of the same family, not just with the same surname, assumed all top leadership positions. The regime has consistently criticized this continuing practice of relatives appointing their own relatives. See Hung-ch'i [Red Flag], 12 (10 June 1962).

65. E. Boserup, Woman's Role in Economic Development (London: 1970), Chap. I.

66. New China News Agency (hereafter NCNA), Peking, 8 March 1956.

67.   "The Unique Wage System of the Ta-chai Brigade," op. cit.

68.   "Women in Kwangtung Make Important Contributions to Social-
      ist Construction," Nan-fang jih-pao [Southern Daily], 8 March
      1963.

69.   Myrdal, op. cit., and interview data.

70.   Letter from Wang P'ei-chin to Ho Yo-hsiu, Chung-kuo ch'ing-
      nien pao [China Youth Paper], 20 February 1964.

71.   M. Spiro, Venture in Utopia (New York: 1964), p. 224.

72.   Interview, 1968: 2.

73.   Ting Ling, "San-pao chieh-yu kan" [Thoughts on 8th March],
      Chieh-fang jih-pao [Liberation Daily], 9 March 1942, p. 4.

74.   Interview, 1969: I.

75.   Teng Hsiao-p'ing, Report on the Revision of the Constitution
      (Peking: Foreign Languages Press, 1956), p. 91.

76.   NCNA, Canton, 7 March 1965.

77.   Heilungkiang Radio, 7 March 1968.

78.   Ibid.

79.   Hofei Radio, 20 August 1969.

80.   Wen hui pao, 14 June 1968.

81.   A. J. Jaffe and K. Azumi, "The Birth Rate and Cottage Indus-
      tries in Underdeveloped Countries," Economic Development and
      Cultural Change, 9 (October 1960), pp. 52-83.

82.   Hou Chi-ming, op. cit., pp. 365-366, 371.

83.   Barry Richman, Industrial Society in Communist China (New
      York: 1969), pp. 304-305.

84.   John P. Emerson, "Sex, Age, and Level of Skills in the Non-
      agricultural Labour Force of Mainland China" (Washington,

D. C.: Department of Manpower, Foreign Analysis Division, mimeographed, 1965).

85. Hou Chi-ming, op. cit., p. 371.

86. Ts'ai Chang, "Chi-chi p'ei-yang ho t'i-pa keng to keng hao ti nu kan-pu" [Actively train more and better women cadres], Hsin-hua pan-yueh-k'an [New China Semi-Monthly], 29 (95), 6 November 1956, p. 99.

87. Ibid.

88. Richman, op. cit., p. 396.

89. Han Suyin, "A Chinese Housewife," Eastern Horizons, 9 (1970), pp. 7-11.

90. Han Suyin, "Family Planning in China," Japan Quarterly, 17 (October-December 1970), pp. 433-442.

Women and Revolution:

The Lessons of the Soviet Union and China

Janet Weitzner Salaff
and Judith Merkle

Rather than simply changing the political system, twentieth-century revolutions have tried to transform the structure of society itself, but unless there are concomitant social and economic changes, the political goals of the revolution are inevitably subverted. The Russian and Chinese revolutions have attempted to mobilize new groups into the political system and to break down old forms of power and authority in society as a whole. In both of these societies, women and efforts to change the position of women have been central to the process of revolutionary transformation.

The destruction of the political power of the old regimes in China and Russia required an attack on the inherited forms of authority in the family, community, educational system and government. While the destruction of traditional social organizations freed both men and women, women and young people benefited more. Women had been particularly oppressed under the feudal legal and economic restrictions of the old system, and one key to the revolutionary political transformation of Russia and China was the change in authority relationships which kept women in bondage. In their traditional positions, women were repositories of old social values; the institutions that most oppressed women, the clan and the family, were the elementary units of traditional authority in the society as a whole.

The status of women was also changed by their involvement in the process of revolution. Mobilizing support for revolutionary change meant involving all oppressed groups in political action;

Reprinted with permission from the Berkeley Journal of Sociology, Vol. XV, 1970.

disruption during the revolutionary period enabled people to escape
from fixed social roles. In the period of revolutionary transformation, women were called upon to perform new tasks and, in their
role as revolutionaries, women could sometimes participate on an
equal footing with men. During the height of revolutionary change
Russian women attained a temporary freedom, even notoriety. This
also seems true of young Cuban women in the first post-revolutionary
decade.[1] A capsule history of the revolutionary role of women in
the Soviet Union and China, however, tells us that even during the
height of revolutionary transformation women played limited roles in
the revolution.

The participation of women in the Russian and Chinese revolutions took several forms. As revolutionaries and political figures
they participated as individuals, as stars and heroines, leaving the
collective power of women unchanged. Alternatively, women were
brought into economic production more fully than ever before but
were left out of the structure of power which grew up during the
revolutionary struggle. Although the economic position of women
improved relative to pre-revolutionary times, women remained largely
in traditional types of work and did not gain control over the means
of coercion that were responsible for the revolution.

After the first stage of revolutionary mobilization and the sei-
zure of power, can we expect continued advancement in the position
of women? In Russia and China, the first stage of revolutionary
victory was followed by a period of concentration chiefly on the
economic goal of increasing production. In the conflict between expanding production and liberation, liberation had second priority.
Women were brought more fully into economic production, the legal
barriers to the advancement of women were removed during this
stage, and individual talented women could rise to new positions.
Women were formally given equal salaries for equal jobs, equal
rights to property, and equal rights to control the means of production. But the oppression of women remained culturally, politically
and economically institutionalized: the traditional image of women,
the subordination of women in the family, and the economic and
political inequality of women were not eliminated by the revolution.

An examination of the fate of Russian and Chinese women may
alert us to the obstacles to liberation even in revolutionary societies;
and the experiences of women in the Russian and Chinese revolutions
may teach us something about the forms of revolutionary participation

most likely to improve the position of women.

RUSSIAN WOMEN: STAGES OF EMANCIPATION

Contemporary materials on the situation of women in the Soviet
Union create the illusion that women's liberation in Russia is a
direct product of the Socialist Revolution and that it has progressed
steadily since October of 1917.   Yet the groundwork for the changes
following the October Revolution was laid over a century before.   In
pre- and post-revolutionary Russia, liberation for women progressed
in waves of alternating freedom and repression.   More than a hundred years of struggle, publicity, and the development of both women's consciousness and men's acceptance of such development preceded the radical changes of October.   While October changed the
terms of women's struggle, it did not end the waves of repressive
reaction to women's attempts to gain freedom, for many of the basic
social conditions remained the same.

Possibilities for the liberation of women were limited by the
general social and economic constraints that restricted the liberty
of all members of oppressed classes.   When a class is unfree, the
women of that class are also unfree; thus the maintenance of an author
itarian state and the existence of oppressed classes set absolute
limits to the progress that women as a whole can make.   The century of preparation for women's emancipation was confined to one
class--the upper class--and this determined the dynamics of post-
revolutionary liberation.   The successes of Soviet women's liberation
depended to a large extent on this period of preparation, and yet to
the extent that these early changes had been limited to a narrow
class, the movement failed to achieve real equality for women.

RUSSIAN WOMEN BEFORE THE REVOLUTION

Three hundred years ago, the women of Russia were the most
oppressed in Europe.   The oppressive legacy of the Mongols had
been added to the common ideology of medieval Europe; no cult of
Mariolatry softened the male orientation of the Byzantine Christianity
of the "Third Rome,"[2] women were not simply maintained in the
legal status of children--they were chattels.   The "Domostroi," a
sixteenth-century book of household rules, supported the absolute
power of the extended patriarchal family, a power modeled on the

fierce and often brutal control of the Tsar, the "Little Father,"
over his people. Women of all classes, illiterate and superstitious,
went in fear of their husband's outbursts of temper; and the day
that a maiden gave up her relative freedom to go and live with
strangers, having been wed at the bidding of others, was traditionally
sad and frightening:

> Don't expect, my dear sister
> That your father-in-law will wake you up gently
> That your mother-in-law will give orders nicely,
> They will howl at you like wild beasts,
> And they will hiss at you like snakes.[3]

The lot of upper class women was, in a certain way, worse
than that of the peasant women because they were even more isolated.
The greater resources of such families meant that, in the "Tartar
fashion," women could be kept absolutely segregated from men in
a special portion of the house, and their ignorance of anything in
the outer world preserved. The husband's horsewhip, which he used
in the "training" of his wife, was customarily hung at the head of the
bed.[4]

Even after Western influence began to change the role of women
among the nobility, much of the traditional authoritarianism of the
Russian family remained. As late as the 19th century, lithographs
of "barbaric Russia" depicted the public punishment of noble women
by flogging. Other observers leave the impression that much of the
primordial brutality of Russian marital relations was unchanged.[5]
The truth of the matter was that in an unfree society women could
not be free either; the state properly considered that the despotism
of men over women, as that of the nobility over the serfs, was an
important support of the despotism of the state over all male citizens.
Russia was constructed like a vast pyramid, based upon the Table
of Ranks,[6] in which the rule of upper class men was made possible
by "binding" those classes lower on the scale to the men who direct
the state. How could women hope to escape the fate of the nation
in general?

In this picture of the relationship of Russian women to the
society, government, and economy, we can discern the basic factors
that shaped the consciousness of women in the nineteenth century and
that continued to restrict their real emancipation even after the
October Revolution. Russia, to compete and survive militarily in the

constant wars of the West, was under the harshest economic constraints. Long before Stalin, the need to "dognat* i peregnat'"
(catch up and overtake) was paramount. Given the backwardness of
the economy, the only apparent solution was for the government
to establish absolute control over the society in order to free the
few available resources by force. While the overriding need for
economic development dictated the preservation of the autocratic
power relationships within society and of the dictatorial power of
the state over society, technology could not develop without Western
education; but Western education was inherently disruptive of these
power relationships. Theories of political and social freedom penetrated Russia along with theories of mathematics and weapons design,
setting up powerfully contradictory forces in Russian society that
have still not worked themselves out.

Prior to the nineteenth century, only an occasional wealthy
woman attained any degree of freedom: the liberation of women
as a social group, rather than as individuals, dates from the development of a Westernized, intellectual class of men who idealized
their own search for liberty from a traditional autocratic state. By
the reign of Alexander I, this intelligentsia, heavily influenced by
European revolutionary thought, was deeply involved with the new
forms of humanism: constitutional reforms, bettering the lot of the
serfs, and the new idea of romantic love. "To love--but whom?"
asked Lermontov in anguish. "In love there must be equality in
physical and in moral feeling."[7] The idealization of Love in place
of Duty created a demand for women with social consciences to be
companions of the young idealists. But while men were educated,
the women of the same class (not to mention those of other classes)
were as ignorant as ever.

"Sometimes, one wants some sort of shelter . . . the
desire takes you . . . to exchange a few words with
some one. Well--would you believe it--you can't,"
remarks a character of Ouspensky. "No development
at all--and in their heads, insanity, pure and simple."[8]

Although the only solution to the search for Love was to find an
intelligent woman and educate her, the conservative forces of the
status quo considered the traditional home necessary for preservation
of society. And to keep women in the home, they were denied any
education except French, a little music, and embroidery. [9] Women
who wanted a real education were forced to flee abroad so that they

could return to Russia as members of the intelligentsia, and thereby try to advance the cause of social justice.[10] As the numbers of emancipated women increased, the image of the emancipated woman, a disheveled figure with masculine habits, who endlessly smoked Russian papirosy and frequently cut her hair short, entered the Russian literature.

As education became more widespread, so did the "Love Problem,"[11] with the result that the increasingly radical intelligentsia included a number of emancipated women that the men considered to be their equals. But the conservative society and the state that represented it did not approve of "emancipated women," and they were subject to considerable harassment and repression. One woman was arrested after the Tsar saw her on the street in mannish clothes, and was forced to sign a statement that she would let her hair grow.[12] Love without marriage was greeted with moral outrage. Some educated women found loopholes that permitted them to enter government employment, but they were fired en masse when discovered by the Tsar. Like the men of the radical intelligentsia, women could find employment only in the rudimentary private economy as writers and teachers and therefore moved into increasingly radical activity.[13]

After the defeat in the Crimea under Alexander II, an attempt was made to "get Russian society going again" by liberalizing it according to the reforms long espoused by the intelligentsia. The serfs were freed, limited local government was established, and an experimental attempt was made to provide professional education for women in the form of a series of medical lectures. The experiment was a brilliant success. Not only did women doctors win medals for their military service, but women entered such fields as mathematics and achieved world-wide reputations.[14] While the women of the peasantry or of the ordinary merchant class were less emancipated than their European counterparts, the intellectual women of Russia were far more emancipated than women in the West. They went everywhere without escorts or fear of the consequences, while young ladies in France went to lectures at the University accompanied by their mamas and young Americans found their reputations "ruined" if they visited a man's room unchaperoned. But when a young woman, Sophia Pirovskaya, was found among the assassins of Alexander II, the subsequent reactionary regime drew the appropriate conclusions. They tried to choke off not only political activity and liberal education in general, but also women's education in particular.

WOMEN IN RUSSIA'S REVOLUTION:
FEBRUARY AND OCTOBER, 1917

As the ignorant, pious, fashionable women became the conservative ideal, the emancipation of women emerged more clearly
as a goal of the revolution. Women were prominent in all of the
socialist movements in Russia, beginning with the agrarian reform
movements and ending with the Bolsheviks. Women participated in
the Narodnik "going to the people" movement--in agitation, and in
every form of political terrorism. They shared exile and prison
with their husbands and earned horrifying sentences of their own as
political assassins. By World War I there were enough women in
the intelligentsia that all reform and revolutionary factions supported
women's rights. But within the Bolshevik Party a centrally located
group of consciously feminist women revolutionaries made the question of women's rights central to the revolutionary program. This
did not happen in the bourgeois parties or the Provisional Government.

Before the revolution, both the bourgeois reformers and the
socialists were interested in The Woman Question (as it was called),
but from different points of view. Wealthy, liberal women, who
identified with the bourgeois reform movement, wished to uplift the
uneducated women of the lower classes. The first political organization for women, the "Union for the Equality of Women's Rights,"
came into being after the 1905 revolution, attained a certain success
in all classes, and presented a twelve-point program to the Duma.
The second women's organization, "The Feminine Progressive
Party," had monarchist tendencies.[15] The women among the Social
Democrats and, later, the Bolsheviks, however, had the more lasting
effect, for they gave shape to vague Marxist generalizations about
changes in family structure and impressed specific plans of action
and their rationale upon the party leaders. As a result the Bolsheviks developed an ideology which saw the liberation of women as
an integral part of the revolution, so important that it was a measure of the success or failure of the revolution itself. Many of
Lenin's specific writings about women on the eve of the revolution
were inspired by the work and thought of his wife, Krupskaya, her
friend, Inez Armand, and Alexandra Kollontai, an ardent women's
rightist in the Party.[16] Although he favored the destruction of the
bourgeois family, Lenin did not approve of militant feminism when
it implied sexual liberation. He found sexual freedom per se dis-

tasteful, and he thought that the substitution of sex for class struggle
could undermine the revolution. Kollontai actually engineered the
coalition between orthodox Marxism and feminism, pointing out that
the concept of women as property was a specific feature of capitalism, and claiming liberty of education, profession, and sexual relationships for the women of the new era.

The upheaval caused by World War I also created opportunities
for women. The terrible losses in manpower put a premium on the
labor of women. As in the West, women organized Red Cross services and relief services and replaced laborers missing from the
production lines. Unlike their Western counterparts, however,
Russian women managed to serve in the military under combat conditions. Dashing "aristos," bourgeois women who romanticized warfare, as well as peasant women defending their homes and families,
served in combat.

One example of military participation by women, the Women's
Battalion, became the sensation of the Western press. Created by
the beleaguered Provisional Government, the Women's Battalion
fought in two battles: in the last Russian offensive of the war
against Germany six women were killed and thirty wounded, and in
the defense of the Winter Palace against the Communists the Provisional Government troops were defeated while the Women's Battalion surrendered without a loss.[17] Its failure is often seen as an
example of the inability of women to unite or to fight together successfully. Louise Bryant, who interviewed the "girl-soldiers" before and after their last battle, concluded that the battalion failed
because of "segregation." Women had been successful in battle
when integrated with the regular troops, and Russian women had
often fought alongside their men. The battalion had developed major
internal crises, and its commander, an "aristo," had cried that she
would never have anything to do with women again, after being beaten
up by the dissident members of her command.[18] The reports of the
Red Guards that the surrendered women had huddled in a back room
to have hysterics[19] confirmed the picture.

Yet the women's own stories create a somewhat different impression. Apparently, the government had undertaken to form the
group, attracting a few "aristo" women soldiers for commanders
and then advertising in the villages for heroic women to replace the
exhausted men at the front. The young village women and city seam-
stresses that answered the call were bitterly disillusioned to find

that there was not enough equipment to outfit them, that they were
to be stationed in the capital, and that the principal reason for
organizing them was not for real duty, but "to shame the men."
Louise Bryant discovered that there were no boots or overcoats for
them, and she found some wearing dancing slippers and frivolous
"French waists" with their men's trousers. The result was a bit-
ter split between the outfitted aristo commanders who continued to
support the Provisional Government when it tried to eliminate the
Bolsheviks, and the young village women, who wanted to go over to
the Bolsheviks.[20] Under these conditions, their defense of the
Winter Palace could only end in failure. The Women's Battalion was
an effort to exploit women for publicity's sake, rather than an organization growing out of the concerns of women themselves. This
group of women, organized by men for symbolic value, is testimony
to the ease with which men can manipulate women for their own ends.
Had the Women's Battalion, or any other group of women organized
for combat, been an autonomous effort by women fighting for women's
rights, they would doubtless have been forcibly disbanded.

In the events of October, the most dramatic military role was
not played by individual women revolutionaries, but by the poor
women of Petrograd who stormed out to defend the Red Revolution
alongside boys of ten and men armed only with shovels. These
women must indeed have been poor, for they were visibly deformed
by overwork and malnutrition and were without weapons or even
adequate clothes.

> Women ran straight into the fire without any weapons
> at all. It was terrifying to see them. . . . The
> Cossacks seemed to be superstitious about it. They
> began to retreat.[21]

The victorious left had pledged to better the lot of just such women
as these. They pledged to let them participate in production under
equal conditions with men, and with equal pay; to teach them to read
and bring them into contact with the culture of the broader world;
to free them from the necessity of continual childbearing, household
chores, and the medieval aspects of marital subjugation. What,
then, was the first response of the men who made the revolution?

In 1918, the Workers' Soviet of Vladimir made a proclamation
which, in the words of the scandalized American press, "nationalized
women." Declaring that the bourgeoisie's monopoly on the means of

production gave them the best looking women of the nation, the Soviet announced that henceforward every woman over the age of eighteen would become the property of the state, being required to register at a central bureau of free love. Men and women both had the right to choose a partner at a rate up to one per month. However, "in the interests of the state," men of 19 to 50 could choose any registered woman without her consent. The offspring of these unions were to be the property of the state.[22] This masculine-oriented version of the "free love" theories of Kollontai was soon squelched on orders from the center, but it indicated the obstacles to genuine emancipation of women prevailing in the population at large.

The same sort of reservations about women's equality could be sensed at the highest levels of the government as well, even during the early days of the revolution. When the Bolsheviks assumed power, a handful of women were installed in leading government posts. While this represented a vast increase in representation over the Tsarist government, some of these posts had already been held by women under the Provisional Government. The difference in the Bolshevik incumbents was their consciousness--do-good Lady Bountifuls like the Countess Panina[23] were replaced by Marxist feminists, such as Mme. Kollontai. Yet it surprised Western feminist observers that a party with the avowed goal of equalizing the position of women, and which possessed such great resources of active, ideologically sincere and talented women, put such a small percentage of women in positions of actual power. Two of the women in the government, Angelica Balabanov and Maria Spirodonova (a revolutionary heroine who had assassinated the governor of Tambov at the age of nineteen), made excuses in terms of the scarcity of women with the proper training and stable temperament.[24] Yet this was an era when untrained workmen and peasants were taking over many of the important tasks of the nation. The subsequent history of women in Russia was to show that the socialist revolution did not eliminate the structure of male supremacy.

AFTER THE REVOLUTION:
THE DESTRUCTION OF VICTORIOUS FEMINISM

The leaders of the Bolshevik Party were irrevocably committed to a program of industrial development that required the imposition of social and economic control from the top. After the revolution,

this emphasis on economic development ran counter to many of the
demands of the very same poor and oppressed groups which had
swept the Bolsheviks into power. The crushing of the Kronstadt
revolt in 1921 was symbolic of this separation of the new Communist
state from its "spontaneous" revolutionary origins and its decision
to impose the "people's" program of economic development on the
people.

Yet Russian society was not immediately prepared for the
strains of rapid industrialization. Revolution, civil war, and the
resulting famine caused incredible suffering, population losses, and
economic setbacks. A decision was made to retreat from "war
communism" and enable the society to repair itself under the com-
parative liberalism of the NEP (New Economic Plan). The Party,
from its "commanding heights," drew up the first five year plan,
and waited for the revolutionary forces to play themselves out during
the 1920s. The "spontaneous" interest groups that had arisen--
trade unions, women's groups, and even "rich" peasants (kulaks)
and private traders (NEP-men)--were not allowed to gain sufficient
power to interfere with the Party's development policy. When these
groups threatened to become too powerful, they were systematically
crushed in order to make way for the rapid industrialization campaign. This process did not originate with Stalin, but it bears his
name because he brought it to completion in the 1930s, and because
many of the most bizarre excesses of the policy can be attributed to
the aberrations of his personality.

The conflicting pressures of "spontaneity" (popular social demands), the need to preserve Party power, and the requirements of
industrial development were the post-revolutionary version of the
age-old social, political, and economic forces that had always determined the fate of Russian women. Looking at these three forces
in relation to feminism, one can see how the defeat of women's
emancipation was engineered.

To begin with, the "spontaneous" demands of the oppressed
classes were for self-determination through grass-roots organization.
Trade unions demanded control of industry: workers, peasants
and soldiers demanded control of the government and economy through
Councils (Soviets) of those directly concerned with each function. The
women of the radical intelligentsia, who were also a suppressed group
drawn into political action by the revolution, made a series of demands
best expressed by Alexandra Kollontai. Mme. Kollontai, a general's

daughter, an emancipated woman who raised her child alone, was
the first (and last) Russian woman ambassador. She was the foremost exponent of the development of a new type of male-female relationship to replace the forms of bourgeois possession characterized
as "marriage." In her famous "glass of water" statement she
claimed that sex is a natural appetite, like thirst, and should be as
easily satisfied. She advocated easy abortions and divorce, since
women should control their own bodies. Characteristically Marxist
was her insistence that women could only attain freedom through
equal participation in production. This participation, however, had
to be backed by adequate maternity leave, child-care arrangements
and mass-household services. Otherwise, she argued, participation
in production would perpetuate the age-old double burden of poor
women who had given birth among the machines and returned home
after work to endless household chores.

For a time, an alliance was formed between the women and
the Bolsheviks. The Marxist "feminists" impressed upon the Bolshevik leaders, especially Lenin, the regressive effects that failure
to liberate women would have on the revolution. The majority of
Russian women were still illiterate and oppressed to a degree un-
heard of in the West. By educating and indoctrinating women, the
Bolsheviks could attack the traditional Russian family and the conservative way of life it perpetuated. To emancipate women would
require the destruction of the conservative power relations which
held them, and through them much of Russian society, in place.
The masses of illiterate women preserved the oral culture, rich in
myth, superstition, and the legendary legitimation of royal authority.
Orthodox religion, a powerful force for conservatism, was preserved
in this "women's subculture" even after it had lost its hold upon
Westernized men. The Bolsheviks had to reach into the home to
weaken the grip of the "women's subculture" by breaking paternal
and marital authority, by educating women, and by bringing them
into the male world of production.

The feminists of the Party were allowed to establish the organizational means for attacking the traditional family. A series of
laws was passed between 1917 and 1921, culminating in the Statute
on the Family, probably drafted by Kollontai. [25] Women were
granted equal rights in work; marriages could be made by regis-
tering at a civil bureau; a wife could keep her maiden name; divorce could be obtained by notification; abortions were made legal;
and the legal distinction between legitimate and illegitimate children

was abolished.   L. Lilina, the wife of Zinoviev, advocated the na-
tionalization of children.   Campaigns for literacy and special education were carried out by the Zhenotdely (Women's Bureaus). [26]

Reinforced by the puritanism of the Party leaders and the tra-
ditionalism of working-class men, the exigencies of industrialization
abruptly stifled women's drive for self-determination.   When such
expenses of liberation as the cost of replacement of women's services and the competition of women for favored jobs became visible,
the men hastened to return women to their traditional place "for the
good of society as a whole."   Male factory workers objected to the
employment of women in any but their usual roles.   In the ruined
economy, most of the work laws (leave, limitations on hours, child-
care) were simply not practical.   Resources were lacking to provide
enough state-operated services such as nurseries and laundries for
the women who needed them.   Finally, the dislocations of the war
had already caused such serious problems as the wild children who
roamed at will living on petty thievery--without the additional dis-
ruptions which would result from liberating women from the traditional family.   When to all this was added Lenin's moralistic opposition to sexual freedom (he denounced the "glass of water" theory,
saying it was driving Communist youth mad), the result was inevitable.

In 1923, a Party resolution was passed against the "feminist"
deviationism of the Zhenotdely: they were accused of turning people
away from class struggle under the pretext of cultural uplift.   The
Party was turning against the equality of women in substance, and
not merely for ideological or moralistic reasons; this retrogressive
policy is indicated by a Party resolution of the following year which
censored the Zhenotdely for excessive complaint about the material
conditions oppressing women.   By 1926, Lenin's view that "feminism"
was anti-Marxist, converting the class struggle to a sex struggle,
finally triumphed.   The family code was rescinded, and a new, conservative code promulgated in its place.   Women were left with the
"right" to work, but with social conditions which made it clear that
the cheap labor of women in the home and the factory was necessary to free resources for the development of socialist society.

The Stalin years replaced "feminism" with a lasting version of
emancipation which was not economically or politically costly.   This
was the "star system," or the elevation of female models, in place
of the equalization of salaries and opportunities for advancement.   A

few highly publicized individuals were elevated to the highest positions in Russian society, and legal barriers to the advancement of
women were removed, but the social conditions of women's oppression
were not challenged. A recent example of the "star system" in operation is the Soviet choice of the world's first female astronaut. Indeed, such tokenism masks the failure to achieve real emancipation
of women. The "star system" combined with Soviet claims about
equality of women, at least begins to change the cultural image of
women, which is more than the United States has attempted.

More common in the Soviet Union is the pattern of professional
"takeover," resembling that in the United States, although the specific professions differ. When women move into a profession which men
abandon, it eventually becomes a "women's job," at which point its
prestige, power and financial rewards decline. In the Soviet Union,
more women work and more professions are open to women than in
the United States. For example, the proportion of Soviet doctors
who are women is very high (about seventy-five per cent), but the
profession of general practitioner is neither well paid nor of high
status.[27] The general practitioners have attained the status of a
skilled trade, in contrast to the highly educated medical researchers,
of whom a higher proportion are men. Similarly, in the diplomatic
corps or the politburo, there are no women. In the military, although
there are many stories of female heroines and there was even a
women's bomber regiment in World War II,[28] there is a pattern of
discriminatory ranks and duties closely resembling the United States
military. In short, women are kept well away from the instruments
of power.

The industrialization begun under Stalin required a reversal of
the liberation begun during the revolution. The legal structure of
the family (e.g., divorce laws) was reimposed, and women were
drawn into the labor force without adequate child care or other support. At the same time, the power of individual women and of
women's organizations was broken by the anti-feminist campaign and
by massive propaganda which urged women to return to traditional
patterns of accommodation.

The revolution vastly improved the lot of many Russian women,
increasing literacy, education and legal rights. Most Soviet women
work out of choice as well as necessity, and child care is available.
But these accomplishments fall far short of the hopes of the women
revolutionaries or the early promises of the revolution itself. Despite

the favorable ideological stance of the Bolsheviks toward women's emancipation, women did not win the power to enforce their interests when these interests conflicted with economic goals, political expediency, or cultural bias. It is clear that without such power revolution alone will not liberate women.

CHINESE WOMEN AND THE REVOLUTION

The twentieth century in China is marked by a radical change in the political and social position of women. The occasional political involvement of uniquely talented women gave way to the broad participation of the hitherto quiescent masses of women. However, the transition was neither easy nor complete. During and after the Chinese revolution, many educated, talented women could take advantage of their new equality before the law and move rapidly, as far as their talents would take them, into new positions in government, politics, and industry. But the mass of women still found their roles structured according to the traditional categories of sex, age, and class. Despite major changes in the position of women in China, the revolution has not eradicated political, cultural and economic barriers to the equality of women.

POLITICAL PARTICIPATION BEFORE THE REVOLUTION

In traditional China, women were denied participation in any political institutions. Leadership in the lineage and village institutions was reserved for men, since this leadership was dependent on the all-male civil bureaucracy. Chinese women lacked legal rights in family councils and in the disposal of property. The kinship structure bound Chinese women to this position of powerlessness and dependency. Political action mystified them, and concerted group action was unthinkable. In fact, their only source of power was the manipulation of kinsmen.

As individuals, however, upper-class Chinese women had traditionally been less confined than women in many other pre-modern societies. Wealthy fathers had their daughters tutored at home, and, where the families were non-Confucian or non-Han, parents allowed their daughters considerable freedom to develop their talents. Those daughters of "boxers" who belonged to Taoist cults and often served as guards even received training in the martial arts. Aboriginal

generals trained their daughters in soldiery along with their sons.
Such women entered the political arena as rebels or bandits. For
instance, during the early stages of the mid-nineteenth century
T'aip'ing Rebellion, men and women were organized into separate
combat units[29] with their own officers. The separation of sexes
was for religious reasons since cultic brothers and sisters were
expected to abstain from sexual relations and to maintain single-
minded devotion to warfare. Although most of the T'aip'ing women's
brigades did work considered appropriate to their sex, such as the
weaving brigades, some women did engage in combat. Contrary to
Chinese practice and unlike the Han women, they fought because
they had martial training at home. The religious crusading spirit
may also have encouraged sexual egalitarianism during the early
years of the rebellion. After the T'aip'ings took Nanking, women
were taken out of combat and placed in secluded quarters of their
own to do "more fitting" work than warfare.

EARLY TWENTIETH-CENTURY CHANGES IN CHINA

The twentieth century saw the introduction of modern educational and political institutions as well as contact with the Western
ideology of sexual equality. Women's political participation changed
accordingly. The first upsurge of the feminist movement occurred
during the bourgeois revolution of 1911. An early effect of the political changes in this period was that women, particularly from the
upper class, could participate in new realms of activity, even though
their general position remained unchanged. The introduction of
modern schooling enabled women to become teachers, and militant
women teachers were able to mobilize their new constituency of
women students for political action. The schools radicalized students
by age-grading pupils and isolating them from their communities,
and women were turned toward feminist goals by learning ideas
about freedom to love, reading translations of Western romantic
literature and discussing Western suffragettes. The first woman
martyr of the Revolutionary Period, Ch'iu Chin, provides an example
of the political goals and the style of female participation on the eve
of the 1911 Revolution.[30] Typical of many upper-class women of
the time, Ch'iu Chin was the daughter of wealthy literati who had
her tutored in classical education. Unhappy in an arranged marriage to a man of lesser talent, she fled from her husband and two
children to assume a position as headmistress in a Chekiang modern
women's middle school and as teacher in a boys' school. Ch'iu Chin

trained her students in military tactics, until enough parents and girls resisted the training to bring it to an end. Like other militant women, she was influenced by the Russian anarchists and the anti-dynastic revolutionary sentiment in Chekiang. Her goal was to organize her pupils to stage an uprising and end the Ch'ing dynasty. She started the first feminist newspaper. She also attempted to introduce the issue of sex role differentiation into her lifestyle. Wearing Western man's clothes, she rode into town astride a horse, provoking a riot which her students had to quell. Ch'iu Chin's attempt to assassinate the Governor and create armed insurrection in the schools failed, and she died a martyr's death defending the movement. As the first woman to die for the revolution she wanted to prove herself equal in martyrdom itself.

Although many were uprooted by the chaos of the early Republican period and some fought bravely for both feminist and revolutionary goals, the mass of women were not involved in the anti-dynastic struggle. Other women followed Ch'iu Chin's example, including her own students who formed a short-lived para-military brigade to fight in the 1911 revolution to avenge their teacher's death, as well as the militant woman teacher Sophia Chang, who took her name from Sophia Pirovskaya, one of the assassins of Tsar Alexander II. During the 1911 revolution, many women joined the women's brigades of the decentralized revolutionary armies, although the women's army was disbanded after the inauguration of the Republic by decree of the Provisional Government in Nanking. The Government found the military wing of the women's rights movement too threatening. Thereafter they resisted the formation of military brigades of women and deflected them toward the Red Cross.

Through the May 4th Movement, 1919, the women's movement organized around such bourgeois demands as the right to marry freely, vote, be elected to office, own property and be educated. This was later known as the "five proposal movement." Some women's rights organizations petitioned the Provisional Parliament in 1912 and asked that the Constitution grant equal rights to both sexes, but they were ignored. In protest, on May 19, a number of young women stormed Parliament, broke its windows and injured its guards. This was unprecedented, and the women's movement was almost suspended because of it. A final upsurge of feminism in the latter stages of the May 4th Movement found that although some demands were granted in the Constitution due to Sun Yat-sen's insistence, most were promised but not realized. As a commentator of the period noted:

"The women's militia movement was quelled by this legal grant of equality in the constitution as ice melting in the spring sun. . . . Like a waterfall flowing to the plain, the women's movement flowed into eddies and whirlpools and never rose in a wave again."[31]

After 1922, the women's movement split into moderate and re-volutionary wings. The Women's Suffrage Association demanded constitutional equality for women; the Women's Rights League in addition called for women to join the revolution, to overthrow the feudal war-lords, and to struggle for a democratic society.

CHANGES IN WOMEN'S LIBERATION
UNDER THE COMMUNISTS

Communist revolutionaries heralded the revolution of women's rights as part of the destruction of the old social order. Revolution meant the restructuring of fixed social relationships--class, political status, and the clan and lineage systems in the community. For this reason, the revolution promised to give highest priority to women's liberation. Women were to be freed as a means of attacking the extended family and destroying the power of the clan head, the pater-familias.

In fact, while some women were trained as political cadres, and women's labor power was liberated, the Communist Revolution stopped far short of transforming the social status of women. The Chinese Communist leadership regarded women's oppression as a special issue which could only be solved in the larger context of the revolution. In his Report on an Investigation into the Peasant Movement of Hunan, 1927, Mao Tse-tung wrote that women were espe-cially oppressed. One of the goals of the peasant movement was "overthrowing the clan authority of the elders and ancestral temples, the religious authority of the city gods and local deities, and the masculine authority of the husbands." He continues, clearly implying that the oppression of Chinese women is greater than that of men,

> As to women, apart from being dominated by these three
> systems, they are further dominated by men. These
> four types of authority--political authority, clan author-
> ity, religious authority, and the authority of the husband
> --represent the ideology and institution of feudalism and
> patriarchy; they are the four bonds that have bound the
> Chinese people, particularly the peasants.

As the Communists consolidated their power, they promulgated reforms in the marriage law and land reform law. These reforms reinforced each other: the marriage law freed women from the authority of the family by granting them inheritance and property rights in case of divorce, while the land reform attacked the political power of the lineage system (which took male supremacy for granted) and granted important economic rights to women. At least in a legal sense, these laws helped liberate women from the bonds of political, clan, religious and male authority.

The Codes of the Kiangsi Soviet period, 1931, included the first Marriage Law which, in conjunction with land reform, was designed to free women for political action. The first goal was to "activate the emotions of the young women and consolidate their revolutionary determination."

> The most important object of the women's movement
> is to mobilize the broad masses of toiling women to
> join the revolution. Only the land reform, only the
> Soviet Government, can liquidate the feudal forces and
> liberate the women.

The second goal was the liberation of women to participate in production. These two goals, essentially designed to double at one stroke the political and economic power of the movement, were fundamentally contradictory. The political liberation of women turned out to be economically costly. Women were needed in the fields of the villages in the Border Region to maintain production, freeing the men to fight in the People's Liberation Army (PLA). These women were organized into brigades for productive labor, to outfit the five million PLA troops. Women in the north were inexperienced in agricultural labor, and great efforts were made to bring them out of the "small home" to do collective work for the revolution. Edgar Snow translates an instruction regarding mobilization for production in the border region, where the male population had declined as a result of enlistments in the Red Army. The instruction reads:

> To mobilize women, boys, and men to participate in
> spring planting and cultivation, each according to his
> ability, to carry on either a principal or an auxiliary
> task in the labor process of production. For example,
> "large feet" [women with unbound feet] and young women
> should be mobilized to organize production-teaching
> corps, with tasks varying from land-clearance up to

the main tasks of agricultural production itself. Small
feet, young boys, and old men must be mobilized to
help in weed-pulling, collecting dung, and for other
auxiliary tasks.[32]

Bringing women into production was one step in giving them mean-
ingful social tasks and control over their lives. However, as the
above instruction indicates, sex-typed division of labor remained,
even when women were used in production. Women were relegated
to the ranks of old men and children while the men went off to wage
war.

The myth of political participation of women as fighters in the
Chinese revolution is not entirely groundless. Some heroic women
did participate as fighters, but more important was the ideological
emphasis which the Chinese Communists placed on the participation
of women in the revolution and the extraordinary appeal of this idea.
The image of women as revolutionary fighters has a firm place both
in Chinese propaganda and in the chronicles of revolutionary history.
However, only about fifty (out of over fifty thousand) of those who
went on the Long March from the Kiangsi Soviet to the Northern
Border Region were women. Often women were trained as guerrilla
fighters in those villages where there were skirmishes and where the
men were absent. For instance, Li Fa-ku of Kiangsi joined the
Party at fourteen years of age. She participated in the Long March,
in warfare with the Nationalist Army, and rose through the political
ranks in Yenan. During 1934-37 she served as a guerrilla. Her
story, with that of other fighters, including a few women, was reprinted in the Red Flag Waves (Hung-ch'i p'iao-p'iao), a sixteen-
volume collection of memoirs written in Peking in 1957 as a tribute
to the revolutionaries.[33] But most women remained in the rear,
producing for the revolution, not fighting for it. Try as they might,
women in the PLA were not allowed at the front, except in the communications or public health corps or running supplies. K'uo
Ch'un-ch'ing disguised herself as a man and rose rapidly in PLA
ranks; she was awarded the highest award the army could give her,
that of "distinguished serviceman." When she was wounded and her
sex was discovered in the military hospital, she explained that the
reason she had hidden her sex was to remain in the army. However,
she was quickly removed to a more appropriate post in the public
health section of the army with other women. Even though women
were allowed in the PLA, they still performed sex-typed tasks. They
were not allowed to do the actual fighting, and they never gained
control of the means of coercion.

Thus, during the thirty-eight-year series of wars and revolutionary struggles that separated the collapse of the Dynasty and the final victory of the Communists, women were freed from a heritage of oppression. In the areas where the Communists held power, women were granted political and economic rights. Implementation of land reform (or rent reduction), the marriage law, and the initial organization of women into the Women's Association cleared the way for an attack on the private forms of sexual oppression. But legal changes were not always enforced, and formal changes in the rights of women did not attack the structures of authority and the informal prejudices which kept women in their places. The further effort to liberate women would have required costly political struggles that would have slowed down economic production. The tension between production and liberation blocked further efforts to emancipate women during the revolutionary period, and the same tensions recurred in the Communist period.

WOMEN'S LIBERATION IN COMMUNIST SOCIETY

After the revolution, the Communist leadership faced the problem of whether women were a special oppressed group in the new society, or whether their oppression could be ended by improving the economic condition of the entire population. Their treatment of women underwent several changes, depending on the political policies of the moment. In the beginning, the Communists genuinely hoped to change women's roles by implementing the Marriage Law and bringing women into the Women's Association, a mass organization treating the special problems of women. The village structure, customs, and rules made emancipation of women from traditional family and community roles very difficult. The Marriage Law was implemented in mass movements lasting from 1950 to 1953. Its purpose was to establish Communist power by destroying the power of the corporate lineage resting on the patrilineal family structure that denied women legal rights. The Marriage Law granted to women their rights to property, inheritance, marriage without regard for family alliances, divorce, and custody of children.

The means of implementing the Marriage Law changed as the resistance to it increased in the villages. In the first year or so, the law was implemented in a period of revolutionary terror. Women were to be completely liberated from the bonds of the "feudal family" --by divorce if necessary. All marriages arranged by the parents

were subject to dissolution, and these, of course, included the majority of village marriages.   The Marriage Law was commonly
known as the "divorce law."   This period of the law created tremendous resistance in the villages.   The cadres empowered to implement the law refused to take it seriously, and the opposition to
this law by the village men was compounded by the difficulties of
organizing women into collectives.   Further, the economic implications of this law were potentially disruptive.   After divorce,
women were allowed to withdraw from the family all their property,
which was damaging to the village economy, and, if carried far
enough, could have driven the poor peasant supporters of the revolution to destitution.   The first stage of revolutionary terror was
soon halted, and a more moderate tactic to implement the law followed in late 1952.   In place of efforts to destroy the family structure
and the use of violent struggle against family members, mediation
for family problems was encouraged.   We will describe the implementation of the Marriage Law in one village in late 1952, as reported in the press.   Even though implementation was comparatively
moderate by this time, the reform clearly benefited women, particularly by encouraging the political organization of women to attack
family problems.   Given the need to preserve the family and to
maintain most existing relationships, alternative means of reforming
the family were considered.   The Communists developed a unique
approach to political change through the tactic known as "small
groups."   This tactic was designed to unify the women of individual
households and isolated families into a social movement.   The campaign had an ideological component that helped to channel existing
discontent and generated collective energy by relating individual experiences to a "paradigm of experience."   In other words, the movement to implement the Marriage Law used ideology to turn private
grievances into public issues; family structure itself became a political issue.   Mobilization through the movement was also a means
of organizing women and developing leadership for local organizations.

One source[34] begins by noting the resistance to the movement
encountered among the Communist cadres:

> After the Fukien People's Court began revolutionary
> reconstruction in October, 1952, an experimental point
> in Min Ch'ing County was organized to implement the
> Marriage Law.   The work team under the direction of
> the CCP committee of Min Ch'ing spread knowledge of
> the Marriage Law and accelerated an early completion
> of the fall harvest within twenty days.

The cadres expressed concern over possible harm to production.
The defensive tone of the article suggests that the leadership realized
how the cadres used the excuse of production to oppose the movement.   The cadres feared the escalation of a special movement
which threatened their masculine authority in the family and community.

> . . . To meet these objections, the work team first
> studied with the county level committee. . . . They
> then convened an enlarged meeting of the cadres of
> six districts and repeatedly explained both the basic
> spirit of the Marriage Law and even wrote a report
> on the connection of the Marriage Law work with the
> work of gathering the harvest.   Such study finally
> "broke through" the cadres' thinking and overcame
> their deepest concerns that implementation of the
> marriage work was contradictory to harvest work.

Once initial reluctance by the leadership was overcome, the
campaigns were apparently efficient in organizing women.   Mass
action was used to accomplish what the cadres alone could not.   The
new mutual aid teams and elementary cooperatives organized villagers
into groups whose composition differed from the kinship associations.
Meetings of special interest groups of women, youth, and elderly
people provided another way for villagers to initiate discussion of
family problems.

> Sixteen work groups were organized, comprised of county,
> district and village cadres.   Expanded cadre meetings
> discussed the thorough implementation of the Marriage
> Law in the villages.   Finally, the cadres and activists
> convened an old people's meeting, a women's meeting,
> youth meeting, and meeting of the peasants' association
> in the village.   The work group participated in harvest
> work while they propagandized the Marriage Law and
> activated the masses.   The peasants discussed the
> Marriage Law in their work groups during rest periods
> at least twice. . . .

The report continues to describe how the dynamics of the movement reformed family relationships.

> Once the masses were mobilized we began to evaluate
> concrete family conditions, a good way to clarify the

implications of the Marriage Law. We spoke of five
kinds of families--model households, ordinary households,
households with marital discord, acutely inharmonious
households, and those in which there was mistreatment
of a criminal nature. We evaluated these families according to the spirit of the Marriage Law. In every
village we convened a movement to evaluate the masses'
own families. After evaluation we held a village meeting
and organized "speak bitterness," developed the struggle
further, and thoroughly aroused the masses' activism
against the feudal marriage system.

(Because the leadership preferred to mediate all difficulties rather
than to send families to the divorce court, only five per cent of the
marriages were declared unreconcilable.)

We praised the model husbands and wives and model
households, and then called meetings to democratize
the inharmonious households. Then the work groups
held mediation committee meetings, and the Women's
Association set up a temporary court to handle each
article of the Marriage Law. Many activist elements
appeared in the course of the movement, and all were
brought into the leadership structure of mediation and
the Women's Association.

The mobilization crystallized the hostile sentiment of women toward
the feudal family, and aroused women's anger through the group discussions and "speak bitterness" meetings. The work groups assisted
family members in resolving interpersonal tensions. Women were
organized and many assumed leadership in the new associations.

The movement to implement the Marriage Law was a political
movement that fundamentally changed the position of women in the
village community and the family. But this movement ended with
the onset of the first Five Year Plan of 1953-57. Political mobilization and struggle in the village and family were economically
counterproductive. For the next decade the struggle to improve
women's condition was absorbed by the struggle of the Chinese people
to improve productive conditions. Many national political goals were
subordinated to the overriding national policy of meeting new quotas.
It was now claimed that women were "liberated," or as the Chinese
said, women had "turned over" (fanshen). It was true that women

were liberated in two new senses. First, the discriminatory laws favoring men over women in wages and family matters were ended. Second, individually talented women were allowed to rise in the political and economic hierarchies as far as their training and talents would take them. Higher status women in fact complained bitterly that there was job discrimination, but on the basis of political connections, rather than sex. During the "Let a Hundred Flowers Bloom" period of 1957, individual women registered their complaints of political discrimination in job assignment, and leaders in the Women's Association complained that wives of cadres were given preference in administrative positions.[35] The freeing of women to rise individually did not alter the fact that the status of women was not equal to that of men.

From the first Five Year Plan to the Cultural Revolution, bringing women into production was the dominant policy of the Communist regime, although implementation varied according to the rate of economic growth and the priorities of various sectors of the economy. Day nurseries were few, jobs in industry fewer, and it was not always possible to find working capital. In the Great Leap Forward, roughly 1958-59, a social movement of intense pressure propelled women into the labor force to work in small-scale handicraft enterprises. But the emphasis on production within the accepted framework of the sexual division of labor served to veil the special authority structures that exploited women. Following the economic disaster of the Great Leap Forward and the ensuing three years of bad harvest, energy was directed toward restoring past production levels, not establishing new ones. When jobs were few, there was a reassertion of traditional structures, and women were encouraged to go back into the home. Women were discouraged from becoming politically organized during the period of recovery, 1961 to 1964. While some media were concerned with the women problem and stressed several aspects of it during this period, they all neglected the reality of persistent male supremacy in the home and local community. The propaganda of the period, as seen especially in short stories and literature, emphasized respect for the aged, the reassertion of the importance of kinship obligations, and awe toward the paterfamilias.[36] The unique importance of women in reproduction and household economy was emphasized in China's Women, journal of the Women's Association. The drive to raise agricultural production in this period dampened the drive to alter the collective image of women.

Beginning in mid-1966 the Cultural Revolution again revived concern that the tight family authority structure, the hierarchical relations of social deference, and obligations between the generations and sexes hindered political participation. This problem had not been dealt with for over a decade, but the political exigencies of the new struggle demanded increased political participation. The upsurge extended to all areas of power relations: it dictated that women unite politically to attack the authority of the bureaucracies with which they had contact--the urban residential administration in particular.

Women had been out of the political arena as an organized group for so long that they had neither developed new leadership nor prepared themselves for political discussion in the home. Nevertheless, two themes emerged during this phase of the Cultural Revolution. One was that women must be politically mobilized, the other that women must participate in economic production for the public good. The economic policies emerging from the Cultural Revolution required total involvement of women.

The journal of the Women's Association came under attack for its previous policies. In its last issue before it ceased publication (August, 1966), China's Women issued a self-criticism of its previous six years of underplaying the political role of women:

> Tung Pien [the editor], the black gang element, under
> the pretext of helping women cadres and women staff
> and workers handle the "contradictions between family
> duty and children and revolutionary work," massively
> proselytized such bourgeois and revisionist fallacies as
> "women live for revolution as well as for husband and
> children"; "to have a warm small family is happiness
> itself"; to bear and nurture children is women's "natural
> duty"; there must be "common feelings and interests" in
> selecting lovers (spouses). These absurd views were
> intended to create ideological confusion so that women
> cadres and women staff and workers would be intoxi-
> cated with the small heaven of motherhood, bearing
> children, and managing family affairs, and sink into
> the quagmire of the bourgeois "theory of human nature,"
> forgetting class struggle and disregarding revolution.
> This is an echo of the reactionary themes advocated

by modern revisionism such as "feminine tenderness,"
"mother love" and "human sentiments.". . .

The black gang element Tung Pien overtly distorted
the policy of the party by turning on the green light for
the demons and snakes and by introducing in undisguised
form such extremely reactionary and feudalistic con-
ceptions as respecting men but denigrating women and
demanding obedience at the three levels (obedience to
father, son, and husband) to spread massive doses of
poison in her publications. Under the pretext of pre-
senting opposite views in discussions, she published,
without any criticism, such reactionary articles as
"For Women to Engage in Enterprises Is Like Flying
Kites Under the Bed," "Women Live for the Purpose
of Raising Children," "Women Should Do More Family
Duties," thus openly attacking and insulting all the
women of new China. . . .[37]

The article condemns the fact that women's role in political struggle
was ignored and points out that they are a major labor resource.
Political struggle serves a double goal: organized collectives outside the home not only raise the level of women's political activity,
they liberate women for production as well. The implication is
that political liberation encourages rather than conflicts with economic
production.

The Cultural Revolution stressed women's political liberation
as part of an attempt to shake up the entrenched power structure.
Requiring the participation of all groups, the Cultural Revolution
also encouraged women to participate in political activity. Women
are encouraged to engage in study, small group political work, and
criticism of their families. For example, women can use Mao's
work to criticize domineering family members, such as parents,
in-laws, or husbands; and they are to persist until they have reformed exploitation and prejudice. Articles in the press include
the following statements which encourage the women to criticize
family members in study sessions.

Over thousands of years our family relations have been
that son obeys what his father says and wife obeys what
her husband says. Now we must rebel against this idea.
. . . We should make a complete change in this. . . .

It should no longer be a matter of who is supposed to
speak and who is supposed to obey in a family, but a
matter of whose words are in line with Mao Tse-tung's
thoughts. . . .

Articles emphasizing women's participation came to the fore in
the Cultural Revolution when a concerted attempt was made to break
down the rigid political and social structure. This timing indicates
the link between women's liberation and revolutionary change: the
fact that women neither generally participated in political action as
women nor questioned the authority of the household head and male
political leadership was seen as jeopardizing the goals of the political
struggle.

The course of the Chinese revolution suggests that the cause
of women's emancipation is advanced when broad popular revolutionary
participation is the policy. When economic goals are stressed, political activities are subordinated to production and, in consequence,
women's emancipation is minimized. While the same relationship
between economic priorities and women's liberation has held true in
the Soviet Union as well, only China during the Cultural Revolution
has been prepared to sacrifice any measure of economic efficiency
in order to maintain the impetus of revolutionary popular participation.
The current period of participation, because it includes the encouragement of female collectives, also seems to be a period in which
male supremacy is attacked. However, whether Chinese women
could retain their level of participation if economic needs were restored to the highest national priority is still unclear.

CONCLUSION

The crumbling of the old regime creates a potential for women's
liberation which cannot exist in pre-revolutionary society. To the
degree that women are oppressed by the same authority that keeps
men in their place and maintains traditional government (such as
lineage systems or village hierarchies), revolutions that attack this
authority will liberate women. Likewise, when the conditions that
oppress women can be attributed to exploitative economic structures,
then revolutionary efforts to change the economic system will also
liberate women. Thus, in Russia and China, the revolution, as it
broke apart the old order, freed women, primarily by removing the
legal restrictions which bound them to the family and kept them from
participating in production.

But women's oppression is not simply a result of general social and economic oppression; it is, in addition, a special form of oppression resulting from the unique conditions which affect women alone of all social groups. The oppression of women inheres in the most intimate, private areas of life, pervades cultural tradition and historical experience, and profoundly benefits men. Thus, it is in the interest of the revolution to liberate women to the extent that this liberation helps to destroy the traditional social structures which support the old regime. But this process will stop short of the additional effort required to liberate women from their special oppression. The costs are too great.

One of the major reasons that the post-revolutionary regimes in Russia and China have not been willing or able to make the effort required to liberate women fully is that both societies have suffered from pressing economic scarcities. In both cases, attempts to change the position of women were blocked when they became too costly either in terms of direct economic costs such as child care and household services or political resistance and disruption resulting from attempts to change the family or to bring women equally into production. It may be that women have a better chance for liberation in revolutions occurring in advanced industrial societies rather than in revolutions which set traditional societies on the path of modernization.

In Russia and China, two special forces worked for women's emancipation: the feminists themselves and the revolutionary ideology which they in part influenced. The feminists, a small group of competent and militant women, fought for the liberation of women within the context of a new and free society. The revolutionary ideology insisted that the liberation of women was necessary to create that new society. The conflict of these forces with the exigencies of the revolutionary regimes led to a curious synthesis: the liberation of women remained a central ideological premise in both revolutions even when attacks on oppression of women in the family and on inequality in economic and political life declined. Simultaneously, a "star system" with the double advantages of co-opting the minority of active talented women and providing propaganda support for the ideology of women's liberation came to absorb the energy of the feminists' drive for the emancipation of all women. Despite the crucial symbolic role played by feminist revolutionaries and the importance of the ideology of women's liberation even now, the outcome has been a system in which individual women are elevated as

symbols of the fulfillment of revolutionary promises rather than a
substantial commitment to end the oppression of women <u>as a social
group</u>. This post-revolutionary synthesis appears to result from the
fact that women were not organized <u>as women</u> during the revolutionary
period. A militant minority, primarily from privileged bourgeois
or aristocratic backgrounds, pressed the demands of women, but
women were not united in pursuit of equality. Because women did
not form a definite power bloc, neither the revolutionary feminists
nor the ideological commitment to women's emancipation were powerful enough to maintain the impetus for change when the costs became
high.

The inevitable conclusion produced by study of these two major
social revolutions is that, given the many obstacles to liberation and
the conflicting demands of different oppressed groups during the revolutionary period, women must win and hold power themselves during
this flexible transition phase. <u>Legal or even substantive changes in
women's position cannot replace the necessary ability to enforce their
interests even in the face of rival interests and demands.</u> In particular, women in Russia and China, despite their heavy contribution
to the revolution, never gained control of the means of coercion--
armed force--which would have guaranteed their power. In addition,
they did not develop mass political power or political leverage through
the control of key positions in the economy, party or state apparatus.
Without a power base, the demands of women were met only when
their liberation was beneficial to the political and economic interests
of the revolutionary regime.

[Authors' note: This paper was not written as the work of two area
specialists who happen to be women. It is an effort by women who
happen to have access to relevant data to answer questions of interest
to women. We felt that only the cooperative effort of women could remove the male bias in the materials of the area specialists and give
a picture of the problems of women in revolution that would reflect
women's own interests in the cultural and historical questions involved.
Much of the work on this paper was joint work. Specific credit shot
go to Janet Weitzner Salaff who prepared the materials on China, to
Judith Merkle who prepared the materials on Russia, and to Ann
Swidler who, as editor, helped to clarify and unify the paper.]

NOTES

1. Chris Carnavano, "On Cuban Women," Leviathan II, No. 1
    (May 1970):39-42.

2. Moscow--The phrase is Ivan the Terrible's, referring to Moscow
    as the last home of orthodoxy (after Rome and Byzantium).

3. An old Russian wedding song quoted in Henrietta Yurchenko,
    "Introduction," in A Russian Song Book, ed. Rubin and Stillman
    (New York: Random House, 1962), p. x.

4. L. Tikhomirov, Russia, Political and Social, Vol. II (London:
    Swan Sonnenschein and Company, 1892), Chap. II, "The Woman
    Question."

5. Sergei Akaskov, The Family Chronicle (New York: E. P.
    Dutton & Co., 1961).

6. The Table of Ranks (17th century) was established by Peter the
    Great as a series of civil service and military ranks for the
    upper class, which he required to enter universal state service.
    To economically free this class for service, the serfs were
    bound back to the land. The subsequent history of the Russian
    nobility consisted of their attempts to free themselves from
    state service while keeping their legal rights to serf labor.

7. Tikhomirov, op. cit.

8. Ibid.

9. A. S. Rappoport, Home Life in Russia (London: G. P. Putnam's
    Sons, 1906), Chap. XVII, "The Education of Women," notes that
    this pattern of learning was first encouraged by Catherine the
    Great. Its rationale was: French for the unity of the family;
    piano for the pleasure of the husband; and knitting and embroi-
    dery for surprises [sic].

10. Ibid.

11.   Tikhomirov, op. cit.

12.   Ibid.

13.   Ibid.

14.   Ibid.; Hélène Zamoyska, "La Femme Soviétique," in L'Histoire
      Mondiale de la Femme, ed. P. Grimal (Paris: Nouvelle
      Librairie de France), Vol. III, p. 387; Rappoport, op. cit.,
      Chap. XVIII, "Literary Women."

15.   Zamoyska, op. cit.

16.   Ibid., p. 390; Louise Bryant, Six Months in Red Russia (New
      York: George H. Doran, Co., 1918), Chap. X.

17.   Ibid., Chap. XXI.

18.   Ibid., p. 397.

19.   John Reed, Ten Days That Shook the World (New York: Inter-
      national Publishers, 1967), p. 105.

20.   Bryant, op. cit., Chap. X.

21.   Ibid., p. 178.

22.   Zamoyska, op. cit., p. 390.

23.   Countess Panina tried to lock up the funds of the state welfare
      organization to keep them out of the hands of the Bolsheviks.

24.   Bryant, op. cit., p. 169.

25.   Zamoyska, op. cit., p. 395.

26.   Ibid., p. 393.

27.   William M. Mandel, "Soviet Women and their Self-Image,"
      (Paper delivered at the Far Western Slavic Conference,
      University of Southern California, May 1970).

28.   Novyi Mir, Nos. 5 and 8 (1969), cited in ibid., n. 48.

29.   William James Hail, Tsêng Kuo-fan and the Taiping Rebellion
      (New York: Paragon Book Reprint Corp., 1964), pp. 125-140,
      285-286.

30.   Mary Backus Rankin, "The Revolutionary Movement in Chekiang:
      A Study in the Tenacity of Tradition," in China in Revolution,
      ed. Mary Clabaugh Wright (New Haven: Yale, 1968), pp. 319-
      365).

31.   Ch'en Tung-yuan, Chung-kuo fu-nü sheng-kuo shih [History of
      the life of Chinese women] (Shanghai: Chung-kuo wen-hua shih
      ts'ung shu, 1937), pp. 358-360.

32.   Edgar Snow, Red Star Over China (New York: Grove Press,
      1961), pp. 232-43.

33.   Summaries of these memoirs are in Robert Rinden and Roxane
      Witke, The Red Flag Waves: A Guide to the Hung-ch'i p'iao-p'iao
      Collection, China Research Monograph, No. 3 (Berkeley:
      University of California Center for Chinese Studies, 1968).

34.   Fukien Jih Pao, 9 January 1953.

35.   Roderick MacFarquhar, The Hundred Flowers Campaign and the
      Chinese Intellectuals (New York: Praeger, 1960), pp. 229-30.

36.   Ai li Chin, "Family Relations in Modern Chinese Fiction," in
      Family and Kinship in Chinese Society, ed. Maurice Freedman
      (Stanford: Stanford University Press, 1970), pp. 87-120.

37.   Chung-kuo Fu-nü [China's women], No. 8, 1966.

A Response to "Women and Revolution"

Nancy Milton

At a time when American women are actively seeking answers
to the particular problems of their own liberation, a discussion of
the experiences of the women of China and Russia is most welcome.
However, it is unfortunate that the authors of one of the first such
articles, "Women and Revolution: The Lessons of the Soviet Union
and China," approach so lightly the demands of both history and
scholarship. For although Janet Salaff and Judith Merkle state that
their intent is to demonstrate that ". . . the experiences of women
and the Russian and Chinese revolutions may teach us something
about the forms of revolutionary participation most likely to improve
the position of women . . . ," their ethnocentric and ahistorical
point of view, combined with a quite remarkable absence of evidence,
either documentary or experiential, not only fails to exorcise old
misconceptions, but generates some new ones as well.

Although Merkle's section of the article on Russian women
appears to suffer from some of the same weaknesses as the China
section, I shall limit my discussion to the latter, for it is through
the experience of living and working in China from 1964 through 1969
that I feel impelled to reply to what strikes me as a surprisingly
confused view, not only of the present position of Chinese women,
but also of the history of their struggle.

Salaff's view is confused in part because of problems of data.
However, underlying her criticism of the position of Chinese women
are several assumptions that would better have been explicitly stated
since they appear to form the basis of her conclusions as to the
failure of the Chinese revolution to eliminate "the economic and political inequality of women." These assumptions appear to be the

Reprinted with permission from Socialist Revolution, November-
December, 1970.

following: (1) The maintenance of the nuclear family in China constitutes a failure of Chinese women to achieve liberation. (2) The
central requirement for the liberation of women is their dominant
role in the military and their control of what Salaff calls "the means
of coercion." (3) Women's participation in production is good when
it specifically aids them "as women," but is alienating when its
primary function is to promote the general welfare.

If Merkle and Salaff wish to argue for these positions in terms
of their relevance to the present struggle of American women, they
should do precisely that. But the retroactive imposition of the theories
of one section of American women upon the demands and historical
necessities of the Chinese women's century of struggle does not constitute serious revolutionary criticism or historical analysis. The
women of China cannot be accused of failure because they didn't
find they needed what Merkle and Salaff thought they ought to have
needed, nor because they didn't get what they didn't ask for.

I shall try to avoid the temptation to reply to generalizations
with generalizations. Nevertheless, for anyone, particularly a woman,
who has worked closely with contemporary Chinese women, it is
difficult to avoid making at least an initial definitive statement --
namely, that the emancipation of China's women, whether judged in
the light of their own historical advance or in comparison with that
of women of other countries, is a miracle of social change and perhaps one of the most remarkable achievements of the Chinese revolution. Certainly, to women from other countries, it is one of the
most impressive aspects of present-day Chinese society. And I
believe that the primary reason for the pervasiveness of this impression
is, ironically, the very irrelevance of one of Merkle and Salaff's
main tenets -- that is, the existence of a "star system" which they
claim gives the impression of liberation where in general reality it
does not exist. China has its female stars of course. But I would
agree with Merkle and Salaff that it is not among them that one must
look to draw conclusions about the general advance of women. Rather
I would argue that it is in the area of basic level day-to-day leadership that fundamental change most sharply manifests itself, not only
in social, economic and political position, but in the more subtle and
elusive realm of the "informal prejudices" that Salaff talks about.
Here, the empirical evidence is most impressive.

My own experience, I think, is somewhat revealing. During
one of my teaching years in Peking, I worked with a teaching group

of about thirty teachers, approximately half men and half women.
Within this group, virtually all specific leadership was in the hands
of women, not because they were women, but because it happened,
in each case of teaching specialization, political leadership or whatever, a woman had superior qualifications of experience, ability,
training or knowledge.   Perhaps what was most significant, considering the less than twenty-five years of China's new society, was
the relaxed acceptance of women's leadership by both men and the
women themselves.   No one seemed to regard the situation as particularly remarkable except perhaps myself, and I too came to take
it for granted.   It is really only now, encountering flat statements
that the revolution has failed to end the oppression of China's women,
that I am struck by its significance.

Nor during that year of close working relationships with both
men and women teachers did I encounter either the open or subtle
manifestations of male supremacy that one might expect to find in
such a situation.   That is not to say that such phenomena did not
exist in the society or that anyone pretended they did not.   We are
discussing historical process after all, not absolute truths.   However,
I recall as exceptional a conversation with several women teachers,
all in their early thirties, about a male colleague of about the same
age.   They referred disdainfully to his superior attitude toward women,
but spoke of him with some amusement and seemed to regard him
more as a fool than a threat.

Obviously, urban intellectuals are likely to be socially advanced
if anyone is, but I am convinced from other experiences in China that
this type of small group authority structure existing among university
instructors was characteristic of the working relationships developing
among men and women in other occupations and in other parts of the
country.   Among peasants with whom I visited and worked in the
outskirts of Peking, leadership of basic level production units by
women, some of them only in their late teens, seemed to be common-
place.   And the increasingly important productive and political role
of women had its concomitant effects upon the question of domestic
labor.   In the household where I stayed, the fact that the husband,
a hard-working young brigade party secretary, was at home at every
mealtime to share the food preparation with his wife, then pregnant
and not participating in field work, was apparently a matter of interest
only to their western visitors.   "But all of the men in this village
cook," my hostess told me quite matter-of-factly.   Yes, they had
had communal dining rooms, but most of the villagers expressed their

preference for meals at home en famille, and so the men also cooked. The significance of all this lies not in comparison with the West, but with China's own history.

Salaff deals with the historical position of Chinese women in a paragraph of remarkable brevity in which she states that "in tradi- tional China, women were denied participation in any political insti- tutions." This is truly a marvel of understatement to describe a social, political and economic institution -- the traditional Chinese family -- which, for over a thousand years, by means of an ethic both personal and official, denied women virtually all legal, economic, social and personal rights -- the right to the choice of a husband (in a system in which marriage was the only means of economic survival), the right to divorce, to remarriage if widowed, to their own children, to education, to property, to uncrippled feet, and most emphatically, to control over their own bodies, not only sexually, but sometimes simply in terms of the right to life. Thus, the observation that "po- litical action mystified them" seems at the least gratuitous, for whether or not it mystified them, in a social structure in which women were denied even the privileges that many other traditional societies gave to them as daughter, wife, or mother, political action was quite sim- ply impossible.

In China, social institutions more than formal legalisms were responsible for the maintenance of the social order, and the family and kinship system, inextricably tied to the economic and political workings of the social system, had among its basic premises the subordination of the young to the old, of women to men. Only when a woman reached the status of mother-in-law in her husband's family did she achieve the possibility of some degree of power, and even that power extended largely to her dominance over the younger females of the family. The unhappy wife was advised to console herself with such folk adages as: "When you marry a chicken, stick with the chicken; when you marry a dog, stick with the dog." For those who were not consoled, the only escape from their highly institutionalized oppression was suicide. The national literature contains stories without end of wives who threw themselves down the household well in a form of suicide which became as ritualized as the marriage system which begot it, while others, with perfect explicitness, hanged them- selves from the connubial bed in their wedding clothes.

Salaff devotes the major part of her section on women's political participation before the revolution to strangely atypical sections of

Chinese society -- families who were "non-Confucian or non-Han"
and the daughters of "aboriginal generals." In a country which was
overwhelmingly Han and Confucian, in which even today the minority
population is less than six per cent, such an emphasis seems somewhat capricious. However, the assumption that military training is
a prerequisite to revolutionary struggle leads one into some obscure
corners. The great Taiping Rebellion (1850-1864), which the Chinese
today regard as the beginning of their one-hundred-year revolution,
was an ideological and philosophical revolution that had a profound
influence throughout the following century. Equality of the sexes and
the prohibition of foot-binding were part of a program that also demanded the distribution of land to the peasants, opposition to foreign
domination, and the overthrow of bureaucratic officials. It would be
difficult to overestimate the influence of these ideas on all Chinese
revolutionary programs in the succeeding century, but the participation of women in the Taiping Rebellion was not predicated upon the
military training of a few women of the time. The writer comes
closer to the point when she says that "the religious crusading spirit
may also have encouraged sexual egalitarianism during the early years
of the Taiping Rebellion."

To say that ". . . the mass of women were not involved in the
anti-dynastic struggle" of the early Republican period is only to state
what should be obvious from any study of the traditional position of
Chinese women. The overwhelming majority were illiterate, and
were oppressed politically, economically, and personally. Clearly it
was only the few who escaped by means of their education and class
position who were able to engage in political struggle. However,
throughout the Republican period (1911), the period of the May 4th
Movement (1919) and into the 1920s, the "family revolution," as it
was called, was never the concern of women alone. The pivotal
relationship of the Chinese family structure to China's political and
economic system was such that any revolutionary, or even reformer,
was forced to concern himself with the change of the family structure,
and hence with the question of the liberation of women. To be sure,
profound differences of opinion developed as to just what this meant,
but it is misleading, particularly on the basis of such inadequate
historical analysis, to state that "through the May 4th Movement,
1919, the women's movement organized around such bourgeois demands as the right to marry freely, vote, be elected to office, own
property and be educated." None of these demands in China could
have been, or were, remotely possible without a radical overturning
of all property and power relationships, and although they might
technically have been "bourgeois" demands, certainly, in light of

the profound social change that they implied, they were revolutionary demands even throughout the period when they were backed up by revolutionary law.

In considering the centrality of the woman question to other revolutionary issues of the May 4th period, it is interesting to re-call that some of Mao Tse-tung's first well-known essays were di-rected to this problem. The story reported in the local newspapers of a certain Miss Chao Wu-chieh of Changsha was not in itself re-markable -- of a young woman forced into an incompatible arranged marriage who on the day of her marriage slit her throat with a dagger concealed in the bridal chair. But Mao's nine articles on Miss Chao in the form of "case studies" which were both literarily traditional and sociologically new in China had a stunning impact upon the revolutionary movement of the period. In the series of articles, he developed his analysis of the relationship of the Chinese social structure to the personal tragedies of thousands of women such as Miss Chao. His writings were then followed by dozens of other such studies by young revolutionaries throughout the country. In his role as editor and contributor to the radical journals of the important Hunan student movement, Mao was to deal repeatedly with the problems of Chinese women.

If we are to assume that he and other revolutionaries, men and women, were correct in their analysis of the relationship between the social structure and the oppression of women, it is absurd to say that "women were to be freed as a means of attacking the extended family and destroying the power of the clan head, and the pater-familias." The implication seems to be that the liberation of women was thus a mere tactic. By such reasoning, one could just as easily reverse the equation and say that "the extended family was to be attacked and the power of the clan head destroyed as a means of freeing women." In fact, of course, the goals of attacking the ex-tended family, liberating women and overturning the traditional so-cial, economic and political structure were part of the same his-torical problem, each aspect inseparable from the other.

It is difficult not to feel that much of Salaff's analysis of the changes in the position of women during the course of the revolution is characterized by a tendency to force the facts into her thesis that the revolution was a failure for women. She states on the one hand that reforms in the marriage system and the land reform implemented one another in the liberation of women. Quite true, of course. It is thus difficult to follow her reasoning when she then says that the two goals " . . . of liberating women politically and for production were fundamentally contradictory . . . ," for the entire history of the struggle during this period is testament to the necessity of integrating the two. Salaff's own interpretation of the one source quoted in her discussion of this question raises some doubts as to her understanding of what she is reading. The instruction quoted from Snow's Red Star Over China states:

> To mobilize women, boys and men in spring planting
> and cultivation, each according to his ability, to carry
> on either a principal or an auxiliary task in the labor
> process of production. For example, "large feet" (women
> with unbound feet) and young women should be mobilized
> to organize production-teaching corps, with tasks varying
> from land-clearance up to the main tasks of agricultural
> production itself. Small feet, young boys and old men
> must be mobilized to help in weed pulling, collecting
> dung and for other auxiliary tasks. [my underlinings]

The quote is, in fact, an effective argument for the position that policy clearly did not maintain traditional sexual division of labor. "Large feet" and "young women" (all of whom would have had unbound feet) means women; "small feet" means crippled women, the victims of traditional oppression. Normal women are included in all tasks up to the "main tasks." But Salaff's interpretation is that " . . . the above instruction indicates sex-typed division of labor remained, even when women were used in production. Women were relegated to the ranks of old men and children while the men went off to wage war." It would seem that her interpretation of the passage is affected by her ambiguity toward the question of women in production.

In light of some of Salaff's own information, it is also difficult to know what to make of the following statement: " . . . formal changes in the rights of women did not attack the structures of authority and the informal prejudices which kept women in their places." Both the Marriage Law and the distribution of land to women were radical attacks of staggering significance upon the authority structures of Chinese society. In every village in which they were implemented, they were accompanied by fierce struggles against both the formal and informal prejudices that kept women in their places. Salaff herself states that " . . . the law (Marriage Law) was implemented in a period of revolutionary terror." One could disagree with her terminology, but not with the essential sense of that statement. That was precisely what the difficulties of implementation were all about -- an attack on "the structures of authority and the informal prejudices. . . ." And further to say that ". . . legal changes were not always enforced" is a meaningless description of an infinitely difficult and complex process in which there were gains and losses, advances and retreats, but a consistent movement forward.

The same tendency to see historical change, not as a process, but in simplistic and absolutist terms, is characteristic of the section dealing with the early period of the Marriage Law. It is turning the matter on its head to say that "the means of implementing the Marriage Law changed as the resistance to it increased in the villages." The resistance did not, in fact, increase, but consistently decreased. Perhaps it would be worthwhile to examine the process of development.

The Marriage Law, which gave to Chinese women, for the first time in their history, rights in regard to marriage, divorce, child custody and property ownership, represented in China an earthshaking change in one of the oldest continuous forms of family structure in the world. That many older peasants in particular saw it as a violation of ethics, morality and justice is hardly surprising. That some would resist it is certainly to be expected. But to state that ". . . in the first year or so, the law was implemented in a period of revolutionary terror. Women were to be liberated from the bonds of the 'feudal family' -- by divorce if necessary . . ." is ridiculous. The legal possibilities for the liberation of women from oppressive family relationships existed, but it was hardly a question of their waiting "to be liberated" by divorce via revolutionary terror. The struggles that took place in those Chinese villages and, in the last analysis in each family, had to be carried on primarily by the women themselves. As some of the problems of these women began to be resolved, often by divorce, naturally the intensity of the struggles began to subside. At the same time, as the Marriage Law increasingly became accepted as a part of the new social organization (which also brought with it the economic possibilities for a different family structure), resistance to it steadily diminished. And obviously, the vast majority of women and young people supported it at all stages.

Salaff states: "In place of efforts to destroy the family structure and the use of violent struggle against family members, mediation

for family problems was encouraged." There were neither policies
nor attempts aimed at destroying "the family structure," but at destroying the old family structure to be replaced by one based on
sexual equality. Nor can one speak in such general terms of
". . . violent struggle against family members." Accounts of the
period record incidents of women tortured, imprisoned, and killed
by family members -- parents, parents-in-law, husbands -- who
resisted the woman's demand to choose her husband, divorce him,
keep her child, remarry when widowed, retain her own property.
It was against such family members that struggles were conducted.
And it should be mentioned that in the now traditional Chinese Communist method of struggle, much of the violent struggle was struggle
by violent talk.

All this being the case, it is impossible to accept the sinister
implications of the statement, "Given the need to preserve the family
. . . alternative means of reforming the family were considered."
Here, Salaff is interjecting her own position on the question of the
family. There is no evidence that the demands of revolutionary
Chinese women, either before or after liberation, ever included the
abolition of the family. It was entirely a question of doing away
with the old, feudal, patriarchal family and creating the social, political, economic possibilities for a family based on equality of the
sexes and freedom of choice in marriage and divorce. It is subjective
in the extreme to imply that the shift from widespread divorce to
attempts to bring about reconciliation was a step backward. The
goal, after all, was not universal divorce, but successful marriages
and families. The high rate of divorce in the early years of the
Marriage Law was the heritage of a history of arranged marriages,
not the first step in the destruction of the nuclear family, as Salaff
apparently thinks it should have been.

The ethnocentricity of Salaff's view is particularly evident in
her dissatisfaction with the period from the First Five Year Plan to
the Cultural Revolution. Perhaps it would not be inappropriate at
this point to mention a few of the realities in China during that period. The Chinese Communists inherited, among other problems, a
backward agriculture, an undeveloped industry, a huge and uneducated
population, an inflated economy, a severe shortage of technically
trained personnel, etc. ad infinitum. During the period of the twenty
years under discussion, they suffered the war in Korea, trade embar-
goes, some of the most serious natural disasters in a hundred years,

a Russian pull-out of technicians with their blueprints in the very
middle of hundreds of construction projects -- all this during a period of virtually unprecedented social change. And somehow, the
problems of food and clothing were fundamentally resolved, literacy
became practically universal, an industrial base was laid -- and
women moved consistently forward socially, economically and politically. That during these two decades they did not reach the millenium of female emancipation in a country that is still struggling
to electrify all of its villages gives rise to a disappointment pecu-
liarly American.

To remark, for example, that "day nurseries were few, jobs
in industry fewer . . ." in reference to a country in which over
two-thirds of the population, men and women, are still peasants, is
meaningless. Obviously there are not "enough" jobs in industry for
anyone. My stress on economic realities does not constitute an
acceptance of Salaff's thesis that the true liberation of women can
take place only in advanced industrial societies, however. Rather,
I wish to point out that one cannot assume that the measuring sticks
of an advanced industrial society -- "day nurseries, jobs in industry"
-- are necessarily reliable indices of the liberation of women in a
society very different from our own not only politically and economically, but culturally as well. For example, day nurseries, though
increasing, are indeed few, but this has not kept mothers from
working. In the interim, children in China are cared for in a multitude of ways -- by grandmothers and grandfathers, by neighborhood
nurseries, or, in the countryside, by the whole village keeping an
eye on things. All of the women teachers with whom I worked had
children, but none of them struggled with the day-to-day child care
problems of American working women. An excellent and inexpensive
nursery (either by the day or the entire work week) was available
a few steps from their classrooms, but in just as many families,
grandparents solved the problem. At any rate, I never heard of a
woman who wanted to work having to stay at home for lack of child
care facilities.

Since the Cultural Revolution, in its early stages at least, was
an ideological revolution against feudal and bourgeois vestiges affecting
the socialist superstructure, it is quite logical that problems concerning women and the family should have been on the agenda. However, Salaff's article contains a number of misconceptions in regard
to both the form and content of these problems raised during the
Cultural Revolution, and once again, she presents little evidence.

She remarks that "women had been out of the political arena as an organized group for so long that they had neither developed new leadership nor prepared themselves for political discussion in the home." During the two years before the Cultural Revolution that I spent in China, women's organizations as such existed, but in areas in which women had already achieved an advanced position, women operated within the same vocational and political framework with men. And, as I have already mentioned, there seemed to be little problem of new leadership. If it is true that women were not prepared for political discussion in the home, they certainly were prepared for it outside the home, as anyone will testify who has been exposed to the thousands of hours of Chinese political discussions involving everyone.

It is true that women were encouraged to ". . . unite politically to attack the authority of the bureaucracies with which they had contact . . . ," but so was everyone else who fell into the broad classification of revolutionary masses. I at no time encountered or even heard of the concept of women ". . . participating in political action as women . . ." nor of the women's collectives of which Salaff speaks, except in those instances in which women simply happened to be in occupational groups made up entirely of women -- an increasingly unusual phenomenon affecting mostly older women -- who joined together in "housewives' groups." The vast majority of women assumed their natural collective to be among those with whom they worked and with whom they were in political agreement, and the women who rose to positions of mass leadership in the Cultural Revolution did not lead women, but women and men. To have suggested that it be otherwise (and once again, I never heard even a suggestion of such an idea) would, I'm sure, have been regarded as the most shocking form of male supremacy. The mass leader regarded as the earliest rebel of the Cultural Revolution was a woman, Nieh Ren-tzu, a forty-year-old Peking University philosophy professor, who remained one of the most influential leaders of students and teachers in Peking throughout the Cultural Revolution. She was not regarded as a women's leader, but as a woman leader, and by most people simply as a leader.

Some comment is necessary upon the long reference from the August 1966 issue of China's Women which the authors present as their definitive proof that the preceding decades had left women pretty well where they found them. Sociologists would do well to approach a social movement of such complexity as the Cultural Revolution with a degree of caution, and specifically, to analyze the characteristics of its different stages, not to mention its cultural particularities. August 1966 was the period of the opening of mass attack on virtually all institutions, hierarchies, bureaucracies and bureaucrats, and was characterized by its fierce criticism and explosive rhetoric. An examination of any periodical dealing with any subject in China during that period will reveal editorials virtually identical to the one quoted from China's Women. This is not to say that the allegations made are untrue or even exaggerated, but simply that they may be expected to be one-sided and will certainly stress every negative aspect of the workings of the particular institution for the previous fifteen or twenty years. A survey of the field during that month, if taken entirely at face value, could only force one to conclude that industry, agriculture, education, foreign relations, scientific research, and the manufacture of teacups had all been total disasters. Probably much, if not all, of the criticism contained in the China's Women editorial was true. The Chinese have never claimed that in twenty years they have swept their society clean of the effects of a millenium's subjection of women. However, one editorial from the period of August 1966 is simply not acceptable as the primary documentary proof of the policy of the preceding decades.

A final generalization demands comment. Just as it is not generally true that women were organized in women's collectives during the Cultural Revolution, it is equally incorrect to state that ". . . women were not organized as women during the revolutionary Period." It was precisely during the long revolutionary period when the struggles of women often involved their specific problems as women that such organization did take place. Any examination of instructions or policy documents will reveal that one of the first organizational tasks of the revolutionary army upon entering an unorganized village was to see to it that women's collectives were set up. It should be fairly apparent from Salaff's own discussion of the struggle for women's liberation during the revolution that the implementation of such radical changes in their lives as the Marriage Law and the distribution of land to women would have been impossible without women being organized into their own groups for discussion and action. However, at the present time, as women come to play an increasingly equal role in society, their problems become less specifically women's problems and their need for women's collectives becomes less. Nobody says that the problems of women as women have disappeared and neither have women's collectives, but certainly the trend is in that direction, not the other way around.

Merkle and Salaff's stress upon the military role of women takes them finally to their conclusion that the failure of Chinese women to achieve real liberation is because " . . . women never gained the means of coercion -- armed force." But, in the realities of the real world, if the Chinese Revolution had had to wait for women to achieve the leading military role Merkle and Salaff designate for them (which, after all, has not yet been accomplished anywhere) Chinese women might still be forced to solve their problems by jumping down wells.

However, in regard to the importance placed upon the specifically military role of women, it is interesting to note that one of the most important, popular, and widely known events of the stage in China, the ballet "The Red Detachment of Women," is, as its title would indicate, a tale of a heroic detachment of women guerrillas during the First Revolutionary Civil War (1927-28). Women guerrillas operating from a village base were at least as common throughout the entire Chinese Revolution as they are in Vietnam today. There is probably no one in China who has not seen "The Red Detachment of Women" in either the stage, film or television version, and probably not a young person who is not able to sing the songs from it, hum the tunes or do some of the dances. The other two contenders for the top three cultural events are two Peking operas, "The White-Haired Girl" and "The Red Lantern," both of which star militant though admittedly non-military heroines. It may be that the authors will see this as part of their "star system" theory, but at any rate it is difficult for a male supremacist in China today to go to the theater or even watch television without being bombarded with stories of heroic women.

At the same time, on the non-star level, the inclusion of young women in the militia is universal. At the language institute where I taught it was taken as a matter of course that young women students would take military training in line with their militia responsibilities. And there certainly are more women, young and old, in China than anywhere else in the world who have been trained in the use of weapons.

I have concerned myself primarily with what seem to me to be scholarly and historical weaknesses in Merkle and Salaff's article, but there is another aspect of it that is at least as disturbing. There is much talk in the American women's liberation movement today about sisterhood, but it is precisely this element which is absent from "Women and Revolution." Whatever oppression middle-class

American women suffer, it does not approach the degree of oppression institutionalized in China for centuries, and it has been by their own struggles and sacrifices that Chinese women have fought their way out of that oppression. With guns and without, they have carried on these struggles in conjunction with the rest of China's oppressed through twenty-five years of continuous war with its accompaniment of prison and torture for many, staggering poverty and overwhelming social problems. Whatever degree of liberation they have achieved by today has been gained at a fearsome price, and the women of China by the millions have paid that price.

The authors comment that "it may be that women have a better chance for liberation in revolutions occurring in advanced industrial societies rather than in revolutions which set traditional societies on the path of modernization." It may be. But it seems a precarious thing to count on, now that history has shown rather definitively that a powerful economic base does not turn out to be the answer to everything. Perhaps the human elements that manifest themselves in struggle -- the qualities which make possible the sacrifices willingly made in revolution -- are at least as significant as the national steel production. The tendency of capitalist ideology to turn everything, including all human feeling, into commodities may indeed turn out to be a more difficult obstacle than the lack of heavy industry. It is the element of feeling -- of compassion, warmth, respect -- that is so strangely absent in an article entitled "Women and Revolution," written by women.

Women Hold Up Half the Sky

Jane Barrett

Recently, someone asked Carmelita Hinton (China-born daughter of William Hinton) what her initial impressions of the United States were upon her arrival here last year. Her reply -- "the incredible waste everywhere and the outlandish way that American women dress." For the American visitor in China, the first images that flash past the bus windows as you roll into Canton are just the opposite -- clean streets free of the neon honky-tonk syndrome, simply dressed men and women free of class and sexist distinctions. At first, the city seems austere to American eyes, and the street scenes are drab, if dignified, largely for lack of decorative women. But gradually the cultural blinders begin to fall away, and the eyes learn to look for a quick smile, an eloquent shrug, a nervous tic, and a thousand other gestures that make each Chinese completely unique. The crowds are alive with a happy hustle bustle that the Chinese call jenao.

As a nation, the Chinese exhibit a vitality and a strength of character that make middle class Americans look positively anemic, and nowhere is this more apparent than among Chinese women. They are generally forthright, self-confident and strong. Unfettered by a role of passive seductiveness, they enthusiastically chat about their work and their lives without self-consciousness. Street chauvinism as we know it -- whistles, stares, suggestive glances -- are nonexistent. One day in Shanghai, a member of our delegation with waist-length blond hair was shocked to hear a wolf whistle in her direction. Whirling around, she saw a carload of European sailors hanging out of a passing car, leering and waggling their fingers at her. The fact that such an incident is extraordinary is some indication of the quantum leap women have taken in the last fifty years, from a society where women hobbled on systematically broken feet, in subservience to husbands, fathers, and a host of other males.

193

We saw women mend high-tension wires with the current on, weld steel plates onto ship hulls, and operate huge cranes. Of course, there's nothing revolutionary about women doing manual labor per se; the real question is how well women are integrated into the entire labor force and power structure. But still, it's startling to see women doing jobs that our society reserves exclusively for men. The Chinese record in employment is uneven. In heavy industrial enterprises, like petroleum refineries and iron and steel complexes, women comprise about one-third of the labor force, often in support services like clinics, day care centers and canteens. In a large Shanghai shipyard, only 800 of the 6,000 workers were women. In light industries, particularly textiles, the record is better -- 50% or more of the labor force are women. Although there are virtually no institutional barriers excluding women from specific jobs, some sexually segregated patterns do emerge. I saw no men working in day care centers with pre-school children. In an embroidery factory in Tientsin, 90% of the workers were women, supposedly because "women are better at fine work; they're cleaner and more careful." Our Chinese guides seemed to find nothing objectionable about such attitudes; the most important accomplishment in their eyes was the fact that women had been organized into any kind of production, rather than sitting at home. And the women themselves said repeatedly, "Before Liberation, we couldn't go out into society." No one said, "Before Liberation, I never could have had this kind of job." Situations like this made me understand more clearly the dramatic qualitative change that Chinese women have experienced in the last 25 years. It was not simply a question of upgrading their position, but of freeing them to enter into a society larger than their immediate household circle. The impact on their lives has been so momentous that our questions about "how many men, how many women work here" struck them as rather meaningless.

Ideas of what constitutes "women's work" seem more definite in the countryside than in the city. First of all, the rural wage pattern contains a built-in disadvantage for women; work points are assigned to each task largely on the basis of how much physical strength is required to accomplish it. Although occasional teams of "iron girl" labor heroes will manage to earn the maximum 10 points a day, the majority of peasant women earn up to 8 points a day. The Chinese say that "pay according to ability" within strict limits is the heart of their socialist economic policy, despite the fact that it puts a substantial part of the population at an economic disadvantage (albeit a minor one). This means that more equalized

pay for men and women hinges on that far-off day when Chinese agriculture is extensively mechanized.   The problem is compounded by
the occasional use of women's inferior strength to bar them from
more challenging and important tasks.   A young peasant activist in
Hopei told us that a number of young women in her brigade wanted
to work on an extension of the Red Flag Canal, but the brigade leadership told them to stick to "regular farmwork."   The activist organized a study group of women which focused on Mao's doctrine of
sexual equality, and after a while confronted the brigade leadership
with charges of male chauvinism.   The leadership relented, and allowed the women to work at the canal site, doing simple tasks like
loading stones into carts.   In their spare time, they watched the
older workers and practiced hammering spikes into rocks, tamping
dynamite, and lighting blasting caps.   The older women of the village rallied behind the team, bringing them food at work and donat-
ing the electric wiring from their own houses, so the young women
could work at night.   After some heroic acts during a blasting ac-
cident, the team became one of the first "iron girl brigades."

Peasant women are also hindered in their work by child care
and housework arrangements.   In urban centers, excellent day care
is available for the children of working mothers, usually right at
the factory or the office.   Most urban women also get 56 days paid
maternity leave.   Rural women get no paid leave, are assigned
lighter tasks during the later months of their pregnancies (resulting
in a work-point drop of about 15%), and often work only part time
after they give birth, resulting in a further income drop.   Although
Ta-chai and a few other "first line brigades" have day care centers
and some payment to women for housework, in most brigades the
traditional arrangement still exists.   If a husband is progressive
and/or his wife is assertive, such duties may be more equitably divided.   Commonly, a granny or elderly aunt lives with the young
family and takes charge of a good deal of the child care.

I agree with Nancy Milton that abolition of the family cannot be
considered the sine qua non of women's liberation in China.   The
problem lies not in the institutions of marriage and family themselves,
but in the social and cultural nexus in which they exist.   Certainly
the Marriage Law of 1950 had more potential impact on Chinese
women than any other institutional change made in the young nation,
but the freedom to choose one's own husband was rather meaningless as long as parents were reluctant to let their daughters meet
and work with men in a variety of settings.   Consequently, arranged

marriages in the countryside were reported as late as the 1960s.
In the same way "abolition of the family," presumably involving universal day care, will not free women if such institutionalized child
care is still considered "women's work." There is no reason why,
given the structure of Chinese society, men can't share household
and child care duties now, and in fact some younger progressive
families do just that. But a conservative concept of the family has
not yet died away. In Tangshan we had a special meeting with a
group of men and women about women in China and the U.S., during
which we repeatedly asked why rural women were paid less and
weren't paid for housework. Finally, one man stood up and explained
that "In every family, there are men and women, so that families
are equal as a whole . . . we view husband and wife as equal; we
do not look at it only from an economic point of view." In other
words, he did not think of women as independently entitled to absolute economic equality, but rather as a married unit. It is the
weight of traditional attitudes like these, particularly in the countryside, that is delaying complete sexual equality. The Chinese have
approached this problem slowly and cautiously. In my view, one of
the Cultural Revolution's shortcomings was a failure to adequately
deal with women's issues. Almost every other aspect of Chinese
society was closely scrutinized and invigorated in those tumultuous
years, but there were very few protracted struggles over feminist
issues. This is not to say that women weren't active in the Cultural Revolution, or that they didn't make some gains, but women's
rights were never more than a secondary issue. Now, in the last
year, several major articles in Peking Review indicate a renewed
interest in women's liberation.

Interestingly enough, there has never been any official doubt
about the importance of marriage for everyone. We never heard
single life mentioned as an alternative lifestyle. Everyone, male
and female, gets married sooner or later (and that may mean as
late as 35). Chinese marriages seem both more flexible and harmonious than American relationships. Because people marry later,
they have a stronger sense of identity and commitment to their jobs,
political activities, and other group activities like amateur cultural
troupes or sports teams. This is particularly important for women,
who may have to cope with the pressures of an old-fashioned mother-
in-law. Moreover, couples get to know each other over long periods
of time at work and in political study groups, so they aren't likely
to rush into ill-fated matches. The criteria are mutual interests
and political attitudes, comparable cultural levels, personality and

"looks," although the Chinese hastened to assure us that outward appearance is nowhere near as important as it is in the U. S. Because
couples have well-developed interests and friendships with others before marriage, the emotional burden that American marriages struggle under is somewhat diffused. Since what we would consider "interpersonal conflicts" (e. g. egotism, selfishness) might take on political
connotations in China, there is all the more reason for a couple to
seek the help of others in resolving their problems. Career demands
frequently split up families for long periods of time, but people don't
seem to mind. The attitude is "I'll go where I'm needed." Perhaps
for some couples, such separations provide a welcomed respite from
married life.

Next to organizing women into production, the government has
devoted most attention to developing women leaders. The numbers
are low but rising. Everywhere we went, we asked about the sex
breakdown on revolutionary and party committees, and almost everywhere men predominated. The extreme case was the embroidery
factory in Tientsin, where 90% of the workers were women, but a
single man occupied the top positions on both committees. Certainly
there are women in top positions, brilliant personable women like
Li Su-wen, finance minister of Liaoning Province and member of the
Central Committee. Li and the other women leaders we met displayed neither defensiveness nor aggressiveness toward their male
comrades. They were completely relaxed and open. But in order
to get to the top, many women must struggle against residual chauvinist attitudes. The pre-Cultural Revolution film called "The Red
Blossoms of Tienshan" details the trials and triumphs of a young
woman who becomes brigade head in a commune on the western
grasslands. She confronts the village elders who doubt her compe-
tence and a capitalist-road saboteur who tries to persuade her husband to whip her, and even humiliates her own husband in public
when she discovers that he made a private profit from selling brigade property. Once she has met these challenges, the whole brigade hails her as a hero.

The Chinese explanation that work is assigned "according to
needs and talents, not sex" sounds a little thin in the face of male
predominance in leading bodies. Like the U.S., China is currently
experimenting with "quotas." District Revolutionary Committees in
Shanghai have set a 20-30% bottom limit for female members. In
some quarters quotas are opposed as an artificial solution, by people who advocate bringing women up through the regular channels of
political activity.

It is quite common to see a woman in her early twenties in charge of a large number of workers; it seems that the younger generation is less affected by the negative self-images and low expectations that Chinese society used to condition into women. The gap in historical experience struck me clearly at a ping-pong match between Sweden and China in Peking's Capitol Auditorium. Since the tickets came through a friend at the Swedish embassy, the seats were in a special VIP section, complete with red carpets, armchairs and ashtrays. Sitting and chatting in front of us was a group of plump balding army men in their sixties. As each new arrival stepped into the box, they greeted him like a long-lost friend, and spent more time talking than watching ping-pong. This group of generals undoubtedly wield a great amount of power, power they acquired through decades of armed struggle in an era when women were involved in troop support rather than active military duty. I felt the same way then that I felt in Miami during the Republican Convention, when the Vietnam Veterans Against the War politely but firmly asked all women to go to the back of their parade column. They weren't purposely discriminating against women; it was simply an historical fact that women haven't shared the first-hand trauma that binds the VVAW so closely.

Chinese women live and struggle in the shadow of similar historical facts. Today, despite the high goals that have been set for women's liberation, and the mushrooming number of women activists at the low and middle level, there remains a de facto monopoly on skills and experience at the top. It is particularly important to break down male supremacy in the army, both because it has been more solidly dominated by men than any other organization, and because of its tremendous power. The army, more than any other institution, is squarely confronted with the contradictions between "red" and "expert," and the various resolutions of this tension will profoundly influence China's future development. Chinese women can't afford to be shunted into support services like medical and clerical units. It isn't enough that all high school students receive some military training; women should have equal access to all the skills and power of the PLA, and at the present time, they don't have it.

One of China's most popular revolutionary ballets, The Red Detachment of Women, reveals some ambivalence about women in a combat role. The women learn to use rifles (they are taught by men), but they also repeatedly sew on buttons and mend uniforms for the soldiers. They are organized and led by a dashing male commissar. When some of us visited the Peking Ballet Troupe, we discovered that historical investigation had proved that the commissar was actually a woman, that the women had taught themselves to use guns, and that Hainan Island was the home of some extremely militant women, many of whom were sold as child slaves to landlords. The ballet troupe explained that the commissar was changed to a male for "artistic reasons, because there weren't enough male leads." We couldn't elicit any "political" explanation for the switch.

The Chinese are making strong attacks on chauvinist attitudes in schools. We got only a superficial glance into primary and secondary education, with lots of visits but no extended classroom observations. It seemed, though, that girl students were just as active as boys, showing us around their school, reciting in class, and fixing flywheels and lathes in campus workshops. In one of the first "cultural performances" that we saw, a Tibetan dance in Canton's Number 61 Middle School, teenaged boys and girls danced enthusiastically, with a total lack of self-consciousness. All of us were struck immediately with the realization that most American boys wouldn't be caught dead in such a performance. In sports and after-school activities, however, students often broke down into male and female groups. Boys played rougher games than girls. In a "children's palace," a kind of hobby center, girls were doing intricate embroidery, while boys were making model boats. Of course they chose their activities themselves, and the teachers explained the "boys just don't like to do embroidery." They thought it was a trivial matter.

In conclusion, it seems logical to ask what lesson American women can learn from the Chinese experience. First, we must recognize the difference in the two situations. American women enjoy many more institutional rights than Chinese women did in pre-Liberation China: the right to vote, the right to hold property, divorce, universal education, etc. We have never been as totally oppressed by the family structure. Thus the American brand of feminism has concentrated much more heavily on analyzing role differences, whereas the main target for the Chinese has been the patriarchal system of authority.

The first major lesson to be drawn is a negative one. Sexual equality does not come automatically with a socialist revolution. While socialism sets up ideals and the framework within which to achieve these goals, women will still face discrimination and chauvinism until the old attitudes are changed. Therefore, radical women should concentrate on raising their own feminist consciousness and others', regardless of whether they feel the major contradiction in American society to be racial, economic, or sexual. The main reason that China hasn't made more progress toward full equality is the heavy burden of old ideas.

On the positive side, the Chinese have implemented a wide range of nuts and bolts programs, like day care, paid maternity leave, free birth control and some cooperative housekeeping services, that have done a tremendous amount to free women to fully participate in society. But more than this, they have set very high ideals for women's liberation, and these ideals can't be shoved aside. One thing about Chinese society that is very different from American life is its moral quality. By and large, things happen the way they are supposed to. Because there is relatively little discrepancy between ideals and reality, the Chinese are not cynical. They are accustomed to challenges and difficulty, but they feel all obstacles will eventually yield in the face of persistent struggle. Women's problems can't be ignored. Too many people have been brought up to believe in total equality, in a social milieu that demands that revolutionary principles be put into practice. Many of the women we met in China had already achieved this goal and are models of what free women can be like -- relaxed, capable, unpretentious, and a lot of fun.

Women's Liberation

Soong Ching-ling

History has proved that Women's Liberation in China--women obtaining equal status with men--began with the democratic revolution, but will be completed only in the socialist revolution.

What is the democratic revolution? It is a revolution to overturn the feudal rule of a landlord class, a revolution participated by the people at large under the leadership of a political party. It first took place in China in 1911, when a monarchy was overthrown, the emperor -- the biggest landlord in the entire land -- was dethroned, and the aristocracy was dispersed. But this revolution was not completed until 1949, when about that time the land of all big landlords was confiscated. Peasants and landlords were hostile to each other. The former participated in the revolutionary movement in 1927, and only after a long period of class struggle did they succeed to overturn the latter.

What has the overturning of the landlord class to do with the Women's Liberation Movement? In the spring of 1927, our great leader Chairman Mao Tsetung clearly gave us the correct explanation: "The political authority of the landlords is the backbone of all the other systems of authority. With that overturned, the clan authority, the religious authority and the authority of the husband all begin to totter. . . . As to the authority of the husband, this has always been weaker among the poor peasants because, out of economic necessity, their womenfolk have to do more manual labour than the women of the richer classes and therefore have more say and greater power of decision in family matters. With the increasing bankruptcy of the rural economy in recent years, the basis for men's domination over women has already been weakened. With the rise of the peasant movement, the women in many places have now begun to organize

Reprinted from Peking Review, No. 6, February 11, 1972.

rural women's associations; the opportunity has come for them to
lift up their heads, and the authority of the husband is getting shak-
ier every day. In a word, the whole feudal-patriarchal system and
ideology is tottering with the growth of the peasants' power." Needless to say that before the democratic revolution the women in China,
with the social status, were in various ways oppressed and exploited.
Women of the richer classes and even the majority of the poorer
classes were occupied in their families and maintained no social occupation. Women employees, especially the domestic ones, received
very low wages. Indeed very few women maintained their economic
independence! Meantime, very few girls were enrolled in schools.
The women graduates by and large returned to their homes, only a
very few turned to be teachers in primary schools and girls' middle
schools.

The pace of the Women's Liberation Movement closely followed
the advance of the democratic revolution. Women's status in China
was apparently raised by 1930, on the eve of the war against Japanese
aggression. There were already at that time colleges and even middle schools where co-education was established. Women graduates,
not a few of them, were employed as teachers, medical doctors and
hospital nurses. Most of the graduates from Christian missionary
schools and colleges, however, did not take up any occupation and
remained in their families to become "social vases," then a nickname
for those who were busy in social entertainments but had no profession
of their own. These women, married or single, free from feudal eti-
quettes, turned out to be social toys and bourgeois parasites. At this
time, there were many women engaged in textile industries, but they
were under capitalist exploitation, receiving low wages and suffering
from poverty.

At the end of the war against Japanese aggression and occupation, the Chinese people under the leadership of the Chinese Communist Party accelerated the revolutionary movement. Thus numerous
women threw themselves into all kinds of revolutionary work, some
of them joined the military services. They gained their economic
independence. Party members devoted themselves to propaganda
work, in villages and factories. Many of them were women graduates from middle schools. By doing their work women won the
equal status with men. They were very active in the land reform
movement, they helped to do away with the land ownership of the
big landlords. They were eagerly devoted to their various tasks,
with self-sacrificing spirit to fulfill the orders given by the Party.

It was upon the basis of this democratic revolution that the Chinese people could and did initiate the present socialist revolution.

When in October, 1949, with the defeat of the Japanese military forces, with the Chiang Kai-shek dictatorship overthrown, with the imperialistic foreign agents cleared off, the People's Republic of China was proclaimed, our democratic revolution came to its conclusion. From then on our socialist revolution began. At the very beginning of the present regime, the Minister of Justice and the Minister for Public Health were both women. Many other women entered government services in Peking as well as in the provinces. In the administration of various public utilities there was no lack of women cadres.

Within the last twenty years, more and more women enlisted themselves in the army, navy and air forces. They voluntarily entered these services after having passed a physical examination. More and more women joined agricultural field work, pasturage, mining, foundry, irrigation, communication, transportation, all kinds of factories, commerce, shop-work, and various other public services. Since 1966, the first year of our Cultural Revolution, which is a part of the socialist revolution, the number of women doctors and nurses has been greatly increased. In very recent years, in a few large cities, all healthy women under forty-five have been given work in manufacture, commerce, communication, transportation, and other services for the people. Middle school graduates, boys as well as girls, have been allocated to work in factories, fields and shops. Whatever men can do in these services women can equally do. By and large every woman who can work can take her place on the labour front, under the principle of equal pay for equal work. A large majority of the Chinese women have now attained their economic independence.

If we ask, however, whether the Women's Liberation Movement in China has come to its end, the answer is definitely no. It is true that the landlord system has been abolished for nearly twenty years, but much of the feudal patriarchal ideology still prevails among the peasants, or rather, farmers. This ideology still does yield mischievous things in the rural places and some of the small towns. Only when the feudal-patriarchal ideology is eradicated can we expect the sexual equality to be fully established.

In order to build a great socialist society, it is necessary to have the broad masses of women engaged in productive activity. With men, women must receive equal pay for equal work in production. Today in our country there are people's communes in rural places where women receive less pay than men for equal work in production. In certain villages patriarchal ideas still have their effect. Proportionately, more boys than girls attend school. Parents need the girls to do household work. Some even feel that girls will eventually enter another family and therefore it would not pay to send them to school. Moreover, when girls are to be married, their parents often ask for a certain amount of money or various articles from the family of the would-be husband. Thus the freedom of marriage is affected. Finally, as farmers want to add to the labour force in their families, the birth of a son is expected while that of a daughter is considered a disappointment. This repeated desire to have at least one son has an adverse effect on birth control and planned births. A woman with many children around her naturally finds it too difficult to participate in any productive labour. Another thing hampering a working woman is her involvement in household work. This prevents many women from full, wholehearted participation in public services.

From the present situation it is not difficult to understand that genuine equality between the sexes can be realized and the Women's Liberation Movement will be ended when and only when, led by a Marxist-Leninist political party, the process of the social transformation of society as a whole is completed, when the exploiting class or classes are exterminated, and when the feudal-patriarchal and other exploiting-class ideologies are completely uprooted.

Liberation of Women

Lu Yu-lan

I have grown up in the new society. My village -- Tungliu-shanku Village in Linhsi County, Hopei Province -- was liberated in 1945 when I was five years old. We girls, like the boys, went to school. After I completed primary school, I did farm labour and joined in revolutionary work, cherishing the ideal of building the new socialist countryside.

Many ordinary working women in our Linhsi County have matured and become leading cadres. Women account for 30 per cent of the county's Party and government cadres today, and many of them hold principal leading posts at various levels. This shows the status of women in socialist New China. Like their men folk, women are managing state affairs. They have been emancipated politically.

TRANSFORMING SOCIETY AND FAMILY

The road of women's emancipation, as I recall, was not a smooth one. At first some did not understand the relationship between the improvement of women's position in the family and participation in society's class struggle, and they thought that as long as women got power in the family the liberation of women was completed. To assert their rights, they often quarrelled with fathers-in-law, mothers-in-law and husbands. But this adversely affected amicable relations in the family and failed to win public sympathy.

Later, the Party organizations led women to study Chairman Mao's teachings on women's emancipation. Chairman Mao pointed out in the 1950s: "Genuine equality between man and woman can

Reprinted from Peking Review, No. 10, March 10, 1972.

be realized only in the process of socialist transformation of society as a whole. " This helped women take a broader view. They understood that to achieve women's genuine liberation they must consider things in terms of the whole society. The family is a cell of society and only by transforming society can the family be transformed. After women have gained their position in society, changes in family relations will ensue. Equality between man and woman will be put into effect.

I was engaged in women's work in my village in 1955. After I had talked it over with poor and lower-middle peasants, we set up an agricultural producers' co-operative. I also persuaded women to go out and take part in collective productive labour. At that time some people still held to the old idea that "the man goes to the county town but the woman remains in the home" and were unwilling to let women go out to take part in activities. There was a just-married girl in a family. Her elder in-laws were strict and wouldn't let her go outside. I used to go to their house in the evening and learn needle work from her. Taking this as an opportunity, I chatted with them and explained the meaning of women's emancipation. I told them: "Wouldn't it be wonderful if women took part in collective productive labour and both men and women were co-op members!" She was very pleased with this and afterwards went to take part in farm labour. She worked well and got her earnings just like male members. Her in-laws and husband no longer opposed what she did. Thus, more and more women in our co-op took part in collective labour and worked with increasing vigour.

To transform our poor village which had lots of sandy land, I and a dozen or so women organized a "March 8" afforestation team. There were no saplings at that time so we travelled scores of li every day to collect tree seeds. In three years we planted over 110,000 trees on more than 300 mu of sandy waste land. By 1971 our village's women and poor and lower-middle peasants had planted more than one million timber and fruit trees on 3,300 mu of sandy land. This checked wind and sand and ensured rich harvests for years running. The per-mu grain yield never exceeded 100 jin in the past, but it topped 650 jin last year. People gradually changed their view, saying that when women took part in collective production, they surely fulfilled half the task.

CHANGES IN ECONOMIC STATUS

Day in and day out, women with children were tied down by household chores. Farm collectivization changes the old relations of production. With the consolidation and development of the people's commune, more and more welfare and maternal and child health establishments have been set up and their services steadily improved. Maternal and child health centres and short-term kindergartens during the busy farm seasons, flour and rice-husking mills equipped with machines and tailoring groups serving commune members have socialized a lot of household labour and thereby created conditions for women participating in collective production.

Women doing collective labour get equal pay for equal work. Having received their own income, women's economic position changed. Family relations also changed accordingly. At the Sunchuang Brigade in the Lipochai Commune, the Lin family has 13 persons belonging to four generations. Lin Chin-lan, her elder sister-in-law and her mother make up an important part of the family labour force. What they get for their labour forms a major part of the family income. This has changed the custom of the old society whereby women asked men for the money they needed. All major spending in the family is decided through democratic discussions. Their food and clothing have improved over the past few years. Chin-lan and her sister-in-law proposed building some new rooms, to which all the family members agreed. So the Lin family added eight new brick rooms. By respecting the old, caring for the young and helping each other, the family lives amicably and happily.

Women have gradually mastered different kinds of production skills and become an important contingent in production. Everywhere in the countryside women are tending pumps, driving tractors or operating flour mills and crushers. They have also made contributions to agricultural scientific experiments. At the Peihsingyuan Brigade in the Hsiapaoszu Commune, there is such an experimental group which was formed by 15 women. The leader is Yang Ai-lien, a deputy secretary of the brigade Party branch, and deputy leader Liu Huan-chin, daughter of a poor peasant family. Both are graduates of the primary school and were less than 20 years old when the group was founded in 1967. Both have not had much schooling, but they have kept the spirit of "the Foolish Old Man who removed the mountains." While experimenting, they have raised their educational level and learned the necessary skills. Over the past few years

the group members cultivated more than 30 fine strains. Apart from
making a contribution to the state and the collective, they also won
public acclaim.

GROWING IN STRUGGLE

The more important thing for women in gaining emancipation
is to be concerned with and take part in political struggle. Owing
to the influence of old ideas and old traditions, not many women
took part in political activities or were firm in waging struggles.
Plunging into political struggle to brave storms and face the world,
women have acquired a better understanding of revolutionary principles, raised their political consciousness and gained experience
in struggle.

Many women activists and cadres in our county have grown in
the course of political struggle. Take the five women members on
the Party committee in our county for example. Hei Yueh-ching,
now a 37-year-old Hui nationality woman, led the Hui poor and lower-
middle peasants to set up people's communes in 1958 in warm response to Chairman Mao's call. This promoted the all-round development of farming, forestry, livestock breeding and side occupations. She has grown into a fine woman cadre. Hsia Hsiu-mei,
Yang Ai-lien and Yang Hsiu-chih are 21 or 22 years old. During
the Great Cultural Revolution, they waged a resolute struggle against
Liu Shao-chi's agents and unreformed bad persons, exposed and criticized their crimes of restoring capitalism in the rural areas and
thereby defended Chairman Mao's revolutionary line.

I have also experienced quite a number of political struggles
in my work. In 1959 a rich peasant in our brigade colluded with
capitalist roaders in the Party to fell and sell more than 100,000
young trees which were planted by the "March 8" afforestation team.
They also slaughtered the collective's pigs and sheep. This seriously
undermined the collective economy. Together with the poor and lower-
middle peasants, I struggled against them.

When the brigade Party branch committee was reorganized, I
was elected secretary. Soon afterwards they spread lies and slanders,
such as "If a woman is in command, trees won't grow" and "When
a woman takes the lead, there will be bad luck." At the same time
they also made up a list of my "crimes" in a vain attempt to get me

thrown out of my post. In studying Chairman Mao's teaching "What is work? Work is struggle" at that time, I felt I really understood its meaning. I knew very clearly that what they hated was not me but the socialist road which I and the poor and lower-middle peasants followed perseveringly. I was determined to struggle against them resolutely. With the support of the poor and lower-middle peasants we triumphed in the struggle.

Experiencing a storm was a good tempering. Since that struggle, the brigade's work has been done better and I also have made new advances.

The Status of Women in Taiwan:
One Step Forward, Two Steps Back

Norma Diamond

This paper is concerned with the status of women in Taiwan, with the advance and retreat of feminist ideology and the opening and closing of opportunity for women to move beyond the domestic sphere. To begin, let us look at two fairly typical upper-middle class families:[1]

> Mr. and Mrs. Kuo, both in their thirties, live in a
> modern duplex with their two sons, ages 12 and 8, and
> Mr. Kuo's widowed mother. Mr. Kuo's father was a
> doctor, and the elder Mrs. Kuo continues to work as
> a nurse at a public health center. She is less edu-
> cated than the younger Mrs. Kuo, who has a senior
> high school diploma. The younger Mrs. Kuo worked
> for four years in a bank before resigning from her
> job to get married. She met her husband through fam-
> ily arrangement with a go-between, but the couple had
> some say in the decision. She has no regrets about
> giving up her job since she feels that the children need
> her care and also because she feels there is no finan-
> cial need for her to work. Mr. Kuo is a successful
> engineer who also teaches at the local university. He
> is very busy during the week, but tries to be home
> several evenings to be with the family. During the
> day Mrs. Kuo is busy with housework, and in the eve-
> nings she tutors the children, watches television, and
> reads women's magazines. A few times a year, she
> and her husband go out to a movie, and annually he
> takes her to a party to meet his colleagues and their
> wives. She regards only one or two of these women
> as friends, and that because she has known them since
> high school. She has lost touch with other school
> friends, and has not gotten to know any of the neighbors

although they have lived in this house for almost nine
years. She rarely goes out except for shopping and
visits to her brothers and sisters who live in the same
city.

The Wangs, with their two children, live comfortably
in housing reserved for military officers. Mr. Wang
is a pilot, and his high pay (about $200 U.S. a month)
is now supplemented by his wife's typing job with an
air lines company. Mrs. Wang began working only six
years ago when the younger child entered junior high
school. Although almost all the households in the neighborhood are connected through work ties, Mrs. Wang
found it difficult to make friends among the wives. She
felt lonely and bored at home, particularly when her
husband's assignments began to require absences of
four or five days at a time. With her two years of
college and knowledge of a foreign language she was
able to locate this job, which pays about $75 U.S. a
month. Although she is now working, Mrs. Wang feels
that it would be wrong for a woman in her financial
circumstances to work until the children were grown
up, and she emphasizes that she is working only to
provide some luxuries for the family and to pass the
time. The older child is now in the army, and rarely
comes home. The daughter is studying at a senior
home economics school and is not expected to go to
college. Mrs. Wang left college to get married, a-
gainst the wishes of her family. Her father had been
a university professor, and her mother was one of
China's first women to graduate from college, after
which she had a long career as a teacher.

Both of these families typify the new Taiwan urban middle class
in its search for material comforts and economic security, and in its
return of the educated women to the domestic role for at least the
first twelve to fifteen years of married life. The women in these
families are usually educated at the level of high school or beyond,
but their education has become a status symbol rather than a matter
of practical concern. For Mrs. Kuo, absorbed in domesticity, her
mother-in-law is something of an enigma: she finds it difficult to
understand how the older woman can find the interest or energy to
continue working, and views her own education only as the means

for guaranteeing the success of her sons. Mrs. Wang finds some
financial and social gratifications from her work, but is firmly
steering her own daughter toward a completely domestic role. If
in the future Mrs. Wang's daughter wants to follow her mother's
example, she will have no similar skills with which to find a job.
The Wang family is almost a paradigm of recent trends, from the
avant-garde grandmother who struggled for the right to attend a
university and devoted her life to teaching, to the romantic mother
who eloped in the middle of her college training, to the young
daughter whose education prepares her only for the marriage that
awaits her in another few years. We have come full circle over
three generations. In the way that she regards herself and in the
way that she regards her future, the Wang family's daughter is, at
least superficially, more similar to her own great-grandmother than
she is to either her grandmother or even her mother. Of course,
she will have more freedom in choosing her husband, she expects
romance to play an important part in her marriage, she is socially
freer to seek her own friends, and her ideas are taken from popular
magazines rather than from traditional ways per se. But in her
conception of women's role she shares much in common with women
of a past generation, with her less educated present day counterparts
in Taiwan, and with women in many other parts of the world including middle class America.

Taiwan provides us with a good example of a rapidly indus-
trializing small nation within which to view the effects of modernization on women's roles. Culturally, Taiwan shares in the heritage
of Chinese civilization, and the "little traditions" of southeast China
from which some 12,000,000 of her 14,000,000 population is derived.
Taiwan's major settlement took place in the 17th and 18th centuries,
and it was in many ways a frontier area of the Chinese empire.
Political controls were weak, and in 1895 the island-province became
a colony of Japan. At the end of World War II it was restored to
China and came under Kuomintang rule. A second wave of migration
occurred with the consolidation of Communist victory on the mainland
of China, when the defeated Kuomintang government and their follow-
ers retreated to Taiwan. This latter-day migration drew heavily
from the Shanghai-Nanking area, but includes people from all parts
of the country. In general, these later migrants ("Mainlanders")
represent a more urbanized and sophisticated population than the
native-born Taiwanese.

Taiwan took its first steps toward modernization under the
Japanese: the colonial administration introduced electrification,

railroads, modern business enterprises and commercial agriculture, as well as a westernized school system that went up through university level and was open to women as well as men. The modernization process accelerated in the 1950's and 60's, with American economic support for the Kuomintang government of Chiang Kai-shek. Diversification of the economy involved an increasing number of the female potential work force. Industries such as textiles, garment production, electronics, and chemical/drug production came to rely heavily on female workers, and women also entered the work force in large number as sales personnel and office staff. Today, roughly 30% of the work force are women but they are distributed unevenly within it. They tend to cluster in the low-skilled industrial jobs and in short-term service occupations. They appear also in large number in such professions as nursing and teaching at the primary school or junior high school level. Relatively few appear in the prestige professions (medicine, law, engineering, university teaching) or in administrative, managerial or executive posts: at most they are 8% of that upper segment of the work force although many are educationally qualified. Impressionistically, it appears that those women in high-ranking jobs today are considerably older than their male counterparts: they are the women who received their educations in the 1920's and 30's when only a brave handful of women were able to advance beyond bare literacy.

Much has been written about the status of women in traditional China.[2] For thousands of years, China was a male-centered patriarchal society. Women were regarded as an inferior group intellectually and morally, and usually regarded as useless economically. They were disqualified by sex from formal schooling and had no access to positions of political power, occasional female rulers notwithstanding. In times of economic stress, daughters were expendable; they might be killed at birth, given out for adoption to some poor family who wanted a child bride, sold as slaves or as servants to wealthier households, or sold into prostitution. They were not regarded as full members of their family of origin, and they became full members of the family into which they married only after they had given birth to a son who would continue that family line. There were few alternatives to marriage, none of them respectable. One could become a nun, a prostitute, a wine-house entertainer, a beggar, or if lucky, a servant. The rights to divorce were male prerogatives and could be invoked for such faults as talkativeness, failure to bear sons, or incurable illness. The divorced (or widowed) woman was not supposed to remarry, in keeping with the high value

placed on female chastity.   And as if the weight of social custom
was not enough to ensure submissiveness and docility, there was
the practice of foot-binding among the more affluent peasants and
upper classes, crippling the girl child both physically and psychologically by subjecting her to intense and protracted torture.

Foot-binding was made illegal in Taiwan under Japanese rule,
and the rights of divorce, remarriage, education, ownership of
property, and general civil rights were extended to women.   But
custom dies hard and many women remained ignorant of their new
liberties.   Civil law since 1946 has followed the precepts developed
under the Kuomintang government during the 1930's on the mainland
of China. [3]   Divorce by mutual agreement is now possible, and
women may sue for divorce on the same grounds granted to men
(adultery, cruelty, desertion, attempted murder, incurable disease,
imprisonment for more than a three-year period or disappearance,
drug addiction).   However, custody of the children is usually granted
to the father or to his kinsmen.   Bride-adoption is discouraged, and
child marriages forbidden, though both of these have become less
popular anyway due to the demand by young people to have more of
a say in the choosing of a spouse.   The taking of concubines continues in altered and quasi-legal form, with the concubine transmuted
into a "mistress" whose residence is separate from that of the
legal wife.

Women are allowed to retain their family names after marriage,
to inherit property from parents or spouse, and to retain property
and income in their own name if they so desire.   But many women
are unaware of the law's provisions and in actuality, the wages of
young working people are often paid directly to their parents or they
are under social pressure to turn over most of their wages.   As for
ownership of property, many women have not been informed that a
special contract must be drawn up: if it is not, then all property
acquired by them before and during marriage comes under the husband's management and can be disposed of by him as he sees fit.
Women are held responsible for debts they acquire before or during
marriage, and are also held responsible for the husband's debts if
he is unable to make payment.   Still, they have advanced over the
traditional system wherein women were unable to own or inherit
property.   And in the labor market, there are legal provisions for
equal pay and equal hiring policies, although in practice women receive less pay than men, are often subject to dismissal when they
marry, and are not usually hired to fill the same positions as men.

There have been, then, changes in law and custom moving toward sexual equality, and objectively speaking they represent a marked
advance. Yet in recent decades there has been the development of
a peculiar nostalgia for the past, and a romanticized version of what
the past contained. It is a view of the past which describes the role
of women as a life of gracious leisure within the confines of the home,
her only responsibility being the loving care of the children and the
management of the household. Other than these tasks, says this version, she spent her time practicing the decorative arts such as embroidery and brush painting, playing music, reading, and keeping
herself beautiful to please her husband. It is highly unlikely that
more than a tiny percentage of women lived a life of this sort: indeed, it sounds more like the description of the life of a pampered
concubine in a wealthy household, except that we would have to omit
such tasks as child care, cooking, and similar household chores.
The wealthy relegated these tasks to servants, wet-nurses, tutors
and slaves, the wife/concubine retaining only the roles of sex partner,
child bearer, and sometime companion.

The charm of this mythic view of the past is that it meshes
with the structure of the emergent new bourgeois family. It validates
the demands of the present in terms of the past and manipulates the
factor of economically productive work as the crucial variable in de-
termining social status. To be a respectable middle class family in
the modern Taiwan setting means to emulate the traditional upper
class by separating the women from the workaday world. What is
crucial to status is not what the woman does but what she does not
do: she does not work.

Women in the peasant sector and in the traditional business
class of small shopkeepers still work, though the significance and
burden of this work is obscured by its being done within the framework of the family. The tasks of women in these lower classes go
beyond child care and care of the house, and the expectation that they
will do other tasks is so ingrained that their occupations are listed
in the successive household registration records as "housewife." To
be a rural housewife means spending much time in such non-household
tasks as transplanting rice, weeding, harvesting, caring for vegetable
gardens, feeding and caring for livestock, gathering firewood, making clothing, and occasional peddling of produce. In business families,
wives and daughters work in the shop, keep an eye on the apprentices
and clerks, serve as loan agents, and help in the decision making.
In a fishing village where I did research in the early 1960's, most

of the women engaged in some form of petty trade or handicrafts
production for sale, or hired out as day labor to add to the household income.[4] These activities were approved and expected. They
were seen as part of the total "wife role," which may explain why
there is denial that women in the traditional sector "work outside."
In a sense they don't, since much of the work is unpaid labor on
their husband's property. But there is also the prestige factor involved in being able to exempt one's women, and if possible oneself,
from labor. In traditional upper class families the men did not
work either, except as scholars and managers of the family estate,
and they took great pride in their long fingernails and soft hands.
In ordinary households, everyone worked, including women and
children. No one had leisure except the very old, the very young,
and the very ill.

The non-working wife has become part of the picture painted
of the modern family, as the most recent stage of a series of
changes in the Chinese family and its economic setting. In the new
middle class families, the husbands hold professional or white collar
jobs in government and business enterprises. They live in the rapidly growing cities, probably in an apartment or duplex designed for
a small family. They own a few luxuries such as a color TV, a
refrigerator, and a motorcycle. The wife is educated, though she
usually has three or four years less schooling than her husband.
The marriage arrangement is made with the consent of the couple,
even if they met only once or twice in semi-formal settings prior
to giving their aggrement. The children are enrolled in one of the
better schools and are expected to eventually attend college or at
least to finish senior high school. The wife is expected to be a
loving devoted mother, selflessly dedicated to making a comfortable
home for the family. This snug, petty-bourgeois life style is seen
as being both a radical break with the past and as a continuation of
the best of Chinese tradition.

Its radicalness stems from yet another mythical aspect of the
past, the myth of the large family which maintains that all Chinese
(except perhaps a desperate and unfortunate few) lived in enormous
extended families incorporating up to five generations under one roof.
In actuality, as generations of Chinese and Western sociologists have
been pointing out, the overwhelming majority of traditional households
were composed of a married couple and their children, with a surviving parent of the husband resident for the first part of the family
cycle. High rates of infant mortality and short life expectancies

made it unlikely that more than three generations would ever live
together or that one would have to face the intricate social problems
of living together in harmony with one's married brothers.   The
desired model for the modern family is the nuclear family, and it
is consciously seen as an improvement over the extended family
system.   Size and composition thus become another criterion for
status, and among the upwardly mobile families of the new middle
class even the elderly surviving parent may be left out of the household, or shuttled in rotation to the homes of surviving offspring.
The nuclear family seems to be a universal product of urbanization
and industrialization, even in cultures that still pay lip service to
the principles of filial piety.

The traditional aspect of the new middle class family lies in
its spurious resemblance to an upper class life style where the wife
is free from involvement in any kind of economic enterprise and is
confined to the home.   The modern urban housewife in Taiwan is in
many ways more isolated than either her Western counterparts or
her historical predecessors.   Expediency rather than custom restricts
her social activity.   Unlike the upper class woman to whose life
style she has presumably risen, she probably has no servants or
nursemaids to take over the household tasks or provide company
during the day.   Nor are there other kinswomen in the household
with whom one shares the work, gossips, and finds recreation.
Kinsmen may not even be living in close proximity due to the recent spatial mobility demanded by the new society.   And unlike her
peasant or artisan/merchant class forerunners, the new middle class
woman has few ways in which to establish friendships in the community, and little or no role to play in that community.   There are
few equivalents to the clubs, organizations, or networks of wives
that one finds in the United States, which might bring the woman
out of the home for social activity.

In the rural areas, kinswomen and neighbors still work together in the fields, do laundry together at the well or riverside,
sit in the warm afternoon sun to sew and knit, and find various ways
of spending time in the company of their peers.   They also exchange
child care services, freeing each other for work tasks where the
presence of children is inconvenient.   They support each other emotionally and in terms of aid during crisis periods such as births,
weddings, and funerals.   They provide an informal court in which
family disputes and inter-family quarrels are aired and adjudged.
And the women whose lives revolve around the small family business

are in daily contact with customers, wholesalers, and other trades-
people in the immediate neighborhood.

The middle class life style precludes all this. The walled
houses and apartment buildings shut out not only thieves and the
glances of curious passers-by, but also most possibilities for social
interactions with neighbors. The high walls, topped with jagged
glass and barbed wire, turn each home into a fortress, and in the
small sunless gardens behind the walls, one takes the air in total
privacy. People may live on the same street or in the same building
for years without anything but a nodding acquaintance with neighbors
-- as is the case in many other urban settings. In comparison, an
American suburb is a carnival of camaraderie. In the modern
Taiwan cities, in these new middle class areas, there is little visiting or exchange with neighbors. People are hesitant to invite anyone into their home for fear it is not up to standard and reluctant
to call on neighbors for fear of embarrassing them. The wife's
only outing of the day is the morning food shopping in a crowded,
hectic outdoor market, and since the pre-schoolers must accompany
her she is not tempted to linger and chat with the few people she
recognizes there. Visits to kinsmen have declined due to spatial
and social mobility. The wife's core of recognized friends are her
former classmates, many of them now living in other cities or
across town, and she sees them infrequently.

The isolation of the wives is compounded by the failure of
other patterns to change. In peasant and traditional business families, the wife usually knows her husband's friends and work associates, just as she knows the women of the community, through her
daily interactions with them. The higher we go on the social scale,
the less likely it is that the wife will know the members of her
husband's social network, and it is even less likely that she will
know their wives. With the work arena completely divorced from
the home, the husband tends to move in a separate social world.
He sees his male friends at work, dines with them or goes drinking
with them after work hours, and accompanies them to movies or
"girlie-restaurants" for weekend recreation. In the evenings, the
restaurants and coffee houses of the cities are filled with men:
few family groups or couples are in evidence. The closer friends
in his network of colleagues and former classmates call at the home
on occasion, but the wife is not expected to help entertain them beyond serving refreshments and exchanging a few words of polite conversation. Needless to say, they do not bring their wives with them

unless they are paying a formal New Year call. Once a year, in
most business and government organizations, there is a formal dinner to which wives are invited. The women describe these as
strained social situations in which they do not have the chance to
make friends. Wives are also invited to weddings or funerals through
the husband's social ties, but few friendships among women are generated this way.

The women thus cannot depend on their husbands to provide
social activities. Middle class housewives have very restricted social lives, and those middle class women who do hold jobs form
social networks among their colleagues which parallel and are separate from the social world of the husband. The work world and the
domestic world rarely mesh. But while the working wife can find
social outlets, the housewife often finds that it is from the children
and her role as mother that satisfactions must be derived. The
mother in the Chinese family has usually played an expressive role,
and in the fictional literature she is depicted as the loved and loving
parent as compared to the distant and authoritarian father. In the
new middle class, mothering takes on an even greater intensity.

In the modern West, the nuclear family derives much of its
stability from the closeness and love between spouses. In the modern
Taiwan family, it is not the husband-wife tie that functions as the
main tie, despite the romantic hopes for the small family. Ideally,
the modern small family is based on a love match. In actuality, at
least a third of the educated middle class women I interviewed had
had little or no contact with their spouse prior to the wedding.
Another large percentage were allowed to "date" only after the en-
gagement had been fixed. Even those who regarded their marriages
as based on love and mutual attraction found that social pressures
kept husbands from spending much free time with the family. Male
friends will tease and shame the man who prefers going home for
dinner to spending an evening "on the town."

In traditional times, the husband's absence may not have been
so painful. Women had outlets via the kin network and neighborhood,
limited of course to other women. Now for many there are only
the children for company and for gratification. The job of housewife does not bring gratification to all: until some ten years ago,
most household tasks were done by servants in middle class households. The young women formerly recruited as servants are now
being swallowed up in the factories and shops, leaving the housewife

to perform tasks that she (and others) regard as having little prestige. In Taiwan, and other developing nations, where a high school
diploma is a passport to a white collar job and release from manual
labor, it is difficult to convince the women that housework is fun.
Many of the middle class women grew up with servants and the expectation of having servants in the future. They are dismayed to
find themselves doing menial tasks. It is even more difficult to
convince the educated men that they might participate in some of
the household chores. These are defined, by default, as the wife's
responsibility now, even by men who are quite aware that their own
mothers and grandmothers did not do such work unaided.

In an earlier generation, educated women held jobs while the
household responsibilities were taken over by servants or other female members of the household. Now, the press of housework and
child rearing is seen as sufficient reason for women to stay home.
The option of hiring servants is rejected, though admittedly the cost
is now so prohibitively high that the question is an academic one. [5]
Values come into play here. There is much said about the harm
which can come to the children at the hands of some illiterate country girl: she will teach the children bad language or improper dia-
lect, she will not be strict enough or she will be too strict, she
won't understand modern hygiene, she won't love the child, and so
on. Similar objections, more politely stated, are also raised to
explain the disadvantages of having a resident older kinswoman in
the household. The working wives in my sample had few such com-
punctions or apprehensions. They paid over a large proportion of
their salary to a servant in some cases, and they were more likely
to accept the idea of a resident mother-in-law. In some instances,
they incorporated their own mother into the household and transferred
to the older woman the major responsibility for daily shopping, cooking, and child care. [6]

The older generation of educated women, being rather exceptional themselves, tended to marry exceptional men who were open-
minded and willing to experiment with new life styles. Having willingly accepted the idea of having an educated wife engaged in an
outside career, they were also able to reevaluate their own roles
and share in the household tasks. In the earlier part of this century, those privileged to have a Western-style education felt an
obligation to serve the wider society, regardless of sex. The obligation of social service for educated women has only recently been
removed. Some would say that her only obligations now are within

the domestic circle. Continued employment after marriage is taken
either as a sign of financial need, to which no upward mobile family
will admit, or as arrant selfishness on the woman's part.

Concern by a woman for a career and the development of her
own talents is increasingly interpreted as selfish and destructive
behavior. It is seen as particularly harmful to the growing children.
Although some of the school teachers we talked to (themselves women)
felt that the children of working mothers were more mature, responsible, and serious about their studies, and better adapted socially,
it is difficult to convince housewives and most middle class men of
that. The expectation is that the children of working mothers are
"wild," get little attention, and do poorly in school. At the back of
most people's minds in this is their observance or memory of peasant
children and the children of the poor, who do badly in school for
reasons other than their mother's work load outside the home, and
who are, in comparison to middle class children, less well super-
vised. But Taiwan also has its affluent upper-strata delinquents
(t'ai-pao) by now, and there is no indication that the crucial factor
leading to their non-conformist behavior is a working mother.

Be that as it may, the media and public opinion are strong in
the belief that the mother's continuous presence and intensive care
is needed during the first twelve years of life or longer. Previous
generations, and children in the lower classes still, were cared for
by a variety of parental surrogates: grandparents, older siblings,
aunts and uncles, neighbors, etc., but in the new middle class family the mother is the primary caretaker, and to all intents and purposes often the sole caretaker. She is the nurturer and main companion; children in this social class are discouraged from playing
outside on the street with neighborhood children. Dependency on
the mother seems to be prolonged, compared to the lower classes.
Some of the middle class housewives interviewed still found it necessary to give 10 or 11 year old children their evening bath, and
children of 8 or 9 still needed to be dressed by the mother.[7] During
school years, it is understood that children should not have to waste
precious study time on household tasks such as straightening up their
rooms, putting clothing away, or the like. Children in peasant and
poor households are still responsible for a variety of chores including
cooking, house cleaning, care of younger siblings, and a variety of
economic tasks, but the middle class child is left free to concentrate
on studies and the acquisition of skills deemed suitable to his status
(piano, violin, painting, ballet for girls). Even the girls are excused

from all but the simplest tasks through high school, with the result
that many are entering marriage with little idea of how to cook,
maintain the house, or make purchases.

The pre-school phase especially seems to be attenuated in
middle class households. Children are eligible to enter kindergarten
at four, but there is little demand for such services except among
working mothers. Primary school starts at six, but many parents
postpone entrance until seven or eight. This delay is rationalized
in terms of the child's physical stamina or his fear and reluctance
to attend. The latter is understandable with those who have had
little opportunity for interaction with other children. Some parents
delay because they think that the child will do better in classroom
competition if he has the advantage of a year's maturity over his
classmates and a backlog of home tutoring. These values delay the
wife's return to a job, if indeed she intends to return at all.

Education is highly valued in the middle class. For a boy,
it is crucial to his future career. For a girl, it is the means
to securing a high status husband. With a high school degree, she
can expect to marry a college graduate. With a college degree, she
may be able to marry a returned student from abroad with an M.A.
or Ph.D., or go to America herself and marry a promising Chinese
graduate student. Some of the marriages to students overseas are
arranged by the family, some are through free choice or prior acquaintance, but whatever the situation, the girl must have a college
degree (or a great deal of family "pull") in order to get a student
passport enabling her to leave Taiwan. The young women going
abroad to study are more often urged to make a good marriage than
to complete their studies and make a career for themselves. In
recent years this has become increasingly difficult to do: the highly
educated men prefer a wife who has not studied beyond a B.A. degree.

Education is the key to success, but the competition is keen.
Until 1967 there were stiff quota examinations for admission into
junior high school. These have been abolished, but quota examinations still exist for admission to senior high school and university.
This weeding out process in the 1950's meant that only one out of
ten primary school students survived to graduate from senior high
school, and only one out of a hundred entered university, college or
technical two-year college. By 1970, the figures had risen to allow
20% to enter senior high school and 4% to enter college. If the family
is native Taiwanese, the children are at somewhat of a disadvantage.

The language used in the classrooms, from kindergarten on, is
Mandarin Chinese, spoken by most of the recent refugee families
and spoken only as a late-learned second language by most Taiwanese.
Many families speak no Mandarin at home and since use of Taiwanese
is forbidden at school the children have difficulty in following the
lessons in the early grades, fall behind in their work, and become
discouraged. To add to the problem, some underpaid teachers
strive to supplement their incomes by saving their energies for
private after-hours tutorial sessions or private evening cram schools
(pu-hsi-pan). Under these circumstances, the role of the middle
class educated mother is expanded to include intensive coaching of
the children. Most of those we interviewed spent at least an hour
a day going over lessons with each child, helping with homework
assignments in primary school, and some continued these efforts
through junior high school as well. After that, private tutors were
hired, or the child was enrolled in a cram school for several evenings a week. Even when she is not actively involved, the mother
feels that she should be there to assure that the child is really studying the texts or reading relevant materials. When major examinations loom, mother and child are up past midnight every night for
several months, going over lessons.

Though the husbands in these families tend to have more formal
education than the wives, they are rarely involved in this aspect of
parental responsibility. For one thing, they are not home regularly
enough in the evenings, and for another, this aspect is now defined
in the mass media as a womanly-motherly task. It is the raison
d'être for a woman's education. As with the demands made in connection with pre-school care, it serves to keep the woman off the
job market even longer. She cannot be expected to have the time
and energy to hold down an eight-hour job, maintain a household,
and spend her evenings carefully tutoring the youngsters.

The new role expectation then, for educated women, is total
involvement with the children until they are grown. To make this
palatable, there is a great deal of glorification of mother love in the
various media, and it is institutionalized in many ways. Most obvious is the celebration of Mother's Day (a new holiday) when model
women are chosen from various areas of the island and publicized in
the newspapers and on television. The choice is based on the career
success of their children and grandchildren, not on their own educational or professional achievements. Most are housewives, and at
least one is a poor widow who cleverly managed the family property

or worked hard to enable her children to rise in the world. The message is that a woman's most important task is to assure her children's success. The child's future stands or falls on the conscientious and devoted playing of the mother role. International Women's Day, a left-over from the more militant feminist movements of the 1920's and 30's, receives less public attention but again stresses the primacy of women's domestic responsibilities over her other activities.

The mass media present women primarily in their domestic role. The textbooks in the primary schools depict women as mothers and housewives and only occasionally as teachers and nurses. In the local television dramas, the small family is the norm for modern dramas, and the women are housewives. In one popular serial, the heroine was a teacher, but she had been divorced by her husband and replaced by a very glamorous and feminine sister. Also she had been deprived of the right to see her daughter, and the drama revolved around her efforts to help the child, who was not only maltreated by her stepmother but also crippled by polio. The theme of mother love was the crucial one, and in the final episodes, the second wife dies of illness and the husband is reunited with his first wife because of her love for the child which she has demonstrated in a number of ways.[8] Other popular serials, set in the pre-modern period or during the Sino-Japanese war, show women in traditional roles, and if they are working it is clearly because of dire poverty and family crisis. Some American programs are also shown; all seem to involve supernatural females playing domestic roles.[9]

Movie viewing provides more of the same. The Chinese films rarely show women as anything other than housewives if they are dealing with the modern period. In a recent film, Mother and Daughter, the mother is the owner/manager of a nightclub. Expectedly, the daughter has been expelled from several schools, and is on the path to becoming a delinquent. In another recent film, Hotel Esquire, a wife works as the manager of a family-owned hotel; her marriage is a disaster because of her lack of femininity and her refusal to have children. Her personality is harsh and unpleasant, and understandably her husband has taken up with another woman. Only when she agrees to let her husband take over the task of breadwinner completely is the marriage saved and she allowed to come across as a sympathetic human being.

There is a genre of Chinese film in which women are shown as something other than wives and mothers. These are the "swords-

man" films, highly popular historical romances, in which the main
character is sometimes a woman. She rides horseback, fights with
skill and courage, combats the forces of evil and rights old wrongs
done to her family or to innocent victims. She is quite admirable,
but she is also sexless. She is not married, she is not interested
in men, she is in fact quite frightening to men. At the end of the
film she either rides off into the sunset, mission accomplished, or
once in a while she turns in her sword and trousers for a skirt
and a normal life. Often she is handicapped by being blind, or
one-armed and unmarriageable for these reasons. And while she
is admirable in what she does, the message of these films is that
the brave independent woman is not quite of this world. Everyone
knows "it's just a movie."

There are of course foreign films shown in Taiwan, but these
are less popular since it is difficult for most people to keep up with
the subtitles and even six years of compulsory English in high school
does not prepare one for catching the dialogue. War movies, cow-
boy films and children's movies are the most popular fare, and films
that are in any way controversial due to sex, social criticism, and/or
politics are banned.

Newspapers in Taiwan have a women's page -- a single sheet
easily detached from the rest of the paper -- which contains articles
on child care, homemaking, recipes, romantic fiction, family advice, children's stories, and etiquette pointers. The articles generally support the small family system, assuming a nuclear family
structure. Rarely are there articles on how to better relations
with mothers-in-law or sisters-in-law, which were once real problems
for generations of women. The tenor of the discussion on these pages
also assumes that the readers are full-time housewives, and that any
lack of enjoyment they feel with this role stems from their lack of
expertise, or conversely so much expertise that time hangs heavy on
their hands. If the latter is the case, there are suggestions for
gourmet cooking, embroidery patterns, and various handicrafts and
hobbies to fill in the time. Many of these suggestions are geared
to further serving the children, so that they are extensions of the
mother role (toys to make for the children, clothing for children,
special foods for children). At least some of the material seems
to be translated directly from American publications.

The women's magazines mirror these themes, for the most
part. Those geared to younger women give repetitious instruction

on grooming and makeup, advice on how to attract and please a man,
clothing patterns, advice to the lovelorn, romantic stories, and basic
information on potential pen pals. The magazines for the older married women are heavier on recipes, children's clothing, and health
problems. Only one of the women's magazines carries articles
about full-time or part-time careers for women, or feature stories
about women prominent in various walks of life in addition to articles
geared to the presumed interests of the homemaker. In the issues
that appeared in the first half of 1971, it began running articles on
women's legal rights in divorce and articles on day care centers,
the need for legalized abortion, and the women's movement in other
countries.

One is tempted to attribute Taiwan's middle class life style
and ideology to "Americanization." Of course, many of the intellectuals who produce for the mass media have been influenced by
the West, but my feeling is that Western trends in family organization and family roles are not being imitated directly. They are not
the cause. At most, they are being invoked as further validation of
trends underway in Taiwan that are related to the economic changes
taking place since the turn of the century. Contact with foreigners
or with those who have lived abroad is slight. The foreign community in Taiwan, which is mainly American military personnel, lives
isolated in its own compounds or neighborhoods. The wives
have little contact with any Chinese, the children attend American
schools, and the male contacts take place during working hours in
a hierarchical setting which makes unlikely any discussion of personal affairs. A large number of students from Taiwan go abroad
to study each year, most of them going to the United States. But
only 5% ever return and most of the returnees are those who studied
in Japan and Korea, or those who were unable to adjust to life overseas and rejected it. For every 300 students who finish their studies
in the United States, only one will ever return to Taiwan to live for
any length of time.

Moreover, despite the similarities that we have been discussing,
there is one area of family life which has retained its Chineseness
and not been easily influenced by the Western world. This is the
husband - wife relationship. In the traditional family system, intimacy
and closeness between spouses were not required. Indeed, they were
seen as disruptive of family unity and of parental authority over sons.
Marriages were contracted by families, on practical grounds, and
mutual attraction between the young partners was irrelevant. In

modern marriages, it is now thought necessary that the couple meet
a few times before marriage and give their consent, but this does
not mean that they will grow emotionally close after marriage.   As
was mentioned before, the lives of married couples often run parallel, rather than being intermeshed.

Courtship and dating as we think of it in the West is still rare
in modern Taiwan, though slowly gaining currency in the upper middle class.   It is not considered normal for young people to have
close friends of the opposite sex, and any young couple who are seen
frequently together are assumed to be formally engaged.   To be seen
with a number of different companions of the opposite sex leaves one
open to charges of promiscuity or dishonesty.   The fictional literature
today deals with love, but there rarely seems to be a happy resolution to a fictional love affair.   Most end in the tragedies of death
or separation, or the relationship is severed due to total lack of
communication and misunderstandings.

The organization of the educational system probably contributes
heavily to the difficulties in relating to persons of the opposite sex.
Primary school is coeducational, but the girls usually are seated
separately and the children are encouraged to play in sex-segregated
groups on the playground.   Until 1967, all junior middle schools
were segregated by sex.   Now they are coeducational in theory, but
most retain separate classrooms or separate buildings, and there is
no sharing of classes or activities.   Senior high schools remain totally segregated.   Not only that, but evidence of dating or exchange
of romantic letters can mean expulsion from school, temporary sus-
pension, or at least demerits and a stiff reprimand from the authorities.   In addition, there is strong pressure from one's peers, and
few youngsters will risk the laughter and shaming by their friends.
Though some of these students are already 18 or 19 years old, the
society's values hold that they are too young and socially immature
to be involved in dating and romance.   The more liberal parents in
the middle class allow their high school age children to attend movies
or go on outings in a mixed group (the boys are usually brothers or
cousins of the girls . . . but one can always meet someone else's
brother on these jaunts).   Going out in couples, however, is radical
behavior, engaged in by those considered delinquent youth.

This attitude extends into the college years as well.   On college
campuses the students come together for the first time since primary
school, but the coeducation is more apparent than real.   Due to

differences in curriculum and guidance, the boys are predominantly
enrolled in the physical sciences, mathematics, engineering, law,
medicine, and political science. The girls are channeled into the
humanities and the social sciences. Study in one's major field begins in the freshman year, and there are no required general courses
taken by all students outside their major fields. The result is that
one can go through four years of college without seeing more than
one or two members of the opposite sex in one's classes. The
college program is rigorous, and if one has any hopes of receiving
scholarships and permission to study abroad, concentration on one's
studies is as intense as it was in high school days. There is little
time for extra-curricular activities, and as a result, little campus
life that would enable students to get to know each other in a relaxed
and informal situation. Social activities are conducted by cliques of
friends who knew each other in high school, and the pattern of group
outings continues. Only the most adventurous and non-conformist
students attempt to emulate a Western dating pattern during the college years. Many students are shocked by the comparatively free
and easy social relations displayed by Chinese from Hong Kong or
the Philippines who have come to study in Taiwan. Even those attending missionary-run colleges, where Western influence is strong,
are not easily persuaded to make friends across sex lines.

Throughout adolescence then, and into young adulthood, contact
with opposite-sexed peers is limited to siblings and cousins. The
close emotional relationships one has during those years is with
same-sexed peers. The schoolmate (tung-hsueh) bond is a strong
and important one, expected to last a lifetime, and it is invested
with much of the intensity of American teen-age cross-sex relationships. The schoolmate bond stops short of overt sexuality, though
it permits considerable physical contact. It is appropriate for school-
mates to hold hands in public, to walk with arms around each other,
and girls are allowed an even greater degree of emotional demon-
strativeness in frequently touching each other, clinging to each other
or embracing. It is difficult to say how frequently the relationship
may move beyond that into overt sexuality. A recent popular novel,
Outside the Window[10] paints a lengthy emotional picture of such
friendships in a girls' school. In it there are several conversations
in which the heroine and her best friend bemoan the fact that one of
them is not a man so that they could marry each other and never
have to separate. The omission of overt homosexual themes in the
literature may be a result of censorship, of course, and not a re-
flection of reality. Taiwan's fiction and movies have almost no
sexual content at all, heterosexual or homosexual.

Sexuality of any sort is played down during adolescence and young adulthood. Boys are required to wear drab khaki uniforms similar to army dress, and to shave their heads or wear their hair closely cropped. Girls' hair must be worn short, in a "dutch bob" style with shaved necks. All makeup is forbidden while a student, and dress must be the uniform prescribed by one's school. All schools seem to favor drab colors such as khaki or black; some schools insist on trousers for girls while others allow skirts that come well below the knee. The girls' uniforms are successful in transforming nineteen-year-old women into the appearance of pre-pubescents.

Faced with the attractions of the women shown in the movies, on TV, and in advertising, or even the imitations of these attempted by her working class non-student sisters, the middle class girl student has serious doubts that any man would ever be attracted to her. She does not use the adolescent years to test her womanliness: on the contrary, she is taught to be ashamed of it. In hygiene class she may be told that the onset of menstruation does not normally occur until 16 or 17, and that only among "foreign barbarians" does it come earlier. This is in contradiction to reality. When I was interviewing junior high school girls of 14 and 15 it became apparent from their answers to one of our questions that most had already started menstruating, and they were very concerned and upset about it. Body shame is learned for other things as well, particularly the appearance of pubic hair and hair on legs and underarms on the assumption that this too is "un-Chinese." Certainly, Chinese are less hirsute than Europeans, but some body hair is no abnormality or indicator of recent racial admixture. There is a great deal of variation, as the sales of depilatories in Taiwan attest. [11] Skin color presents another problem. Genetic heritage combined with a semi-tropical sun could produce a tanned, ruddy-cheeked population, especially among the native-born Taiwanese and other South Chinese. But while relative darkness of skin tone is acceptable for men, the ideal for women is whiteness. This may go back to traditional ideals of beauty, when the most praised women in the literature were the housebound daughters of the upperclass, their health undermined by foot-binding, lack of exercise, and lack of fresh air. It is also related to differentiating oneself from the daughters of the peasantry. Whatever the cause, no self-respecting middle class girl would go outdoors without a parasol to keep the sun from her face, and the makers of bleach cremes do a thriving business. Another cause for concern are the various adolescent skin problems, which seem to occur with great frequency in Taiwan due perhaps to an oily diet, heavy consumption of starches and sweets, and, again, lack of sun- light. Middle school and college girls feel "ugly," and nothing much is done to persuade them otherwise. They lack the self-confidence to deal with boys, and find it more comfortable to cling to a school- mate who shares the same awful problems.

The school experience also manages to communicate to the girls that they are intellectually and emotionally inferior to boys. It does not help that the overwhelming majority of teachers at the primary school level are women. One such teacher I interviewed said frankly that she spent most of her time and energy working with the boys in her classes, since they were naturally more intel- ligent and the bright girls were an exception. Any evidence of good work on the part of girls she attributed to rote memorization and long hours of study -- an explanation one hears over and over again[12] to explain the success that young women do have in their studies. It seems that the girls do study harder: their parents are much less likely to spend money on tutors and private schooling for them, and they must do better than their brothers in order to be allowed to continue in school.

By junior high school, the children are no longer getting quite the same curriculum, and the girls have become pessimistic about doing well in sciences and mathematics. They "elect" a humanities track, which by the time they reach college means that they are in- eligible to take the entrance examinations that would permit them to study in the sciences, professions, or agriculture. By the second year of junior high school, few girls can even fantasize about going into these lines of study: they type them as unsuitable to feminine abilities. [13] Some will abandon the academic track altogether, and finish their education in a home economics program.

Those who continue to college are usually assigned to the less prestigious departments and to those which do not lead to high-paying or high status jobs. At the end of four years of literature or anthro- pology, the girl graduate will at best end up teaching in a junior high school or working as a secretary in a foreign business concern where her knowledge of English or French is useful. Or she may simply stay at home, waiting for marriage. A large percentage of recent college graduates do not work. This is understandable, since good jobs are harder for women to find, and those that are open to them are of low status. After a year or two of inactivity or a dull, low-

paying job, the young woman is happy to accept someone's offer to
the family to introduce her to a suitable young man. Her Western
education has given her some hope of romantic love in her life, and
the media have exalted the life of the wife/mother. She marries,
hoping that things will turn out ideally, that she will have a happy,
perfect family.

In an earlier generation, when women comprised 10% or less
of college students, retreat into marriage seems to have been rare.
Even women with senior high school degrees were eager to put their
education to use, and found ways of structuring their domestic lives
so that it was possible to have both marriage and an outside job.
We were struck, in our interviews, by the change in spirit of the
educated women. Those who were in their 50s and 60s and held
jobs had almost unbroken career lines; at most, they had stopped
work for a year or two due to health or employment problems. We
tried to find educated women in this age group who were not working,
or who had worked only a short time, and could locate very few
from the household registers. Generally, if a woman had a senior
high school education or above, she was employed and had been
employed since her graduation. Women in their 40s showed more
disruption in their career patterns, and the women in their 30s
and late 20s in our sample were the least likely to have any interest
in continuing work after marriage and the most likely never to have
had any work experience at all.

This is not meant to imply that the decline of feminist spirit
is the fault of the women. On the contrary, it reflects the changing
ideology of the total society in respect to the purpose of education for
women. In the course of the past two decades, education for women
has changed its aims from service to society to self-improvement
and service to the family. Education has also become available to
a wider segment of the population. Almost every child in Taiwan
now is enrolled in the six-year primary school program. Junior
high school education is now on the basis of open enrollment. Senior
high school and university facilities have been greatly enlarged. [14]
However, while the academic track has been expanded, and the percentage of women has risen from 10% to over a third in the universities and colleges, the proportion of spaces for women in the senior
high schools has risen only from 28% to 36% since 1950. In short,
it has become more difficult for women students to gain acceptance
to academic senior high schools. Girls comprise almost one half
of the primary school students, compared to a third in 1950, but

problems of space still limit them to being a little more than a
third of senior high school students. [15]   Recent discussion suggests
returning them to the 10% level in colleges by a fixed set quota.

There has also been expansion of a non-academic track, a
system of vocational schools and five-year high schools that do not
lead to university and college.   Here the sex ratios are more in
balance, though boys still take the lead.   These schools, which teach
agriculture, home economics, commercial skills, and industrial skills
are for the most part dead ends; a few lead to a two-year technical
school beyond the high school level.   The current feeling in Taiwan
is that the expansion of education for women should be along the
lines of home economics schools training girls to be housewives, or
commercial schools that lead to low-rank office jobs.   Most of these
office jobs require the woman to resign when she marries, on the
theory that she will be unable to give her best effort to the job because of the demands made on her at home.   Job training and job
availability are increasingly geared to the unmarried young woman
for the interim period between school and marriage.

Despite the growing economy, competition for good jobs has
become stiffer in recent years due to the growing number of educated
personnel.   Jobs that twenty years ago required only a high school
diploma now ask for a college degree, and jobs that were open to
college graduates now search for people with an MA degree.   Male
resistance to female employment has become sharper as the pool of
qualified personnel has grown.   Even in government bureaucracies
and government operated enterprises where recruitment is by civil
service examination, women find themselves passed over for promotion or assigned to lower-level jobs than their male counterparts.

Moreover, expectations have risen faster than earning power.
Middle class status demands a certain amount of consumerism; a
refrigerator and television set are the minimum in luxuries, and
the cost is high.   Due largely to taxes, a small refrigerator costs
the equivalent of two months' salary for a middle class professional
or white collar worker.   A color television costs at least three
months' salary.   An obvious solution would be to have two wage
earners in the family, but the pressure works the other way.   It
increases male resentment toward women's employment.   Some families solve the problem by the husband's "moonlighting"; if he teaches
in a senior high school he also teaches in an evening cram school.
University professors may actually be under contract to two or three

different schools at one time.   The pressure to maintain a certain
standard of living further serves to cut the amount of time a man
will spend with his wife and children.   At the same time, it can
lead to resentment of the housebound wife and further denigration
of the role that she performs.

If the husband does not feel that his status is threatened by
letting his wife work, there are still difficulties involved in releasing
the wife onto the job market.   With time, she may be able to locate
a suitable job (one that does not plunge her into working class status), but there still remains the problem of child care.   Servants
are increasingly difficult to find.   This is because the one area
where there is a real demand for female labor is in the semi-skilled
and unskilled jobs in light industry.   Local and foreign-owned factories alike recruit girls between the ages of 14 and 21.   Women
workers constituted 40% of all factory workers in 1971, and almost
half of them were under the age of 19.   Other sources of domestic
workers have dried up because of the demand for female labor in
agriculture as sons drift off to the cities in search of better jobs
or are drafted into the army.   Institutionalized child care facilities
are few and are regarded as less healthy for a child than a mother's
care.   The number of private and public kindergarters (for 4 to 6
year olds) has jumped in the past two decades from 28 to 581, han-
dling almost 91,500 children today compared to 17,000 in the early
1950s.   But there are roughly 900,000 children in that age group;
public and private resources combined provide space for only one
out of ten.[17]   There are even fewer resources for children under
four, and most parents I interviewed were very reluctant to send
their children because of the lack of trained child care workers and
poor physical facilities.

If one can generalize, the older mainland-born husbands seem
more willing than either native Taiwanese or the young Taiwan-born
"mainlanders" to go against tradition and share in the household
tasks and child care.   This may be because they are cut off from
family and old friends through migration, and thus do not have to
answer to significant others for their behavior.   It may also be because they regard themselves as temporary sojourners in Taiwan
(though the temporary retreat has already lasted over twenty years!).
Having lost their savings and property during the Communist victory,
they are dependent on the joint financial resources of the nuclear
family to reestablish a secure economic base or see them through
until such time as they can return home.   Some of them had their

early marriage years shaped during the war, when women participated more widely in various activities. Some were influenced by
radical ideology before their departure from China proper. Whatever the reasons, the mainland-born husbands in our sample were
much more active in the household, and more enthusiastic about
their wives' working. In fact, some of the most militantly feminist
native-born Taiwanese women interviewed married mainland-born
men for these reasons. Even though marriage to an outsider had
met with some family disapproval, they felt it was worth the cost
in order to have a life outside the home and a husband who shared
in the home.

However, for men who regard Taiwan as their permanent home,
this accommodation to changing circumstances is not acceptable.
Tension over job availability and the felt need to assert one's masculinity by avoidance of "female" behaviors feeds into the demand
that women return to the home and stay there. Aspects of traditional Chinese ideology (and Japanese teachings from a period when
Japan was under military/fascist rule) are invoked to demonstrate
that this is the natural order of the society. Women in the home,
minus the foot-binding and arbitrary beatings, is the way things ought
to be.

In this regard, the status of women in Taiwan differs markedly
from the situation of women in mainland China today. There too the
economy is expanding and diversifying, but under current social planning the participation of women in the work force is seen as necessary at all levels. Women's participation in the agricultural and
industrial sectors is eased by the existence of child care centers
and flexible working hours, and women are encouraged into many
new fields of activity. The Chinese cultural base, as regards family and the status of women, has been overtly rejected as semi-
feudal or bourgeois. There is no nostalgia for days gone by. Taiwan,
modernizing as a capitalist economy, seems unable to make the
structural changes or ideological changes that would permit women
fuller participation in society. Technological improvements that
lighten the burden of housework are seen in Taiwan as the means
to provide women with more leisure within the home rather than as
a means for releasing women to use their energies elsewhere in
the society, as is the case in mainland China. Education for women
in Taiwan is a route to upper class status and the means to better
performance in the domestic role and/or a means of self-cultivation,
rather than as preparation for a life-long commitment to society.

Only men are regarded as legitimate wage earners in the family;
approval for women working holds only for the years before marriage, or for women who for some reason are disqualified from the
marriage market.

One indicator of the more recent shift in women's status in
Taiwan is the increasing emphasis over the past decade on physical
attractiveness as the means to gain and hold the attention of a husband.   Once student days are over, young women are expected to
bloom, though the blooming may not occur until they are in their
early twenties.   But with the move into adulthood and onto the marriage market, young women are expected to dress in bright colors,
wear heavy makeup, and permanent-wave their hair.   Their bodies
are molded into heavy corsets and padded brassieres, their feet a-
dorned with spike-heeled shoes, and the services of plastic surgeons
are available to reshape eyes and noses to conform to the current
standards of beauty.   From sexless school girl days, women move
into the hard sexual sell, spending hours each week at the beauty
parlor and having makeup applied for them by professionals for important occasions.   It is a sharp contrast to the modest downplay
of sexuality among earlier generations of educated women and in
present times a rather startling contrast to the women of China.[19]
The woman-as-sex-symbol, reserved in traditional times for concubines and professional entertainers, has been extended in Taiwan to
the population at large and taken up not only by young women on the
marriage market but by women in their 30s and 40s as well.   Older
women still find it inappropriate, and this style has not yet fully penetrated into the rural areas.   Some may think that this new style
in dress indicates increased freedom for women, but my analysis
would be that it points up the decline of familial authority in the
arrangement of marriages and the necessity of being well-packaged
in order to be chosen by some young man as a wife on the basis
of only a few meetings.

Taiwan of the 1970's, in its middle class, bears some strong
resemblances to Vogel's description of Tokyo's suburbs of fifteen
years ago, with their educated well-bred wives deeply involved in
child care and domesticity.[20]   There too, social mobility for males
revolved around the passing of examinations to the best schools and
the securing of a stable white-collar job.   Special mobility for women
required only attachment to one of these successful men.   Japan,
like Taiwan, welcomed women into the work force mainly in those
areas of the economy where cheap labor with a rapid turnover made

economic take-off possible. Of course, some middle class women held jobs, but they were deviants from the ideal.

Taiwan's economic boom is dependent upon a cheap labor pool of women and rural migrants. Real trade unions and strikes are illegal under the martial law which has ruled Taiwan for two decades. Young women workers are in demand; they do not have to be paid at the same rates as men with families to support, they do not stay at the job long and thus cannot demand promotion and wage increases based on their experience and tenure, and most importantly they are grateful for the opportunity to earn wages (and escape a little from parental authority). Their low pay in industry ($20 to $30 per month) is justified by the fact that they are women. This also tends to keep male wages down, but men, even though underpaid, can console themselves by knowing that they receive more than women workers and that the better jobs and advances are reserved for men. For the aspiring middle class men, there is the added comfort of knowing that one is competing almost solely against males. Really good jobs are hard to find, and one may not be fully compensated after the long academic struggle, but at least the competition for jobs is kept down. The middle class jobs will probably necessitate moving to a new city and living among strangers, but there will be a secure home base for the little family, with a wife to shoulder all of the domestic tasks. They know that it is unlikely that they will have to learn to deal with female colleagues after a lifetime of apartness from women, and highly improbable that they will have to relate to a female superior.

In the expansion of the universities and colleges, for example, there has been no attempt to increase the proportion of women teachers in relation to the increase of trained female personnel, or even to preserve the ratio of the female teaching staff. Just in the past five years, the percentage of women professors has declined from 9% to 6%. And though a much larger percentage of women now go through the university system as students, one would never guess that a third had been women if one looked at the appointments at the junior levels. Women's appointments at the lowest ranks still fluctuate around 18%, and in the junior college system hiring of women has declined from one-fifth of the total to one-sixth over the past five years. The same holds in other professions.

The gates of opportunity that two decades ago were still open to educated women have been closing in recent years. There is no

official pressure to keep them open, as there is in China. On the
contrary, there is talk of setting a low fixed quota for women's
admissions to college, and there is a great deal of social pressure
to re-create and maintain a male monopoly for the more prestigious
jobs. After a brief burst of egalitarianism which left Taiwan with
women judges, newspaper editors, architects, doctors, business
executives, and politicians -- all now well advanced in years --
things have come around to de facto exclusion of women. Ideally,
women stay in the home. If they participate in the work force it
is on the lower rungs of the ladder. There are more educated
women than ever before, and still some who try to make a life for
themselves beyond the domestic sphere. But they meet with greater
opposition from society, including their educated male counterparts
and educated sisters who have retreated into domestic life. For the
less well educated middle class women, whose education stopped at
junior high school, there are few job possibilities in accord with
their social standing. They have no option but to immerse themselves in home responsibilities. For those who are more educated,
the alternatives have become fewer. Ideology has been mobilized,
combining traditional and recent definitions of women's talents and
abilities to rationalize a second-class status for women, one that
permits them low paid jobs before marriage and defines them as
a source of domestic labor after marriage, regardless of training,
talent, or social class.

ADDENDUM

Shortly before this volume was to go to press, I had the opportunity to read the recommendations presented to the Sino-American
Conference on Manpower held in Taiwan in late June 1972. The paper on women, prepared by the Chinese members of the conference,
presented a strategy for the coming decade which would bring women
into the work force as 40% of the overall participants despite the
expected decline of manpower in the rural sector. However, their
increased participation would be in the areas of semi-skilled and
low-skilled factory work and in the areas of services and sales.
In the rest of the labor force, women's participation would actually
decline, both absolutely and relatively, through manipulation of the
school system. Specifically, it was recommended that the enrollment of women in the colleges and junior colleges be cut 2/3 from
the current level of graduating women so as to fix yearly female
admissions at around 4000 students. These survivors in the system

would be encouraged into fields where a labor shortage is expected, such as engineering, agriculture, medicine and business -- all fields where women are currently under-represented. But given the drasticness of the cut in female enrollments overall, they would still continue to be under-represented in those fields, and the effect would be to reduce both the absolute numbers and the percentage of women in most white-collar and professional jobs including nursing and teaching. No corresponding cuts were advised for male enrollments or overall college enrollments, suggesting that at the least male admissions will remain the same, and possibly increase to fill the vacancies left by the departing women students.

The report further recommends a similar, though unspecified, cutback in female enrollments in senior vocational and technical schools and the transfer of these students into a generalized liberal arts program at the middle school level. This presumably means the conversion of some of these schools into girls' senior middle schools since the current facilities are already packed to capacity. Again, no such recommendations are made for boys' schools. The effect of this is to further assure the monopoly of white-collar and low-level managerial jobs by men.

If these recommendations are put into practice, and given the mood in Taiwan it appears likely that they will be, there will emerge a small elite of highly educated women dispersed across a number of fields that are now still closed to them, who will have won these privileges through a much stiffer competition. They will be the "exceptions," while a much larger group of women will be unemployable except in the working class jobs that carry low salaries, little or no prestige, and no hope for advancement. The women in the growing middle class will be able to maintain that status only through marriage to a middle-class husband and total commitment to the domestic role after marriage.

NOTES

1. The materials on Taiwan's women were collected over a period of 16 months of field research during 1969 and 1971. Support was made possible through the American Philosophical Society, the Rackham School of the University of Michigan, and the American Council of Learned Societies-Social Science Research Council. The opinions and views expressed in this paper are my own, and these agencies are in no way responsible for the content.

2. For readings on traditional China and the transitional period, the following books are recommended reading: Olga Lang, Chinese Family and Society (New Haven: Yale University Press, 1946); Marion Levy, The Family Revolution in Modern China (New York: Octagon Books, 1963); and C. K. Yang, The Chinese Family in the Communist Revolution (Cambridge, Mass.: The M.I.T. Technology Press, 1959).

3. See V. Y. Chiu, Marriage Laws and Customs of China (Hong Kong: New Asia College, 1966).

4. N. Diamond, K'un Shen: A Taiwan Village (New York: Holt, Rinehart and Winston, 1969).

5. Teaching jobs are the most easily available, but they are low paid and the wages for a full-time servant would take about half of this income. Wages for educated women range between $60 and $150 per month. A servant costs $20 to $30, plus room and board.

6. Some 20% of the working wives in our sample had their own mothers living in the household. This is not to be confused with the old practice of an "adopted husband," brought in by sonless families to carry on the family name and take over economic responsibility. It seems here to be more a matter of expediency, i.e. no other place for the older woman to live, or a result of strong ties between mother and daughter. Nowadays, older women may prefer to live with a daughter than with a potentially hostile "modern" daughter-in-law.

7. One of my research assistants, living at my house, became
    upset at the prospect of having to wash her own hair. At age
    21, she had never had occasion to do it by herself before,
    since her mother always did it for her.

8. Comments on Taiwan TV are based on monitoring of popular
    programs in 1971. Since about 1967, most families have had
    access to a TV set. Neighborhood shops and snack bars pro-
    vide viewing for those who don't own their own.

9. American selections consisted of "Nanny and the Professor"
    "Bewitched," "I Dream of Jeannie," and "The Lucy Show," all
    somewhat remote from reality.

10. Ch'iung Yao, Ch'uang-wai (Taipei: Crown Magazine, 1969 edi-
    tion). Since 1963, this novel has gone through 25 printings and
    is still selling strongly.

11. Prostitutes in Taiwan usually shave off all body hair, including
    pubic hair. In addition to aesthetic appeal, this is also said
    to be done for reasons of hygiene.

12. In 1969, there was considerable distress over the results of
    the island-wide college entrance examinations when it was found
    that over 50% of those who had passed for admission to the top
    university were women. A number of press articles insisted
    that they not be admitted since they had merely memorized the
    material and were not really qualified to do advanced study.

13. These comments are drawn from a paper in progress on ca-
    reers and aspirations of Taiwanese youth.

14. In 1950, Taiwan had a total of 7 universities and colleges, with
    a student body of 6,665. In 1970, there were 22 universities
    and colleges, plus 69 junior colleges, with a total enrollment
    of 184,215. Enrollment of women had risen from 726 to
    65,260, half of these in junior colleges. See Educational
    Statistics of the Republic of China 1970, Taipei, Ministry of
    Education. Female enrollment in the academic senior high
    schools during the same period rose from 5,111 to 59,195.

15. This further explains the uproar when 50% of the top examinees
    for the best university turned out to be women, since they were
    outnumbered by boys two to one in the competition.

16. See Quarterly Report on the Labor Force Survey in Taiwan, Republic of China, January 1971, Taiwan Provincial Labor Force Survey and Research Institute, Taipei.

17. See Educational Statistics of the Republic of China 1970, Taipei, Ministry of Education.

18. There was a crèche located on my street which seemed to provide custodial care only. The children were confined in their cribs all the time, given no toys, never taken outdoors, and ignored except at feeding times.

19. One of my assistants sent off a photograph to relatives on the mainland, showing herself in her made-up best. She was quite hurt when their acknowledging letter to her parents asked why the daughter was dressed like a prostitute. The tone of the letter was one of concern, not malicious intent, one hopes.

20. Ezra Vogel, Japan's New Middle Class (Berkeley: University of California Press, 1967).

Taken by Louise Bennett in 1972 near Anshan, Liaoning Province.
Woman worker repairing insulation cups on live high tension wire.

Bibliography

WOMEN IN TRADITIONAL CHINA

Ayscough, Florence. Chinese Women: Yesterday and Today. Boston, 1937.
Discusses the "breathtaking change" in the status of Chinese women from 1905 to 1920 by contrasting their past and present social and political positions. Sections on childhood, marriage, education, professions, the Soong sisters, Communist women, and women as warriors.

Burton, Margaret E. Women Workers of the Orient. West Medford, Mass., 1918.
Published by the Central Committee on the United Study of Foreign Missions, this missionary picture of the working lives of Indian, Japanese and Chinese women is useful for its information (albeit unsystematically presented) on the kind of work done by women in these three societies. It is well illustrated.

Chao, Buwei Yang. Autobiography of a Chinese Woman. Trans. by Yuen-ren Chao (her husband). New York, 1947.
Describes B. Y. Chao's life from her childhood in China to her roles as teacher and wife of one of China's eminent linguists (from 1898 - 1945).

Chin P'ing Mei: The Adventurous History of Hsi Men and His Six Wives. New York, 1949.
Introduction by Arthur Waley.

Ch'u T'ung-tsu. Law and Society in Traditional China. Paris and The Hague: Mouton, 1959.
See particularly the sections dealing with family law.

Conger, Sarah. Letters from China. Chicago, 1909.
Wife of an American Minister to China, Mrs. Conger was

particularly interested in the state of Chinese women. Her
letters home are interesting for their direct observation of
such elite Chinese women as she met (including the Empress
Dowager) as well for what they reveal about the foreign female community in Peking.

Diamond, Norma. K'un Shen: A Taiwan Village. New York,
    1969.
    An anthropological case study of a Taiwan fishing village. It
    includes the village setting and history, the economy, the life
    cycle, family, community and religious life. See Chapter 3
    for an excellent treatment of the role and socialization of
    women, and Chapter 4 for the effects of this socialization
    on them.

Fielde, Adele M. Pagoda Shadows: Studies from Life in China.
    London, 1887.
    A Christian woman missionary who lived in China and wrote
    on the status of women, infanticide, foot-binding, various
    "autobiographies" and "Native female Evangelists."

Freedman, Maurice. Family and Kinship in Chinese Society.
    Stanford, 1970.
    Eleven essays on the Chinese family and kinship system. In-
    cluding child training, family relations and a comparison with
    Japanese kinship.

Gernet, Jacques. Daily Life in China in the Thirteenth Century.
    New York, 1962.
    A preliminary survey of Chinese sex and society ca. 1500 B.C.
    until 1644 A.D. See chapter on women's roles, and precepts
    of the idealized Confucian view of family life (pp. 98-106).

Highbaugh, Irma. Family Life in West China. 1948.

Hosie, Lady Dorothea [Soothill]. Portrait of a Chinese Lady and
    Certain of her Contemporaries. New York, 1930.
    Somewhat longwinded and chatty sequel to Lady Hosie's earlier
    Two Gentlemen of China (which bears the wonderful subtitle --
    "An Intimate Description of the private life of two Patrician
    Chinese families, their homes, loves, religion, mirth, sorrow
    and many other aspects of their family life").

Hsiao Kung-chuan. <u>Rural China: Imperial Control in the Nineteenth
    Century</u>. Seattle, 1960.
    A voluminous, thoroughly documented analysis of "self-govern-
    ment" organizations during the Ch'ing government as instru-
    ments of political and ideological control, and of the deterio-
    ration of the Imperial government's efficiency in local govern-
    ment in the 19th century; an important contribution to the
    understanding of the Confucian governmental system. The
    role of women and the family in rural Imperial China is not
    dealt with but there is a great deal of material on the clan
    as a political and economic force.

Hsu, Francis L. K. <u>Under the Ancestor's Shadow</u>. New York, 1948.
    An anthropological field report on a Yunnan town, emphasizing
    ancestor worship and other aspects of folk religion. Research
    conducted in 1941-1943. See index under women, girls, family
    for specific references.

Kuo, Helena [Ch'ing-ch'iu]. <u>I've Come a Long Way</u>. New York, 1942.
    Autobiography of the daughter of a rich Chinese businessman
    from Macao. Gives an interesting perspective on a young girl's
    educational experiences in early 20th century China.

Lang, Olga. <u>Chinese Family and Society</u>. New Haven, 1946.
    One of the most comprehensive descriptions of the Chinese
    family system.

Levenson, Joseph. <u>Liang Ch'i-ch'ao and the Mind of Modern China</u>.
    Cambridge, Mass., 1959.
    Particularly relevant to women: Chapter II, the breakdown of
    the Confucian world; and Chapter IV, the substitute for tradition.

Levy, Howard S. <u>Chinese Footbinding: The History of a Curious
    Erotic Custom</u>. New York, 1966.
    A profusely illustrated and footnoted account of the custom of
    foot-binding from the court dancer of the Sung dynasty to the
    emancipation movements of the 20th century.

Levy, Marion J., Jr. <u>The Family Revolution in Modern China</u>.
    Cambridge, Mass., 1949.
    A standard sociological/anthropological account of the family
    system.

Li Ju-chen. Flowers in the Mirror. Translated and edited by Lin
    Tai-yi. Berkeley, 1965.
    An early champion of equal rights for women, Li, a Chinese
    scholar (1763-1830), wrote in the 1820s. This is a marvel-
    ous satirical novel of fantasy, a combination of Gulliver's
    Travels and Alice in Wonderland.

Li Yu. Jou Pu Tuan [The Prayer mat of flesh]. New York, 1963.
    A classic of Chinese erotic literature and a document of man-
    ners and morals in the form of a novel by Li Yu, a Ming dy-
    nasty writer. It is a handbook of love concerning a student
    who devotes himself to a life of utter eroticism and six women.

Lin Yueh-Hwa. The Golden Wing: A Sociological Study of Chinese
    Familism. New York, 1948.
    A sociological study (written in the form of a novel) of two
    families -- the Hwang and the Chang -- in a Fukien village. It
    is the story of the business success of the Hwang family and
    the failure of the Chang. For the woman's role in agriculture
    see p. 74, and for her role in the economy see pp. 77-80.

Lin Yu-tang. My Country and My People. New York, 1935.
    A prolific interpreter of China to western audiences. Chap-
    ter 5 offers his views on "Women's Life."

_____. Widow, Nun, and Courtesan: Three Novelettes from
    the Chinese. New York, 1951.

McAleavy, Henry. "Certain Aspects of Chinese Customary Law in
    the Light of Japanese Scholarship" in Bulletin of the School of
    Oriental and African Studies. London, 1955.
    A review of recent Japanese findings about traditional legal
    relations within Chinese families.

Ning Lao T'ai-t'ai. A Daughter of Han: The Autobiography of a
    Chinese Working Woman. Ed. Ida Pruitt. New Haven, 1945.
    The story of a Chinese peasant woman who worked as a ser-
    vant for officials, military officers, and missionaries from
    the 1870s to 1938. A highly recommended account of her
    childhood, marriage, child-bearing, grandchildren, ideas on
    the Japanese invasion, domestic work, travel, and personal
    strength.

O'Hara, Albert, S.J. The Position of Woman in Early China.
Translation of Lieh Nu Chuan [The Biographies of Chinese
women of the former Han dynasty by Liu Hsiang]. Washington,
1946.
One hundred and twenty-five short biographies of women from
legendary times to the Han dynasty, of all classes, locales,
and types. Written by a Confucian scholar, it became the
manual for the correct conduct of ladies for centuries.

Quayne, Jonathan. Diary of a Concubine (The Jasper Gate). New
York: Lancer, 1969.
Probably an authentic life-history of a prostitute.

Schurmann, Franz and Orville Schell. The China Reader. Three
volumes. (Imperial China, Republican China, Communist China).
New York, 1967.
In volume 1 there are articles concerning women: Mencius on
the family, pp. 13-21; Confucianism and kinship by Fairbank,
pp. 36-56; women's attire by Wang Hsi-chi, pp. 122-126; and
the position of women in the Taiping rebellion by Franke,
pp. 186-187.

Smith, Arthur H. Village Life in China. New York: Fleming
Revell, 1899.
A knowledgeable missionary's description of rural life, with a
sympathetic chapter on women.

Ts'ao Hsueh-ch'in. Dream of the Red Chamber. Trans. by Arthur
Waley. New York, 1958.
China's great eighteenth century novel about the house of Chia
in Peking and the innumerable relatives and servants in this
complex and fascinating household. An extremely important
novel not only for its literary merit but sociological picture
as well.

Van Gulik, R. H. Sexual Life in Ancient China. Leiden: E. J.
Brill, 1961.
Despite the title, this is for the most part a survey of the
status of women and views toward women through different
periods of Chinese history with material drawn from literature, poetry, painting and "pillow books."

Wang, Elizabeth Te-chen. Ladies of the Tang. Taipei: Heritage
    Press, 1961.
    Translations of famous T'ang dynasty stories, many of which
    continue into the present time as opera/drama or in the oral
    tradition.

Wolf, Margery. The House of Lim: A Study of a Chinese Farm
    Family. New York, 1968.
    An anthropological study done in story form about an extended
    family in Taiwan. Especially interesting are the stories of
    the daughter who becomes a prostitute and her later familial
    relations.

_____. Women and the Family in Rural Taiwan. Stanford,
    California, 1972.
    In this superbly written and empathetic anthropological study,
    the ways in which women resist oppression within the tradi-
    tional family structure are imaginatively explored.

Wong Su-ling and Earl Herbert Cressy. Daughter of Confucius.
    New York, 1952.
    Autobiography of Chin, a girl from the gentry class, born in
    1918 in Fukien.

Yang, Martin C. A Chinese Village. New York, 1945.
    Account of the author's own village in Shantung, and his ex-
    perience growing up there. Good on the intra-family relation-
    ships.

WOMEN IN REVOLUTIONARY CHINA

All China Democratic Women's Federation.   Chinese Women in 1950.
Peking, 1950.
A collection of articles on women centering around the 1950
marriage laws.   Contains "China's women -- active builders
of new China."

_____. Documents of the Women's Movement of China.
2nd ed.   Peking, 1952.
Outlines Chinese Communist policies on women, especially
women's role in the economy.

Belden, Jack.   China Shakes the World.   New York, 1949.   Reprinted:
New York, 1970.
A journalist's first-hand account of the Chinese civil war from
1946-1949.   Gives a detailed account of both peasant life and
reactions to the societal turmoil.   Excellent chapters on women
and revolution.   See especially "Goldflower's Story."

Chesneaux, Jean.   The Chinese Labor Movement 1919-1927.   Trans.
by H. M. Wright.   Stanford, California, 1968.
In the words of Mary Wright, who wrote the foreword, "one
of the very few seminal works on the history of China in the
twentieth century, and a pioneering probe into the vast unex-
plored realm of twentieth-century Chinese social history."   The
best -- in some respects the only -- book to consult on the
number, nature, condition and structure of women industrial
workers in this period.

Chiang Kai-shek, Madame (Soong May-ling).   We Chinese Women.
New York, 1943.
A collection of speeches and writings given during the first
United Nations Year (12 February 1942 to 16 November 1942).

Chin Ai-li S.   "Family Relations in Modern Chinese Fiction," in
Family and Kinship in Chinese Society.   Edited by Maurice
Freedman.
Focusing on the nature of family relations, she compares lit-
erature of the May Fourth period and of the early 1960s in
Taiwan and the People's Republic.

Chinese Women in the Great Leap Forward. Peking, 1960.

Chou Shu-jen [Lu Hsun]. Selected Works of Lu Hsun. 4 vols.
     Peking, 1956-1960.
     On women see especially "The New Year's Sacrifice" and
     "The Divorce" in volume 1. Excellent short stories by a
     famous Chinese writer of the early 20th century.

Chou Sui-ning Prudence. "The Chinese Communist Policies Toward
     Rural Women from 1949-1955." Unpublished thesis. Univer-
     sity of California at Berkeley, 1968.
     Mostly devoted to a discussion of the implementation of the
     new marriage laws which were crucial in the changing of
     peasant women's status both within the family and in society.

Chow Tse-tsung. The May Fourth Movement: Intellectual Revolution
     in Modern China. Cambridge, Mass., 1960.
     Recounts the events of the May 4th movement (1917-1921) and
     examines in detail its currents and effects. Chow sees the
     rising tide of "feminism" as one of the primary sociopolitical
     consequences of the May 4th movement.

Cohen, Charlotte Bonny. "Women in China." Sisterhood is Power-
     ful. An Anthology of Writings from the Women's Liberation
     Movement. Edited by Robin Morgan. New York, 1970.
     A sketchy history of women in China from traditional China
     through 1969.

Crook, David and Isabel. The First Years of Yangyi Commune.
     London, 1966.
     As in Ten Mile Inn (though perhaps not as dramatically) the
     Crooks offer close observation of social, economic and polit-
     ical changes in southern Hopei. They are constantly aware of
     the special position of women and both books are essential to
     an understanding of revolutionary policy toward women before
     and after 1949.

_____. Revolution in a Chinese Village. Ten Mile Inn.
     London, 1959.

Cusak, Dymphna. Chinese Women Speak. London, 1959.
"A sympathetic report of eighteen months spent in Communist
China with character sketches of numerous women encountered:
not scholarly, and not entirely objective; but showing many
aspects of what modernization and communication have done
to Chinese women's lives and attitudes."*

Hahn, Emily. The Soong Sisters. New York, 1945.
An elegant account of these three powerful women.

Han Suyin. The Crippled Tree. New York, 1965. A Mortal Flower.
New York, 1965. Birdless Summer. New York, 1968.
The daughter of an upper-middle class family -- Chinese
father and Belgian mother -- tries to reconstruct her family
history in China. A personalized story of China during its
transition, with particular attention to Kuomintang attitudes
towards women.

_____. "Family Planning in China," Japan Quarterly,
17:4 (Oct.-Dec. 1970).
A systematic study of planned parenthood in China for fourteen
years (1956-1970).

Hinton, William. Fanshen: A Documentary of Revolution in a
Chinese Village. New York, 1955.
A classic account of social revolution in a Chinese village which
treats the participation of women with enormous understanding.

Ho Ching-chih. The White Haired Girl: An Opera in 5 Acts.
Peking, 1954.
". . . about a servant girl who was raped, and whose father
is a murdered by an evil landlord and the eventual triumph of
justice upon 'liberation' by the red army."*

Hsia C. T. "Residual Feminity: Women in Chinese Communist
Fiction." The China Quarterly (Jan.-Mar. 1963).

Hsieh Pingying. Girl Rebel. Trans. by Adet and Anor Lin. New
York, 1940.

_____
*Quoted from Charles Hucker, China: A Critical Bibliography,
Tucson, Arizona, 1962.

The autobiography of Hsieh Pingying with extracts from her
New War diaries. This is a story of a woman's struggle to
free herself from the repression of a traditional family, prin-
cipally relating to the 1920s.

Hucker, Charles. China: A Critical Bibliography. Tucson,
Arizona, 1962.

Israel, John. "The Red Guards in Historical Perspective: Conti-
nuity and Change in the Chinese Youth Movement." The China
Quarterly, No. 30 (1967).

_____. Student Nationalism in China, 1927-1937. Stanford,
1966.

"Li Shuangshuang." The People's Comic Book. Trans. by Endymion
Wilkinson, with an introduction by Gino Nebiolo. New York,
1973.
A fascinating moral tale of familial conflict on a commune in
which the problems of an activist peasant woman are seriously
examined and happily resolved. The book also contains a comic book version of the famous revolutionary opera, "The Red
Detachment of Women."

Mao Tse-tung. "Report of an Investigation into the Peasant Movement in Hunan." Selected Works. Vol. 1.
Written in 1927, Part 7 is of particular importance to women.

Michael, Franz, and Chung-li Chang. The Taiping Rebellion:
History and Documents. Vol. 1 of 3 vols. Seattle, 1966.
A concise documentary history of the Taiping Rebellion. The
radical policy of Taiping rebels towards women is among the
most fascinating aspects of this great nineteenth century uprising.

Myrdal, Jan. Report from a Chinese Village. New York, 1966.
Descriptions of the villagers of Liu ling in Northern Shensi,
plus records of the experiences of the villagers in their daily
lives during the upheavals of the Chinese revolution. Interesting character sketches of women.

Myrdal, Jan, and Kessle, Gun. China: The Revolution Continued.
   New York, 1971.
   A return visit which focuses on the effects of the Cultural
   Revolution. Wonderful photographs.

New Women in New China. Peking, 1972.

Orleans, Leo. "Evidence from Chinese Medical Journals on Current
   Population Policy." The China Quarterly, No. 40 (1969).

Pa Chin [Li Fei-kan]. The Family. Peking, 1958.
   The first novel of a trilogy published in 1931 is a passionate
   indictment of the tyranny of the authoritarian Chinese family
   system. The spokesman for youth during China's stormy
   transitional period, Pa Chin (took syllables from the names
   of Bakunin and Kropotkin, Russian anarchists) felt that the
   road for young people lay in resistance, struggle, and revolution.

Rankin, Mary. Early Chinese Revolutionaries. Cambridge, Mass.,
   1971.
   See especially Ms. Rankin's description and analysis of the
   revolutionary martyr, Ch'iu Chin.

Rowbottham, Sheila. Women, Resistance and Revolution. A History
   of Women and Revolution in the Modern World. New York,
   1972.
   A descriptive history of feminism which explores, in various
   countries and time periods, the complex relationship between
   feminism and social revolution.

Schurmann, Franz. Ideology and Organization in Communist China.
   Berkeley, 1968.
   Excellent book to understand the construction and transformation of Communist China, however, it does not present much
   material on women. See pp. 7, 377, 392, 425, 479. Women
   in the labor force: pp. 355-356, 397.

Sidel, Ruth. Women and Child Care in China. New York, 1972.
   A firsthand, illustrated account with chapters on pregnancy
   and childbirth, marriage, women's liberation and some com-
   parative discussion of Israel and the Soviet Union.

Smedley, Agnes. Battle Hymn of China. New York, 1943.
    Agnes Smedley was, in some respects, the keenest and most
    lyrical observer of the Chinese revolution. A working class
    feminist herself, Smedley's descriptions of Chinese women are
    vivid and directly moving. Few reporters have put us so im-
    mediately in touch with the realities of the situation of women
    in China.

_____. Chinese Destinies. New York, 1933.

Snow, Edgar. Red Star Over China. New York, 1961. 1st revised
    and enlarged ed. 1968.
    One of the best reports on China in the 30s, which includes a moving
    account by Mao of his childhood and revolutionary development.

Snow, Helen Foster. Women in Modern China. The Hague, 1967.
    Though culturally biased, Snow offers important information
    on women's struggle for emancipation in China. Includes
    sketches of ten famous Chinese women in the twentieth cen-
    tury, such as Soong Ching-ling, Teng Ying-ch'ao, Ting Ling,
    and Ts'ai Ch'ang.

Strong, Anna Louise. China's Millions: The Revolutionary Strug-
    gles from 1927-1935. New York, 1935.

Teng Ying-ch'ao. "The Woman's Movement in New China." People's
    China. 1 March 1952.

Tsai Ch'ang. "The Party's General Line Illuminates the Path of
    Emancipation for our Women." Women of China. No. 1
    (1960).

Vogel, Ezra F. Canton Under Communism: Progress and Politics
    in a Provincial Capital, 1943-1968. Cambridge, Mass., 1969.

Wales, Nym. [Helen Foster Snow.] Red Dust: Autobiographies of
    Chinese Communists. As told to Nym Wales. Stanford, 1952.
    Introduction by Robert Carter North. Twenty-four short auto-
    biographies collected in 1937. Includes two narratives by
    women: T'sai T'ing-li, an editor and writer on women's
    problems; and K'ang K'e-ch'ing, a guerrilla fighter and wife
    of Chu Te.

Wang, Simine. Le Travail des femmes et des enfants en Chine.
    Paris, 1933.

A sympathetic survey of the conditions of labor of women and children.

Wei, Yu-hsiu Cheng. My Revolutionary Years. New York, 1943.

Witke, Roxane. "The Transformation of Attitudes of Women During the May Fourth Era of Modern China." Unpublished dissertation. University of California at Berkeley, 1970.

The Woman's Representative: Three One Act Plays. Peking, 1956. Three one-act plays dealing with the love and family life of the new Chinese women.

Women in New China. Peking, 1950. Contains two articles published by the People's Republic on women.

Wright, Mary C., ed. China in Revolution: The First Phase, 1900-1913. New Haven, 1968. New studies on the 1911 Revolution. Professor Wright's introductory essay takes full account of the participation of women in the revolution. See also Professor Mary Rankin's fine study of Ch'iu Chin.

Yang, C. K. The Chinese Family in the Communist Revolution. Cambridge, Mass., 1959.

_____. A Chinese Village in Early Communist Transition. Cambridge, Mass., 1959. Both of these books by Professor Yang are essential to a fuller understanding of the way traditional Chinese family structure has been changing. Both deal extensively with women.

Yang Mo. The Song of Youth. Peking, 1964. A novel by a major woman writer dealing with the radical student movement of the 1930s, with an emphasis on women students.

Zen, Sophia H. Chen. [Mrs. Heng-che.] The Chinese Woman and Four Other Essays. Peiping, 1934. A western-educated Chinese feminist's views on China in transition.

Notes on Contributors

Jane Barrett visited the People's Republic of China in spring 1972, as a member of the Second Friendship Delegation of the Committee of Concerned Asian Scholars. A graduate of Vassar College, she is currently completing a master's degree in Chinese studies at the University of Michigan and plans to enter law school in the fall of 1973.

Delia Davin is a Lecturer in economic history in the Department of Economics, University of York, England. She taught English at a college in Peking for two years in the 1960s. She is currently preparing a book on the women's movement in the People's Republic of China.

Norma Diamond is presently an Associate Professor in the Department of Anthropology, University of Michigan. She has made several field trips to Taiwan, studying both peasant and urban communities. Among her publications is K'un Shen: A Taiwan Village. She is currently working on materials dealing with the status of women in China since the early 19th century.

Linda H. Erwin received a bachelor's degree from Duke University and is currently a graduate student in Chinese studies at the University of Michigan. She is employed by the Center for Chinese Studies.

Penny T. Greene received her bachelor's degree from Cornell University. She is now a graduate student in European history at the University of Michigan and is employed by the Center for Chinese Studies.

Suzette Leith received her bachelor's degree from Stanford University and her master's degree in Chinese studies from the University of Michigan. She is now working in journalism.

Lu Yu-lan has been chairman of an agricultural producers' cooperative and secretary of a production brigade Party branch under
a people's commune. She attended the Ninth National Congress
of the Chinese Communist Party in 1969 and was elected a
member of the Party's Central Committee. She is Secretary
of the Linhsi County Party Committee and Deputy Secretary
of the Hopei Provincial Party Committee.

Judith Merkle holds a master's degree from the Harvard Center for
Soviet Studies and is currently teaching at the University of
Oregon while completing a dissertation in political science at
the University of California at Berkeley. Her activities in the
women's movement at Berkeley led to an investigation of socialist women's movements and to a collaboration with Professor Salaff. Her other publications are on post-industrial bureaucracies.

Nancy Milton teaches English to foreign students in the San Francisco
Community College district. A teacher at the Peking First
Foreign Languages Institute in China from 1964 to 1969, she
is an editor, with Naomi Katz, of Fragment from a Lost
Diary and Other Stories, Women of Asia, Africa and Latin
America.

Janet W. Salaff, Ph.D. Department of Sociology, University of
California, is an Assistant Professor at the University of
Toronto. She and Judith Merkle wrote "Women and Revolution" when the "Cambodian crisis" raised sharply the issues
of women's ability to defend their political viewpoints, and
the women's movement was concerned to search out previous
historical circumstances when women did so defend their
right to rebel. Professor Salaff is currently studying the
reasons for the delay of marriage in Hong Kong.

Soong Chingling (Sung Ch'ing-ling) is the vice-chairman of the
People's Republic of China. The widow of Sun Yat-sen, her
career spans the entire half-century of revolutionary change
in modern China. Although her health seems to have been
poor of late, she receives foreign dignitaries, makes public
appearances and, as the current article indicates, expresses
herself cogently on important topics. A selection of her
speeches and articles from 1927 to 1952 has been translated
in The Struggle for New China.

Beth Urdang, the designer of our cover, is an artist and educator
    currently residing in New York City. She is a master's
    degree candidate in painting at Hunter College of the City
    University of New York.

Roxane Witke is on leave from the State University of New York
    at Binghamton. She was a Visiting Associate Professor of
    History at Stanford University in 1972-73, and is currently
    a Research Associate in East Asian Studies at Harvard Univer-
    sity's East Asian Research Center. "Woman as Politician in
    China of the 1920s" is taken from a forthcoming work on
    feminism in the May Fourth era. She is currently preparing
    a biography of Chiang Ch'ing.

Marilyn B. Young teaches history at the Residential College, Univer-
    sity of Michigan. She is a member of the Committee of Con-
    cerned Asian Scholars and the author of Rhetoric of Empire,
    a study of American China policy at the turn of the century.

MICHIGAN PAPERS IN CHINESE STUDIES

No. 1, The Chinese Economy, 1912-1949, by Albert Feuerwerker.

No. 2, The Cultural Revolution: 1967 in Review, four essays by Michel Oksenberg, Carl Riskin, Robert Scalapino, and Ezra Vogel.

No. 3, Two Studies in Chinese Literature: "One Aspect of Form in the Arias of Yüan Opera" by Dale Johnson; and "Hsü K'o's Huang Shan Travel Diaries" translated by Li Chi, with an introduction, commentary, notes, and bibliography by Chun-shu Chang.

No. 4, Early Communist China: Two Studies: "The Fu-t'ien Incident" by Ronald Suleski; and "Agrarian Reform in Kwangtung, 1950-1953" by Daniel Bays.

No. 5, The Chinese Economy, ca. 1870-1911, by Albert Feuerwerker.

No. 6, Chinese Paintings in Chinese Publications, 1956-1968: An Annotated Bibliography and An Index to the Paintings, by E. J. Laing.

No. 7, The Treaty Ports and China's Modernization: What Went Wrong? by Rhoads Murphey.

No. 8, Two Twelfth Century Texts on Chinese Painting, "Shan-shui ch'un-ch'üan chi" by Han Cho, and chapters nine and ten of "Hua-chi" by Teng Ch'un, translated by Robert J. Maeda.

No. 9, The Economy of Communist China, 1949-1969, by Chu-yuan Cheng.

No. 10, Educated Youth and the Cultural Revolution in China, by Martin Singer.

No. 11, Premodern China: A Bibliographical Introduction, by Chun-shu Chang.

No. 12, Two Studies on Ming History, by Charles O. Hucker.

(continued)

No. 13, <u>Nineteenth Century China: Five Imperialist Perspectives</u>, selected by Dilip Basu, edited with an introduction by Rhoads Murphey.

No. 14, <u>Modern China, 1840-1972: An Introduction to Sources and Research Aids</u>, by Andrew J. Nathan.

No. 15, <u>Women in China: Studies in Social Change and Feminism</u>, edited with an introduction by Marilyn B. Young.

*   *   *

MICHIGAN ABSTRACTS OF CHINESE AND JAPANESE WORKS ON CHINESE HISTORY

No. 1, <u>The Ming Tribute Grain System</u> by Hoshi Ayao, translated by Mark Elvin.

No. 2, <u>Commerce and Society in Sung China</u> by Shiba Yoshinobu, translated by Mark Elvin.

No. 3, <u>Transport in Transition: The Evolution of Traditional Shipping in China</u>, translations by Andrew Watson.

*   *   *

Michigan Papers and Abstracts available from:

Center for Chinese Studies
University of Michigan
Lane Hall
Ann Arbor, Michigan 48104
USA